OUT FOR MORE BLOOD

Other Victoria A. Brownworth Books

Out for Blood: Tales of Mystery
& Suspense by Women (editor)

Night Bites: Vampire Stories by Women (editor)

Too Queer: Essays From a Radical Life

OUT FOR MORE BLOOD

Tales of Malice & Retaliation by Women

VICTORIA A. BROWNWORTH
& JUDITH M. REDDING, EDITORS

 Third Side Press

Chicago

Printed on recycled, acid-free paper in the United States of America.
Design and production by Midge Stocker.

Back cover photo credits
  Beth Brant by Denise Dorsz
  Joanne Dahme by J. M. Redding
  Joyce Wagner by Betsy Corsiglia
  Judith Katz by Ricardo Bloch
  Judith M. Redding by Tee A. Corinne
  Lisa D. Williamson by John H. Williamson, Jr.
  Mabel Maney by Dina Wilson
  Nikki Baker by D. Scott O'Brien
  Victoria A. Brownworth by Tee A. Corinne

Library of Congress Cataloging-in-Publication Data
Out for more blood : tales of malice & retaliation by women. /
    Victoria A. Brownworth & Judith M. Redding, editors. — 1st ed.
    p. cm.
    ISBN 1-879427-27-3 (acid-free paper)
    1. Detective and mystery stories, American. 2. American
fiction—Women authors. 3. Revenge—Fiction. 4. Women—Fiction.
I. Brownworth, Victoria. II. Reddings, Mudith M.
    PS648.d4094 1996
    813'.08720809287—dc20   96-32120
                                                                  CIP

Third Side Press, 2250 W. Farragut, Chicago, IL 60625-1802

First edition, October 1996
10 9 8 7 6 5 4 3 2 1

FOR

ROBERTA L. HACKER AND PATTI J. LITTLE

WHO HAVE KEPT US WELL-FED AND MELLOW

IN A HUNGRY AND VENGEFUL WORLD

AND

DR. BEVERLY SHAPIRO

WHO HAS KEPT US ALIVE

WHILE PUTTING MALICE AND RETALIATION

IN THEIR PROPER PERSPECTIVE

CONTENTS

Acknowledgments

Anyone who thinks compiling an anthology is an easy task has never attempted one. But beyond the simple hard work are the choices one makes. The most difficult aspect is choosing from a plethora of intriguing pieces from a range of writers. Many of the submissions we received for this book were interesting and well-written, but didn't fit the criteria of mystery/revenge stories (or weren't written by women). We want to thank those writers, women and men, who submitted work we did not use here. We also want to thank people who helped expedite the process. Ruthann Robson listened to a lot of moaning with characteristic patience and support. J. D. Shaw uncomplainingly retyped edited manuscripts (deciphering VAB's handwriting, an awesome task in itself). Susanna Sturgis offered numerous helpful suggestions from her own vast editorial experience. Lawrence Schimel offered more helpful suggestions from his vast experience, including names of writers. Jane Murtaugh was her usual solicitous and cheerful self in the face of encroaching deadlines; we don't believe she ever gets huffy. And Midge Stocker, as ever, deserves thanks for her commitment to a feminist vision and for continuing to publish feminist writing that refuses simple labeling or pigeonholing. Third Side Press, despite the vicissitudes of an ever-changing publishing milieu, continues to take risks and push the proverbial envelope. We are grateful to Midge and Third Side for another volume in the Out for Blood series.

Introduction

Victoria A. Brownworth

Malice, retaliation, revenge, obsession, hysteria. These words—and their pejorative connotations—have ever been applied to women and their perspective on the world: particularly the emotional and psychological. Women are the "weaker" sex, with all that implies: They have no control over their emotions or psyches; their actions spin out of control as easily as their feelings—and minds.

Thus when women talk to each other it is termed gossip; when they talk about each other it is malicious; when they talk back to men it is called vituperative. When women feel deeply they are "hysterical." When women love, they are called obsessed; when they respond to betrayal, it is termed retaliation or revenge.

Literature, whether classic or popular, is rife with these stereotypical images of women, regardless of the gender of the writer. In fact, the inculcation of these images of women begins early, in the cradle—with fairy tales. Cinderella has three spiteful, vengeful step-sisters; evil female fairies and witches—malicious and retaliatory—populate "Sleeping Beauty" and "Rapunzel"; an obsessional and vengeful queen takes violent action in "Snow White."

These tales all feature an evil, *active* female driven by obsession, malice and revenge against a good, utterly *passive* female who is saved from the actions of the evil woman by the true love of a fearless man. Thus from our earliest excursions into the literary we—female and male—are taught a linguistic and literary subtext in which women who are meek and submissive are rewarded by external forces for not acting, while women who act on their strong feelings are demonized and ostracized.

This internecine—and stereotypically female—web of obsession, malice and revenge forms the foundation of much of classic literature as well as genre potboilers. In Charlotte Bronte's classic novel *Jane Eyre*, for example, the self-effacing Jane is victimized by the demonic first wife of Rochester. Obsessional and hysterical, Bertha Rochester maliciously attempts to steal Jane's happiness at the altar, but settles for true female vengefulness in her violent retaliatory actions against Rochester, torching his estate and blinding him in the process. Daisy Buchanan's thoughtless malice and retaliation leads Gatsby to his death in F. Scott Fitzgerald's novel; Gudrun's malicious unconcern and sexual obsessiveness drives Gerald to suicide in D. H. Lawrence's *Women in Love*. Obsession—sexual and romantic—kills Anna Karenina and destroys the life of Emma Bovary. And what woman in literature could be more steeped in obsessional rage and hysterical revenge than Lady Macbeth (except perhaps Medea)?

Popular fiction and drama yield their own vituperative anti-heroines. Scarlett O'Hara's malice and retaliation cannot rend the Wilkes' marriage, but certainly sunders her own to Rhett Butler. Death follows on the heels of Regina's maliciousness in Lillian Hellman's play, *The Little Foxes*, while malice, retaliation and revenge wreak havoc (and death) on the lives of three people in another of Hellman's plays, *The Children's Hour*. In James M. Cain's *Double Indemnity* an unwitting insurance agent becomes the victim of a beautiful and dangerously malicious woman. Daphne du Maurier explores equally dark terrain in *Rebecca*, where the malicious and obsessional *Rebecca* haunts the second Mrs. de Winter from the grave, with the help of the equally retaliatory-minded and malicious housekeeper, Mrs. Danvers.

In literature, active women—like those characters mentioned above—are often predatory and dangerous: They are evil. Sometimes that evil is complex and predacious and other times it is simple and even off-hand—women are thoughtlessly destructive; they just can't help themselves. Yet in real life, although women are often preyed upon and victimized by malice, obsession and revenge, they are most often perceived as being somehow complicitous in those actions. From the office worker who provokes sexual harassment to the child who provokes incest to the college student who gets drunk at a frat party and provokes her own rape to the girlfriend who leaves a relationship and provokes obsessive stalking to the abused wife who provokes her own murder, women are still rarely seen as blameless when retaliatory violence touches them. Culturally, retaliation and revenge are inextricably linked to the female persona. Feminism has blurred some of the stereotypes of the guilty female victim, but stereotypes are difficult to expunge from society's collective consciousness.

The stories in *Out for More Blood* take that view of women—multifaceted only in the variety of stereotypical images (women as victims, as incapable or incompetent, as sexual predators and violent seductresses, as hysterical, obsessional and vengeful)—and implode it. In these stories betrayed lovers do not throw themselves under the wheels of trains like Anna Karenina, nor do they go quietly and unproblematically mad like Emma Bovary. In these stories women obsessed with their looks take a different tack than the evil queen in "Snow White"; guests left off the party list find different solutions from "Sleeping Beauty." And women's emotions run the expansive gamut: in *Out for More Blood* there are no passive women, because those women who appear to fit the traditionally passive social role search for and find ways to escape. By any means necessary.

Women have long been the mistresses of the craft of suspense and mystery writing. Perhaps because of the very duality of the female persona in literature and in life, the incorporation of the mysterious into both stereotype and reality of who women are, women writers have defined the genre. And it was women writers who created an entire sub-genre of mystery and suspense writing—the "malice domestic," or creepy tales from the home front. *Out for More Blood* continues and (it is to be hoped) expands that tradition.

This collection offers up a variant menu of retaliatory tales. In some the malice is subtly nuanced, in others revenge may be sweet, but it is also bloody. Each story delves into common areas of women's lives: relationships, family, love, sex, work. Race, class, gender, sexual orientation—each finds relevance and explication in these stories. But at the foundation of each tale are women taking charge of their lives—for good or ill—but preferably against type.

There is an essential feminism in these stories. In these dramas women play all the roles: victim, villain, vanquished, victor. The authors cover the racial, ethnic, sexual, generational and geographical map. The stories chart the psychological, social and cultural cartography of women's lives. From the drug-infested side streets of the inner city to the bucolic serenity of small-town America, the landscape of these stories is distinctly and definingly female.

Linda K. Wright and Mabel Maney put a 90s spin on the classic malice domestic. Each covers similar ground in "A Neighborly Gesture" and "Mrs. Feeley Is Quite Mad," but with radically different styles: Two wives in traditional American marriages make similar choices, but with vastly divergent results. Beth Brant and Helena Basket focus their attention on the perils of childhood, also with diverse outcomes, in "Little Girl Tells" and "Catacombs." Brant's story explicates the parallel issues of racism and the victimization of a Native American child, while Basket delves into the terror of a young girl's brutal isolation and how she learns to cope.

The sphere of the home marks familiar territory for women writers and familial bonds form the dramatic nexus in several tales. Joyce Wagner explores the cutting edge of sibling rivalry in "Edna & Carole," while Terri de la Peña elucidates sorrorial love in "Caballito del Diablo." Meredith Suzanne Baird's "Thin Ice" plots the chilling disintegration of a family during a vacation. The birth of a baby spurs a reunion between two old friends in J. D. Shaw's "The Visit," but this meeting uncovers an eerie secret.

Joanne Dahme addresses filial concern in the context of suburban life in "Grandfather in a Box," a story that also raises questions about the role of women's work in and out of the home. Work is also at the root of "An Affinity for

Machines," by Lisa D. Williamson, a tale that will strike a
chord in any woman who has ever faced harassment on the
job. Diane DeKelb-Rittenhouse and Toni Brown also focus
on work and how it connects with love, family, race and
class in "Access Denied" and "Never Too Old." Ruthann
Robson and Nikki Baker detail the hidden dangers of police
work and second sight in "The Death of the Subject" and
"Negatives."

The perils of sexual relationships haunt two women and
take them on very different journeys in Judith Katz's homage
to Franz Kafka, "Metamorphosis," and Amalia Pistilli's
aptly titled "Breasts."

Each of these stories details the elements of violence in
women's everyday lives. As depicted in these stories, that
violence may be relegated to the realm of fantasy, or be
grimly realistic. Those words—malice, retaliation, revenge,
obsession, hysteria—replay again and again as the coda to
these tales. How women cope—if they cope, why they
cope—with both the stereotype and reality of female rage is
catalogued in these stories in compelling and diverse detail.
What women see—the literal and the metaphoric—becomes
clarified in these tales in which some women are believed,
others are not and still others disbelieve themselves. Each of
these stories begs a question of perception—cultural, racial,
social, familial. *Who*, these stories ask, are women; *what* are
their lives about; *how* do they survive the violence—physical
and psychological—of their lives?

Mysterious, suspenseful, ironic, and highly entertaining,
Out for More Blood examines the darker aspects of
women's lives—and of the society in which they play such a
defining, if often unrecognized, role.

An Affinity for Machines

Lisa D. Williamson

The severed finger in the Mr. Coffee was the last straw
for Sue Ellen Cooper. After a couple of minutes trying to fish
it out of the hot liquid without burning herself, she realized
it had probably contaminated the entire pot, so she tossed
the full twelve cups down the drain.

She stretched on tiptoe, pulled a fresh filter from the
cupboard, and measured the water and coffee for the second
time that morning, although it wasn't even nine o'clock yet.
Sue Ellen was very careful not to look up, not to show a hint
of emotion on her face. When they had left the plastic vomit
on her chair her first week of work, she had let out a small
yelp. It had made the young salesmen's day. They still talked
about it, nearly a year later, as if it were a landmark event.
The Pilgrims' landing, the Declaration of Independence, the
first man on the moon, and the day someone put vinyl barf
on the new girl's chair.

When Sue Ellen had started her job as office manager at
Mr. Siple's company eleven months earlier, she was nervous
but excited. Although she was only twenty, she knew it
might very well be the best job she'd ever get. She had heard
about the job by accident, and she might never have gotten

1

up the nerve to apply, but she had grown to hate the
SuperKwik, the grocery store where she'd worked all
through high school. It was hard now to remember which
was worst about working there—the demanding customers,
her cliquish fellow employees, or the dull monotony of
passing tampons, tabloid magazines, and day-old bread over
the scanner hour after hour.

But Sue Ellen knew at the time she couldn't hope for
much better than the SuperKwik. She was not the smartest
person on the face of the earth. It wasn't just that everyone
had always told her so; she knew for herself it was true. In
class at high school, she would stare very hard at her
teachers' lips, as if intensity could draw meaning out of
biology or algebra. Things that seemed to come so easily to
her classmates never came to her at all. Nor would she be
able to skate through life on her looks. She had nothing
much on the inside, and nothing much on the outside, either.
She wasn't ugly—that would have been too much to
take—she was just not pretty enough to be popular. All
through school, Sue Ellen had always felt apart from
everyone else. Like her plain good looks—simply not enough.

At graduation, Sue Ellen's teachers and her friends'
parents congratulated her on already having a career. As if
knowing the price of Kwik & Lite Low Fat Yogurt was the
career all the popular kids had been fighting for, and she was
the lucky one to get it. Sue Ellen's family thought she was
lucky to work at the SuperKwik as well. She had five
younger brothers, all two years apart. They liked that she
brought home past-due Kreme-filled Krescents and Koko
Donuts. Her youngest brother, Billy, had a ten-year-old's
respect for her achievement. He thought it was awesome
that she worked all sorts of interesting machines that beeped
and buzzed. Her mother liked that Sue Ellen got a
thirty-percent discount. At least Sue Ellen assumed she did. It
was hard to know exactly what her mother thought, so Sue
Ellen had gotten into the habit of assigning thoughts to her.

Sue Ellen's father had died shortly after Billy was born,
leaving a hefty insurance policy that allowed the family to
stutter along on the thin edge of lower-middle class—as long
as they had Sue Ellen's SuperKwik salary. Her mother had

checked out around that time, abdicating her maternal role to Sue Ellen, a role Sue Ellen had reluctantly accepted.

Jocelyn Cooper seemed to think that, having given birth to six children and buried a husband, her job was done. She had settled in the corner of the couch in the TV room seven years before and had hardly moved since. Having devoted more than ten years to enlarging her family, Jocelyn was now doing the same to herself. Sue Ellen estimated that her mother—once petite—now weighed close to three-hundred pounds, but it was hard to tell because she never saw Jocelyn move. Only her legs changed position, at different angles during the day, like a bizarre timepiece. Her mother's legs were at their highest every night, propped on top of a pile of couch pillows, when Sue Ellen trudged in from the late shift at the SuperKwik.

♦

One day in late August, the summer after graduation, Mrs. Jenkins, the aunt of a high-school friend, was in Sue Ellen's line at the SuperKwik. She handed Sue Ellen her check-cashing card and told her of a job opening she'd just heard about. Sue Ellen smiled politely and ran the card through the scanner. But Mrs. Jenkins pressed Sue Ellen for an answer. Sue Ellen finally said she didn't think the job sounded right for her. How could she run an office?

"Horse manure," Mrs. Jenkins had hissed, startling Sue Ellen because Mrs. Jenkins had always been one of her more polite customers. "You've been running your mother's household for years. And you're not the smartest girl in town, Sue Ellen, but you're a whiz with machines."

This statement startled Sue Ellen even more than the first, because she had never thought of herself as a whiz with anything. She promised Mrs. Jenkins she'd consider it.

Sue Ellen couldn't get the idea Mrs. Jenkins had planted out of her mind. The more she thought about it, the more it seemed Mrs. Jenkins was right. She *was* good with machines. It was a talent she'd always had, but neither she nor anyone else had ever given it much attention.

At the SuperKwik, she'd gently shoulder Jason aside when he started banging on his register, and with a few deft touches, Sue Ellen had it up and running again in time to prevent a riot in the fast line. At home, she was the only one who could program the VCR, although since she had simply read the manual, she never knew what the big deal was. Mr. Klein, the manager of the SuperKwik, always dragged her into his office when his computer went down. She could fix things in less time than it took to get hold of the store technician and she was a lot cheaper, too.

The more Sue Ellen weighed Mrs. Jenkins' words, the more she like the idea of becoming something more than a check-out girl. And there was another thing. Combined with her newly discovered affinity for machines was Sue Ellen's other talent: she could see a task to its completion. Again, she was baffled by others' inability to do such a simple thing. But she had always been able to take any assignment, start it and see it through, something others—even the popular, smart ones—always found difficult. Surely that would be a valuable asset in an office manager. Sue Ellen spent a long and sleepless night thinking about what she should do. When she came downstairs the next morning—her mom's legs had lowered themselves sometime during the night and were now on the floor—Sue Ellen had decided to apply for the job as office manager at Mr. Siple's Manufacturers' Representative Company.

♦

Sue Ellen arrived for her interview dressed in a crisp, white blouse and a black, pleated skirt, trying to look as much like an office manager as possible. Mr. Siple turned out to be different from the imposing businessman she had pictured during the phone interview. He was short with closely trimmed, grizzled hair. He wore an oxford-cloth shirt and tie, and his charcoal-gray pants were belted tightly under a protruding belly and flapped loosely around stick legs. He ushered her into his office with avuncular solicitousness, bouncing around Sue Ellen, offering her coffee, and chattering at her so quickly she wasn't exactly sure what he was saying. He finally settled behind his desk and looked expectantly at Sue Ellen. Somehow by the end of a half-hour, Sue Ellen was hired. Her hours would be longer and her pay less than her SuperKwik union job, and she had agreed she would work through her lunch hour so the salesmen wouldn't be bothered by ringing phones, but despite all that, Sue Ellen left the office with the absolute conviction that her life had turned an important corner.

◆

From the beginning, Mr. Siple's young turks seemed to have Sue Ellen's number. If she had been a little bit smarter, a little bit prettier, a little more with-it, things might have gone differently. But from her first day on the job, as Mr. Siple led her around and introduced her to the ten or so salesmen working in the office, Sue Ellen saw interest, scrutiny, and dismissal wash through their eyes, the same way she'd seen it all through high school.

In many respects, Sue Ellen felt right at home in the office. The salesmen were all older than she, around twenty-five to thirty, but their behavior was familiar enough. The guys acted very much like her own brothers. She would run around all day, answering their phones and typing their correspondence, only to be treated with contempt. From the first week, their favorite name for her was "Screw-Ellen." Then came the famous plastic vomit incident, when the salesmen learned they could get under her skin. They'd take things from her desk, help themselves to her lunch in the refrigerator, use filthy language, and make her feel she was not one of the guys if she complained.

Then, just when she thought her job at the SuperKwik hadn't been as bad as she remembered, the guys would bring her a Coke from lunch at the diner up the street, or one of them would thank her when she helped him with a computer problem, or Mr. Siple would say crossly, "Ask Sue Ellen. She's the only one in this office who knows anything." Then she would feel needed, an essential part of the organization.

It was just like at home. Her brothers all acted as if she weren't there unless they needed something, like a meal cooked, clothes washed, homework solved. But every once in a while, Billy would snuggle next to her in front of the TV late at night, or Ted would yell, "Sue Ellen, you're the best," as he ran out of the house with the ten dollars she'd given him, and she'd feel that their behavior only masked the real affection that lurked beneath the surface.

Her life as office manager percolated along for nearly a year. Sue Ellen was pretty much used to things, rarely regretting her career move. But it had already been a bad week when Sue Ellen found the severed finger in the coffee pot. Nothing had gone right in the office, at home Billy had been sick most of the week with an ear infection, and her mom was cranky because of the heat—at least Sue Ellen thought it was because of the heat.

Now, after making a new pot of coffee, Sue Ellen calmly picked up the finger from where she had laid it on the counter and silently marched past all the work stations to Mr. Siple's office. She knocked on the door frame and when he looked up, slipped into his room and closed the door.

"Mr. Siple," she said, somewhat surprised at her own nerve, "I need to talk to you."

Sue Ellen hadn't foreseen that she would be talking to Mr. Siple about her difficulties at the office. She had not organized her thoughts or rehearsed what she would say, so all the past indignities, all the slights, all the jokes came tumbling out of her in a chaotic rush. She found herself repeatedly saying, "And another thing . . ." as one experience reminded her of the next. Sue Ellen had never been one to dwell on insults or aspersions, but she now found they must have been stored up somewhere inside her, because they all came pouring out. Mr. Siple sat back in his leather swivel chair, his eyes wide, both hands on his desk as if to prevent himself from being blown away by her outburst.

". . . and I can take the jokes. I don't care if they don't think I'm the smartest or prettiest woman around," Sue Ellen finally finished, "but I don't like being called Screw-Ellen." She looked down and saw she still held the rubber finger. She threw it on Mr. Siple's desk with more force than she had intended. They both watched it bounce and roll toward the edge of the blotter. "And I don't like fingers in my coffee."

The moment she said it, Sue Ellen could hear how ridiculous—how *pathetic*—she sounded. She looked at Mr. Siple, wondering how she was going to get out of his office with whatever was left of her dignity. Then she heard a noise. The blood drained from her face as the noise got louder. She looked at Mr. Siple, who suddenly was looking anywhere but back at her, and went to the door. Flinging it open, she saw the entire office gathered around one of the intercoms, laughing. Not just laughing. Roaring with laughter. Crying with laughter. Holding each other up they were laughing so hard. Sue Ellen looked back at Mr. Siple, who hastily pulled his hand away from the intercom's off button. Sue Ellen stared at him. Mr. Siple shrugged apologetically and said, "It was just a joke, Sue Ellen."

Sue Ellen turned. The salesmen still hadn't seen her. Mason, the heavy hitter of the office, put his hands on his hips and said in a high falsetto, "And I don't like fingers in my coffee." They all roared again. Then one of the salesmen saw her. There was a momentary silence as they looked at her and she looked at them. Suddenly she bolted, running for the door, knowing she had to get out of that office. As she ran to her car, Sue Ellen could hear the laughter start again.

◆

Sue Ellen drove home in a controlled rush, periodically wiping at the tears. She kept playing back in her mind her ridiculous speech, the salesmen's laughter, and Mr. Siple's perfidy, although she would have liked nothing more than to forget the whole thing. It was like having a sore tooth one couldn't help probing, even though it made the pain worse. She didn't know whether the guys she worked with were big assholes, or she had just made an enormous fool of herself. All Sue Ellen knew was that she had once again come up with the short end of the stick.

Sue Ellen entered her house, thankful that Billy's ear infection had subsided. He was in school today, so no one would ask prying questions. She moved past her mother—who seemed mildly surprised to see her daughter home at such an early hour—and into the kitchen. This room had, over the years, become Sue Ellen's domain, her place of refuge when things went bad. And things, right now, couldn't get much worse. Her breath came out in snuffling bursts as she dug into the cabinet beneath the sink and pulled out the cleanser.

"They're all *jerks*," she sobbed aloud, as she scrubbed furiously at a dark stain left by that morning's blueberry pancakes. Then, despairingly, "*I'm* a jerk."

Sue Ellen would have loved to talk to someone—anyone—about her morning. She needed to be told that she had put up with more than anyone should, that it was okay to be angry at all the practical jokes and cavalier treatment. But who was there? Since her job at Mr. Siple's had started, she had drifted away from her SuperKwik friends, replacing them with long hours at work and brainless nights in front of the TV. Her mother was in the next room, watching *Donahue* by the sound of it. But Sue Ellen knew from experience that other people's problems, other people's televised problems, were of more concern to her mother than Sue Ellen's. So Sue Ellen scrubbed. And scraped. And scoured. As if by putting the house in order, she could do the same with her life.

When Billy came home from school around four o'clock, Sue Ellen had managed to regain some of her equilibrium. She had cleaned the kitchen, changed the sheets on all the beds, and done the laundry. She was polishing the furniture in the seldom-used dining room when Billy appeared in the doorway. The mindless chores had calmed Sue Ellen by that time, so Billy noticed nothing unusual in her behavior. She had recovered herself to the point where, when he asked her why she was home early, she could smile at him and say, "Mr. Siple gave me a few hours off today. Wasn't that nice?" And Billy looked at her for a moment, then nodded, satisfied. He asked her what there was for an after-school snack and left.

Sue Ellen was happy that Billy hadn't seen anything unusual. She hoped everyone else would be just as unseeing. That was part of the plan she had gradually arrived at during the long day of cleaning. Sue Ellen had come to many conclusions over the course of scouring and scrubbing. One, they could all make her seem as stupid as they wanted, but *they* were the ones in the wrong. Two, she would not show them exactly how much they had hurt her. And three, her ability to see a task through to its completion had never been so important. Because somehow, no matter how long it took, she would make them pay.

The next morning was one of the hardest in Sue Ellen's life. She paid careful attention to her outfit and makeup and, when she could no longer delay it, drove slowly to work. She arrived before anyone else, made the coffee, filled the copy machine, the printer, and the fax with paper, and was hard at work when the salesmen came in. Sue Ellen's bright, "Good morning," warded off any awkward conversation, although even with all her determination to make the day seem like business-as-usual, she couldn't force herself to look anyone in the eye.

When Mr. Siple came in, she went straight to his office and shut his door. He looked alarmed, as if he expected a repeat of yesterday's performance. Sue Ellen allowed some of the humiliation she was feeling into her face as she apologized for her behavior of the day before, explaining that she had been experiencing horrible PMS. She had figured out this excuse the previous night, knowing the guys would be more than happy to blame *their* behavior on *her* hormones. Mr. Siple blanched at the mention of this most unprofessional of topics but was nevertheless visibly relieved at a problem so neatly solved and, skirting actually discussing Sue Ellen's premenstrual difficulties, told her not to worry about making up the lost hours.

For the rest of the day, Mr. Siple and all the guys treated her better than they ever had. It was ironic, given that Sue Ellen had decided they'd all have to go.

◆

During the next few weeks, the office seemed to be under some sort of jinx. Perry had just entered a great deal of vital sales information one morning when his computer went down and he lost everything. He asked Sue Ellen what had happened and, after many minutes under his desk, she emerged with the cords for a fan, the radio, and the copy machine that sat not far from his work station. Someone had plugged all these appliances into the same outlet with no surge protector, and when Mr. Siple had come out of his office to use the copier, a fuse had blown, erasing all Perry's data. Although Perry furiously interrogated all the other salesmen repeatedly during the day, no one owned up to rearranging the circuitry. Over the next few days, Mr. Siple had as little luck himself trying to get to the bottom of the incident. He finally installed an Uninterruptable Power Supply unit—a UPS—that connected all the computers. He had it installed in the conference room, so it could be locked up every night, to ensure that no one could fool with the data files again.

But the practical joker did not confine himself to the area of computer sabotage. Mason, the most successful of the salesmen, was used to coming in early, before anyone else. One morning, as they all filed into the office, they found Mason lying on the floor, unable to get up. Somehow oil had gotten all over Mason's anti-static mat and when he'd gone to sit down, his legs had flown up and his chair had flown back. The impact had thrown his back out, and Mason had lain there until the other salesmen came in and could help him. No one knew how the oil had gotten on Mason's mat.

But worst of all was when Mr. Siple was in the middle of feverish negotiations for a new sales contract. He had been working on the deal for months, but things had really heated up in the past week. After much work, he had the finished document ready moments before the deadline. He rushed to the fax machine, carefully placed the pages in it, clapped his hands together in ecstatic satisfaction, and watched in horror as his papers came out the other end in ribbons. Someone had taken the old shredder out of the storage closet and replaced the fax with it. Mr. Siple was apoplectic. Sue Ellen thought he might drop over from a heart attack, but no one ever confessed to the switch.

The atmosphere of the whole office changed. There had always been banter and competition, but where before it had been the healthy rivalry of a closely knit family, now suddenly back-biting, suspicion, and sullen anger boiled just under the surface of Mr. Siple's company. Where before in the office Sue Ellen had been the butt of all the jokes and the object of contempt, suddenly she found herself the unwilling confidant, the expert of office psyches, the only loyal friend any of the salesmen had.

"Who do *you* think it is, Sue Ellen?" each would ask at different times of the day, suspiciously scanning his fellow workers. Sue Ellen would shrug regretfully and be rewarded with "You're the only one I can trust."

Mr. Siple was at his wit's end. Despite threats, bribes, and furious private conferences, he watched helplessly as his carefully built company went down the tubes. His salesmen were paranoid, his office equipment in constant need of repair, and his customers getting perilously irate at the unreliable service that was becoming the trademark of his company.

And the mischief continued. The speed dial buttons on the fax were changed so that confidential sales information went not to the customer but to the competition instead. A small magnetic toy was placed on top of Andrew's computer sometime during the weekend and by Monday had erased the entire hard drive. And someone programmed Jim's phone for conference calls so that he found himself talking simultaneously with his girlfriend and his fiancée.

"That's it!" yelled Mr. Siple after the latest incident. "Sue Ellen, tell all the salesmen to be in the office—in the conference room—nine o'clock sharp tomorrow morning. Cancel all sales calls, all trips, all appointments. Tell them to be prepared for a long day. We will be in there until someone confesses. This mischief has got to stop before we don't have a company!"

◆

At around six o'clock that evening, Mr. Siple emerged from his office and caught sight of Sue Ellen working at her desk.

"Sue Ellen, what are you still doing here? Everyone else has already left."

"I'm just finishing things up," she replied. "I'll be done soon."

Mr. Siple walked up and put his hand on her shoulder.

"Thank God you're here," he said. "Sometimes I think you're the only sane one in this office."

She smiled up at him. He patted her shoulder one last time and left.

Sue Ellen waited until she was sure Mr. Siple had gone. Then she took all the things she needed into the conference room. She place the materials and tools on the conference table, a large glass-and-brass affair that had been dubbed the "Smart Table," because it had outlets built into it for phones and faxes and all the other electronic gadgets one might need during a conference. It was completely wired—all one had to do was plug it in. Mr. Siple was very proud of his Smart Table. Sue Ellen clipped off the plug, stripped the cord, carefully unrolled the heavy-duty wire she had brought, and thought of all the times the salesmen had compared their office manager unfavorably to the Smart Table.

"Good thing at least the *table* is smart," they'd snigger.

Sue Ellen smiled slightly as she checked the manual one last time to make sure she was connecting the table to the UPS just the way she wanted. Tomorrow they'd find out that smart is not necessarily the most important virtue for a table. Or an office manager.

It took Sue Ellen a couple of hours before she was satisfied with her work. She had been preparing for this moment for weeks. She had read all the manuals—especially the chapters on troubleshooting and cautions—more than once before she'd come up with what she thought was a foolproof idea. The power came in through the black wire—the hot wire—and sought to go back out through the white—the common wire. Black in, white out. All that was needed was a connection between the two. Anything would do, as long as it conducted electricity. Even a salesman. Sue Ellen smiled again at the circularity, the aptness of her plan. What goes around, comes around, she thought.

How fortunate that Mr. Siple was so gadget-happy—and how fortunate that he'd been so frustrated by the practical jokes that he'd gone overboard and had installed the most powerful UPS on the market. But, she thought, as she carefully set the Mr. Coffee she'd brought into the conference room (and which had a totally new wire connecting its timer and the UPS) to 9:15 a.m., there would have been other ways.

♦

Mr. Siple came in the next morning at 8:45 and was gratified to see Sue Ellen already there.

"Is everything all set up?" he asked her.

Sue Ellen told him regretfully that someone had come in during the night, somehow gotten into the conference room, and soaked all the upholstered chairs with water.

"I checked the computers and the UPS," Sue Ellen assured Mr. Siple, "but whoever it was evidently wasn't after the data files this time. The chairs are too wet to use today, but I pulled those metal folding chairs from the storage closet and set them up. The carpet around the table is still a bit damp, but I mopped up what I could." She paused and said with sympathy. "It looks like someone is afraid of what will happen during the conference."

"And they should be," Mr. Siple said, his color a dangerous purple. "This stuff stops *today*."

When all the salesmen were seated in the conference room, Mr. Siple told Sue Ellen to hold all calls. She told him everything would be taken care of and wished him luck.

"Oh," Sue Ellen added, "I laid out coffee mugs and creamer for everyone. The Mr. Coffee will turn on automatically in a few minutes."

Mr. Siple smiled gratefully at her and went into the conference room. He closed the door and Sue Ellen heard the lock click.

Sue Ellen looked at her watch and continued the typing she'd been doing before Mr. Siple had come in. She could hardly hear herself think with all the bellowing and fist-on-table slamming coming from conference room. Obviously no one had noticed the rewiring or the wet carpet underfoot. At 9:15, the lights of the office suddenly surged brighter and there was an explosive *crack*. The low bass of the shouting went up at least an octave before the office was completely silent. The lights flickered weakly a few times, then went out. Sue Ellen sat for a moment, listening. The office seemed strange without its usual noise, the salesmen talking, the hum of machinery. And instead of the usual smell of morning coffee came the faint waft of bacon left too long in the pan.

Sue Ellen picked up her purse. She looked around the office and, satisfied, left, making sure to lock the door behind her.

♦

Sue Ellen was at the dining-room table, circling interesting-sounding help-wanted ads in red pen when the police came. What only a year ago would have looked like an impossible dream—page after page of pleas for dependable office managers or executive assistants—now looked like ripe picking, what with her expertise. Sue Ellen pushed the paper aside for the moment and let the two officers in the front door. Jocelyn was watching *The Price is Right* in the TV room, so Sue Ellen took the officers to the kitchen, where she made them a pot of coffee.

They asked her about her job and why she wasn't at the office this morning. Sue Ellen told them all about the practical joker who had been plaguing the company and explained that Mr. Siple had called a meeting. The officers had been taking careful note of everything from the moment they'd walked in the house—from Jocelyn, to the clean but hardly affluent house, to Sue Ellen herself. They looked at her in that particular way she recognized.

"Since I wasn't needed," she told the two, "Mr. Siple told me I could have the day off. What's this all about?"

The female officer put her hand over Sue Ellen's while the other told her the news. When Sue Ellen asked what exactly had happened, and why, the other officer nodded somberly.

"Now that you've told us about the vandalism," he said, "it all makes sense. We found some wire fused in the outlets of the table—"

"The Smart Table," said Sue Ellen, helpfully. The female officer patted her hand.

"—and it evidently made the whole table live, frying everyone around it. It shorted out the whole electrical system, not only in the office, but the whole building. The electrical surge was so powerful it melted this box in the corner—"

"The UPS," said Sue Ellen, nodding.

"—and even blew up the damned coffee maker. The sprinkler system kicked in as well. There's water, machine innards, and bodies all over the place. It's a godawful mess," finished the officer.

Sue Ellen sat silently for a moment, picturing the scene. "The jokes stopped being funny," she said, shaking her head. "What goes around, comes around."

The officers agreed. Whoever the jokester was had joked himself into oblivion with the rest of his coworkers. They gave her a moment to compose herself, then asked if she could come with them to help identify the bodies.

"It won't be pretty," the female officer warned her, "but I think you could probably help us."

Sue Ellen agreed and tucked her purse under her arm. On the way to the front door, she picked up the newspaper from the dining-room table, folded it, and put it under the TV stand. She said goodbye to Jocelyn and followed the police out the door. Sue Ellen paused, looking at the newspaper one last time before closing the door behind her, and smiled. She knew, given her affinity for machines, that finding a new, equally challenging position would be a snap.

A Neighborly Gesture

Linda K. Wright

Martha knelt, furiously scrubbing the front porch. According to her friends at The Marble Gates Holy Insanctified Church, her husband Frank was at it again.

Frank's latest infidelity had the ladies buzzing. They had no qualms about simultaneously expressing their dismay at Frank's conduct and conscientiously keeping Martha informed of all the juicy details they'd heard about his latest affair. Martha pressed her thin lips together firmly. Frank was almost sixty years old. With the children gone, Martha'd thought he'd stay home and pay more attention to her. She ridiculed herself for the thought. Frank had always had other ideas.

The sun felt hotter than usual in the hollow today, and Martha heaved a sigh as she finished cleaning. As she stood, lifting the old pail of dirty water in one hand and the scrub brush in the other, she caught a glimpse of turquoise a little ways down the road. The color she glimpsed was on a bandanna worn around the neck of a young girl with flying blonde hair. The girl—who couldn't have been much more than twenty—wore cut-off shorts, sneakers, and had tied the ends of her blouse around her slim, firm waist. When the girl saw Martha, she helloed and waved, speeding her step a bit.

Reaching Martha's house, she gasped, "Boy, am I glad to see you. I been walking the hollow for a while now, and I didn't see anyone or anywhere I could stop."

"We're pretty far away from things out here," Martha said slowly.

"Well," the girl said, "I was just wondering if I could have a drink of water. I'm so thirsty."

Martha hefted her bucket. She thought, well, that girl's sure got her nerve showing up here. Or Frank must not have told her where he lived.

Martha said aloud, "I got some lemonade I was just going to pour. You're welcome to a glass, if you'd like."

The girl climbed the three steps to Martha's porch. She stuck out her hand, saying, "Well, that's real nice of you, I'm . . ."

Martha didn't put down her bucket to shake hands. "I know who you are."

"You do?"

"You're new around here, right? Got a job at that new bar up in Big Fork?"

"The Thirsty Man, yeah." The girl, seeing Martha's hands were full, lowered her hand.

"These parts are kind of small," said Martha, by way of explanation. "News of strangers travels real fast. I'm Martha," she said, knowing if Frank had talked about his wife, he would not have mentioned her first name.

"I guess news does get around." The girl smiled. "Well, pleased to meet you, Martha," the girl bobbed her head in place of a handshake. "I sure would like to take you up on that lemonade. That's a real neighborly gesture."

Martha walked around to the back of the house with the girl following and placed the bucket and the scrub brush on the back porch. There were two wooden chairs, and she motioned for the girl to seat herself while she went into the house to get the lemonade. As Martha pulled the pitcher out of the refrigerator and poured it into two glasses, she thought about the bandanna the girl wore. Martha had last seen it in a gift box in her husband's drawer as she put his laundry away. A turquoise bandanna with a yellow border. Her sources at church had made sure to tell her that Frank had bestowed it upon his newest fling. Martha took the two glasses out to the back porch.

The girl was wiping her forehead with the bandanna and Martha saw its yellow border more clearly. The girl looked over at Martha and stretched out her hand to claim the glass of lemonade.

"Thanks. This'll sure hit the spot."

Martha watched, thinking how greedily the girl drank down half the contents of the glass without even stopping. When she did, she balanced the half-full glass on the arm of the chair as she surveyed the overturned back field.

"Looks like you'll be doing some planting out here soon," the girl said.

"Yeah," Martha said slowly. "I hadn't decided what to plant before today, but now I have." Martha placed her wide body in the other chair and, sipping her lemonade thoughtfully, looked out over the field.

Much later, Martha sat in the rocking chair in her living room, waiting for her husband to come home. The sun had set a couple of hours before. She'd taken a bath and changed her clothes after scrubbing the back porch and planting the field. She wore a short-sleeved dress and flip-flops. She rocked back and forth. A distinctive bandanna tied delicately around her throat highlighted her outfit.

In town, Frank slipped on his loafers as he sat on his latest girlfriend's bed. He'd stayed later than he'd planned and knew he should be getting home. As it was, Martha would be giving him the silent treatment, which included a repertoire of dirty looks and a cold dinner. But he had to stick around long enough to see Debbie get dressed. He always enjoyed that. She was getting ready to go to her job at the Thirsty Man. Something was missing. The bandanna he'd given her.

"Hey honey, aren't you going to wear the bandanna I gave you?"

"Oh, I forgot to tell you." Debbie came over to Frank and brushed her lips lightly against his. "You remember the girl who came into town with me, Jill?" Debbie sat down close to Frank, giving him short kisses on his neck.

"She wanted to go exploring the hollow today. In this heat, I knew she'd need something to wipe her face with, so I lent it to her. I hope you don't mind."

Frank smiled at Debbie as he was leaving. He always had admired a neighborly gesture.

Mrs. Feeley Is Quite Mad

Mabel Maney

for Miss Tinkham and Mrs. Rasmussen

Monday, February 5, Mrs. Feeley, of 37 Badger Avenue, did her wash, as usual. It was a gray day. Mrs. Feeley, as usual, first soaked Mr. Feeley's shirts in a concentrate of Duz detergent, thirty-nine cents for the large-size box *that week only* at the new Piggly-Wiggly. Then she scrubbed the collars and cuffs with a little scrub brush, five cents from the five-and-dime, put the shirts through the hand wringer and hung them on the clothesline out back to dry. There were storm clouds in the eastern sky, so Mrs. Feeley clipped Mr. Feeley's wet shirts to a makeshift line in the basement, something she knew would annoy Mr. Feeley terribly, but couldn't be helped.

"There's a place for everything, and everything in its place," Mr. Feeley had scolded Mrs. Feeley once when he had come home early and found his good shirts hanging in the dark cellar. If they had a telephone, Mr. Feeley could notify Mrs. Feeley that he was coming home at an unexpected hour, but a private telephone was a luxury the Feeleys could ill afford.

Mr. Feeley had put up the clothesline in the back yard himself, thus saving a tidy sum, and so rightly preferred Mrs.

Feeley use it as it was meant to be used and not as a resting place for the chickadees and sparrows that came around looking for bird seed, three cents a pound at Smith's Hardware, paid for by Mrs. Feeley out of her personal allowance with which she purchased stockings, facial powder, and other female fripperies.

Mr. Feeley, who was good with money and other important things, kept track of Mrs. Feeley's expenditures since it was clear that Mrs. Feeley, who had no head for numbers, would give the coat off her back to anyone with a hard-luck story and a sad smile. The coat was a perfectly good red-wool, three-quarter-length overcoat with a smart squirrel collar that was only a little worn in places and with care would see Mrs. Feeley through many more harsh winters.

Mrs. Feeley had never worked in her entire life and so didn't know the true cost of things. Some women like poor Mrs. Bederhoeffer from the Rotary Club had learned this lesson the hard way. Mr. Bederhoeffer had gone hunting one day and never returned, and was later spotted in Chicago with his secretary, Miss Dithers. Mrs. Bederhoeffer would die old and alone in a little room at her sister's. Thank goodness for Mr. Feeley, who was as loyal as the day was long.

Tuesday, after Mrs. Feeley had finished the breakfast dishes, she took Mr. Feeley's shirts from the line and sprinkled them with water from a 7-Up bottle with tiny holes punched through the cap. She had made it herself using a number two sewing needle and a hammer. Making things yourself saves you money. Mrs. Feeley had driven the needle through her nail only once and that had stopped bleeding by the time Mr. Feeley had returned home for supper. Mr. Feeley had been quick to point out that what little Mrs. Feeley had saved she had wasted in bandages for her finger. Mrs. Feeley was to remember that most accidents happen in the home, Mr. Feeley told her.

After Mr. Feeley's shirts were sufficiently dampened, Mrs. Feeley rolled them into tight bundles, squeezed them into plastic bread wrappers and stacked them in an orderly fashion in the giant stainless-steel deep-freeze in the cellar, a gift from Mr. Feeley on the occasion of her sixtieth birthday, almost exactly one year ago. Mrs. Feeley had secretly wished for a modern freezer like her best friend Myra Meeks', which was pink and went so well with her white-and-gold Formica kitchen set, but Mr. Feeley said the large commercial freezer was more economical. Mr. Feeley could bring home entire cows bought wholesale, and Mrs. Feeley could carve them with a large cleaver Mr. Feeley kept razor sharp. Mrs. Feeley often felt faint as she sawed through muscle and flesh, but she knew the savings were great and so never complained.

Mr. Feeley had gotten the idea from their next-door neighbor, Mrs. Mertz, a retired home economics teacher who ran her household as tight as a battleship. Since Mrs. Mertz was a widow, Mr. Feeley helped her with difficult chores. Not only was he a good neighbor, he picked up many helpful household tips for Mrs. Feeley.

The bottom of the freezer was lined with tidy bundles of meat, wrapped in white butcher paper and marked with a big black grease pencil. Flank. Rump. Tongue. Liver. A dozen smaller bundles occupied a corner of the deep-freeze. It was venison Mr. Feeley brought home every week, gifts from the men at work who appreciated Mr. Feeley's careful handing of their money, Mr. Feeley being a loan officer at the biggest bank in town. Some of the meat had been there for a whole year now, but Mr. Feeley had instructed Mrs. Feeley to leave it be. Mrs. Feeley figured the meat was gamy to begin with; otherwise, it would have found its way to the supper table long ago, as theirs was a frugal household.

Mr. Feeley was simply too nice to hurt anyone's feelings by turning down their gift. Besides, the freezer was so big there was plenty of room for the casseroles and vegetables Mrs. Feeley spent her afternoons putting up, not to mention Mr. Feeley's shirts. The freezer was big enough to hold a body, Myra had once pointed out, with a little laugh. It gave Mrs. Feeley the shivers every time she went downstairs.

The freezer had belonged to a butcher driven out of business by the Piggly-Wiggly supermarket and was just a tiny bit stained inside with blood. The prices were better at the Piggly-Wiggly so Mrs. Feeley shopped there now, from a list Mr. Feeley prepared for her before he went to work. It kept her from acting impulsively.

Mrs. Feeley always felt like a traitor when she walked past the small shops owned by people who had always seemed genuinely interested in her well-being. Mrs. Pringle from the bakery had even gifted Mrs. Feeley with a little pink birthday cake on her sixtieth, and everyone in the store had sung "Happy Birthday," but once Mr. Feeley had made up his mind, there was no arguing with him.

"There's a place for everything and everything in its place," Mr. Feeley had said. Clothes belonged on the clothesline, birds in the sky, and money in the bank.

Mrs. Feeley's birthday was Friday, her regular shopping day, and this year she wasn't at all looking forward to it. Last year Myra had given her a lovely rayon housecoat and matching slippers that were far too elegant for someone like Mrs. Feeley. This year Myra was at her daughter's in Cleveland helping with a new baby, a girl, so there would be no one to sing to Mrs. Feeley. Friday night was Mr. Feeley's night out with the boys. Soon Mr. Feeley would retire and be home all day, every day.

Wednesday Mrs. Feeley took Mr. Feeley's stiff, icy shirts from the freezer and, after they thawed, pressed them good and flat with an old iron heated on the gas range. The results were almost as good as a professional presser at no cost whatsoever. Mrs. Feeley sometimes felt as though she would snap in two from the effort.

Mrs. Feeley decided she would ask Mr. Feeley that very night if they could purchase a lightweight electric iron with temperature controls and a durable safety cord. It would be her birthday gift. An advertisement in *Good Housekeeping Magazine* promised it would make her ironing day a breeze. A photograph of skating star Sonja Henie illustrated this point. Mrs. Feeley's iron would glide over the cold, hard mountain of shirts like a lady skater gliding over the ice.

Myra had been a wonderful skater as a girl, so Mrs. Feeley had carefully cut out the photograph and put it in the top drawer of her sewing chest to show her later.

As she ironed, Mrs. Feeley began to smile. She imagined herself perched on gleaming white skates doing figure-eights while the ladies from the Rotary Club applauded politely. Then she imagined she was skating with Myra, her best friend in the world, and almost burned Mr. Feeley's favorite shirt!

Now that Myra was a widow and long out of mourning, she went on glamorous trips to faraway places, often inviting Mrs. Feeley along, free of charge. Short leisure trips interrupted household duties and caused havoc to Mr. Feeley, who relied on Mrs. Feeley to keep the home-fires burning while Mr. Feeley worked hard to ensure them a future in an unstable world. Just that morning Mrs. Feeley had received a postcard from the Snow Carnival in Cleveland, which only reminded Mrs. Feeley again of the electric iron she so badly wanted.

That night when Mrs. Feeley tried to bring up the subject of the iron she got confused and, to her horror, found herself telling Mr. Feeley that she wished to become a figure skater! Mr. Feeley looked alarmed but said nothing. After a while he asked Mrs. Feeley to pass the mashed potatoes. Later, while in the cellar getting sausage for the next day's breakfast, Mrs. Feeley convinced herself that Mr. Feeley hadn't heard her at all. Mrs. Feeley was awfully relieved. Many of the women in Mrs. Feeley's family had lived long, unhappy lives with no one to care for them. Mrs. Feeley was fortunate. She and Mr. Feeley would be together until death.

Thursday, as Mrs. Feeley mended the frayed cuffs of Mr. Feeley's shirts and replaced chipped buttons, she got the surprise of her life. The afternoon mail brought with it a bus ticket and a note from Myra begging her to spend her birthday in Cleveland. In her excitement, Mrs. Feeley, who hadn't gone anywhere since her honeymoon, almost forgot about the prunes stewing on the stove. The bus would leave Friday after breakfast and, after a stopover in Chicago, would arrive in Cleveland at noon. Mrs. Feeley would return first thing Monday morning, leaving plenty of time to start her wash.

Confident that Mr. Feeley would never miss her, Mrs. Feeley packed her suitcase, the same one she had taken on her honeymoon, laid the dinner dishes on the dining-room table, and waited for Mr. Feeley. She spent the afternoon rehearsing her conversation with Mr. Feeley.

But before she could finish telling Mr. Feeley about the free ticket, Mr. Feeley announced that he had news of his own. He was going hunting. He would leave right after work tomorrow and be gone the entire weekend. Mr. Feeley would need his hunting clothes, sandwiches, and beer. While he spent the evening cleaning his rifle, Mrs. Feeley must run to the supermarket before it closed and get some of that tasty spiced ham in a can, for sandwiches. Mr. Feeley didn't intend to come home after work tomorrow. He would take his things with him.

Mrs. Feeley threw on her worn red coat with the squirrel collar and practically ran to the Piggly-Wiggly. Success was assured, for even Mr. Feeley would see how practical it was for her to go away at the same time. She told everyone, even the sour store manager who never smiled at her, that Mr. Feeley was going hunting. The man who sold her the spiced ham stared at her just like Mr. Feeley did when Mrs. Feeley prattled on too long about insignificant things, as she was wont to do.

Mrs. Feeley realized with a start that she had run out of the house without her coupons, and spiced ham was on sale that week, six cans for one dollar *with coupon only.* The store manager promised she could bring her coupon tomorrow and he would give her the extra two cans, but tonight she could only have four. Mrs. Feeley ran home praying Mr. Feeley wouldn't want more than four sandwiches, only to find a startling scene in her kitchen. Her most private things, including the lovely rayon housecoat and matching slippers from Myra, were heaped in a pile on the worn linoleum kitchen floor and her suitcase was nowhere to be found.

Had Mrs. Feeley been robbed?

Mrs. Feeley jumped when she heard someone lumbering about in the cellar. Mrs. Feeley tiptoed down the stairs and was surprised to see Mr. Feeley standing near the stainless-steel deep-freeze, a package of that old venison from the boys at work in his hand. Mr. Feeley was a big man with hands like hams who moved clumsily through the world. Mr. Feeley had blurted out an abrupt proposal of marriage just weeks after his mother's death. No one else had wanted Mrs. Feeley. No one else had even asked.

Her suitcase, the one she had had long before she married Mr. Feeley, lay open nearby, packed with neat bundles of meat. Luckily, Mrs. Feeley's maiden name had also begun with an F, and so she hadn't had to get any new luggage when she married.

Mrs. Feeley cringed. The meat would thaw overnight and ruin her only suitcase! Mrs. Feeley plopped down heavily on the creaky wooden stairs and tried to stop the fluttering in her chest. How could she go to Cleveland now?

"Mr. Feeley, have you lost your mind?" Mrs. Feeley surprised herself by crying out. After thirty-five years of marriage, she knew full well that Mr. Feeley hated to converse after a hard day at work.

Mr. Feeley placed another neat bundle of meat into the suitcase, then turned to look at Mrs. Feeley.

"Mrs. Feeley," he said, running his hand over his faded brown hair, or what was left of it, "Mrs. Feeley, I'm leaving you." He said it in the same tone of voice one might have used when reporting the weather. *Showers are expected for this evening, but look for sunshine tomorrow.*

"You are going hunting," Mrs. Feeley felt confused and flushed. She clutched the paper sack containing four cans of spiced ham to her bosom.

"I am going away," Mr. Feeley corrected her, talking slowly and deliberately as if speaking to a daft child. "You'll find the mortgage papers in my top desk drawer, although they'll be of little use to you when the bank comes to collect its due."

Mrs. Feeley took off her eyeglasses and wiped them on the hem of her cotton housecoat. It was long past time for Mrs. Feeley to get stronger lenses, but she could see Mr. Feeley clear enough. A little drop of saliva clung to his bottom lip, a lip so thin and stretched it looked like an angry red mark in his large, meaty face. Mrs. Feeley must be hearing things, like that girl from Menasha who said a voice told her to jump off the Wanamukka Bridge and so she did.

"You can go live with your brother and his wife," Mr. Feeley added helpfully. "You can have all the furniture and your clothes." He took a freshly starched handkerchief from his back pocket and wiped his high, shiny forehead with it.

Bending over the deep-freeze had caused Mr. Feeley to exert himself unduly.

Mrs. Feeley realized she wasn't dreaming. "But why should I go live somewhere else?" Mrs. Feeley cried aloud. "This is my home."

Mr. Feeley ignored her frightful outburst. Mrs. Feeley obviously didn't understand the ways of the world. Mr. Feeley had done his best to protect her, but there was only so much one could do.

Mr. Feeley threw the last bundle of venison into Mrs. Feeley's suitcase. The bundle broke open, and, to Mrs. Feeley's surprise, a thick stack of hundred-dollar bills spilled out. Mr. Feeley hurriedly swooped up the money and stuffed it into the suitcase. He snapped the lid shut, tied a double length of rope around it, and secured it with a square knot.

"Don't say a word to the police about the money," Mr. Feeley hissed. "It's mine free and clear. By the time the bank misses it, I'll be long gone. They'll never trace it, and they'll never find me," he boasted. "All you know is, I went hunting and failed to return as scheduled. Do you understand?"

Mrs. Feeley understood. Mr. Feeley, it seemed, was a thief. She opened her mouth to speak but nothing came out. Mrs. Feeley sat there in her old red coat, her mouth hanging open like a marionette waiting for someone to supply the voice.

A look of relief spread over Mr. Feeley's doughy face. Mrs. Feeley would let him go without a fight.

Mrs. Feeley felt scared. She had to say something.

"I got four cans of ham," Mrs. Feeley blurted out. "They're six for one dollar but I forgot my coupon, but the manager, who's usually so rude but was quite pleasant tonight, told me I could bring back the coupon tomorrow and he'll let me have the other two cans." For as mute as she was a minute earlier, now she couldn't make herself stop talking. Mrs. Feeley talked on and on, about Myra and the Snow Carnival, the little baby girl, and how last year on her birthday Mrs. Pringle from the bakery had made her a cake, and how much she *really* wanted that new iron. Mr. Feeley looked alarmed, but didn't try to stop her. Excitement welled in Mrs. Feeley's chest. She feared she would be sick all over herself. She felt quite mad. She couldn't make herself stop talking.

"He isn't going to give you two perfectly good cans of ham for nothing. He was lying to get you to shut up," Mr. Feeley finally interrupted angrily. "You probably scared the other customers. You are quite insane, Mrs. Feeley."

"Yes, I know," Mrs. Feeley replied softly. "I am mad."

Mr. Feeley seemed a little startled by this admission. Then he smiled his false little banker's smile. He was done here and wanted business to move along. "Suppose you go upstairs and make sandwiches for my trip. There's no use letting good food go to waste," he suggested.

Mrs. Feeley, to her astonishment, didn't move. She sat still as lamb, feeling the *thump thump thump* of her heart as it beat under the worn wool of her one good coat. She flushed with embarrassment when she realized Mr. Feeley was right about the store manager. She shook her head. "I *am* mad," she said aloud, more to herself than to Mr. Feeley.

Mr. Feeley chortled triumphantly. "Mrs. Feeley," he said, "you have no common sense. God knows what's going to happen to you when I'm gone." Mrs. Feeley took a good look at Mr. Feeley. His forehead was glistening with sweat, much like the fat on a strip of bacon as it sizzled in Mrs. Feeley's griddle. Mr. Feeley liked bacon; he liked it a lot.

"You mustn't believe everything everyone tells you," he added in friendly tone that showed he was full of concern for Mrs. Feeley's welfare. Mr. Feeley prided himself on his ability to steer people in the right direction. It was his job.

Mrs. Feeley smiled. A small smile. "I won't," she assured Mr. Feeley. Then she reached into the paper sack and took out a can of spiced ham, Mr. Feeley's favorite sandwich spread on sale now at the Piggly-Wiggly, six cans for one dollar, and held it in her hand. Mrs. Feeley had never noticed before how closely Mr. Feeley resembled the cartoon pig on the label. She must remember to mention it to Myra someday.

Mrs. Feeley pitched her hand back and hurled the can right at Mr. Feeley, striking him right between his small, watery, blue, close-set eyes.

Mr. Feeley stood there, stunned. A trickle of blood ran
down his bulbous red nose. Mrs. Feeley had surprisingly
strong arms for such a tiny woman. All that ironing.

Mr. Feeley's thin lips fell apart, making a perfect "o,"
but no sound emerged. Mr. Feeley looked just like a goldfish,
Mrs. Feeley decided. She had never really liked fish, they
seemed so cold and slimy. A friendly little dog would suit her
much better.

Mrs. Feeley plucked another can of spiced ham from the
bag and pitched it right at Mr. Feeley's rather large head. Mr.
Feeley stumbled backward, lost his footing, and fell heavily
against the sharp side of the stainless-steel deep-freeze,
striking his head with a loud crack.

Mrs. Feeley sat frozen to the step. After a while, Mr.
Feeley's low moans turned to gurgles and his shallow
breathing stopped. A bad smell wafted toward Mrs. Feeley.
It was the smell of death. Mrs. Feeley was well acquainted
with that odor, having spent many hours in that dark cellar
wielding a sharp cleaver over some poor beast destined for
the deep-freeze.

Mrs. Feeley sighed. She had never wanted this enormous
appliance in her house, but Mr. Feeley had said she must live
with it and so she had.

Friday, Mrs. Feeley, of 37 Badger Avenue, boarded the
bus for Cleveland. This was her first trip since her
honeymoon, when she and Mr. Feeley had stayed in his
cousin's cabin at nearby Bear Lake. This time Mrs. Feeley
might never come back. There was no law against it, after
all. By Tuesday, maybe Wednesday, Mr. Feeley's absence
from the bank would be cause for concern. A bank official
would come to the house and find it deserted. Mr. Feeley, it
seemed, had gone on a hunting trip and had never come
home. His theft would surface eventually, but by then it
would be too late. Mr. Feeley would be long gone.

The house would be sold to pay the back taxes. The
threadbare furnishings would be hauled away by the junk
man. Mrs. Mertz, who had taught home economics for
thirty-five years and so knew all there was to know about
spoilt food, would keep the rump roast Mrs. Feeley had
wrapped for the deep-freeze only last week but would know
to throw away the large quantity of three-year-old pork,

marked in Mrs. Feeley's tidy hand. Mrs. Mertz would think
Mrs. Feeley had fallen down on her duty as a homemaker,
keeping old meat like that around, but it couldn't be helped.

Mrs. Mertz would find four empty cans stacked neatly
on the drainer, but no other sign of the Feeleys. While it
would come as a shock that Mr. Feeley was a thief, it would
surprise no one that Mrs. Feeley had disappeared along with
him. She always was such a devoted wife.

Mrs. Feeley smoothed the skirt of her one good suit, a
lightweight black crepe she took out of mothballs only for
weddings and funerals, and tucked her shoes out of sight
under her seat. They were so worn the leather was
paper-thin and cracked in places. She had had no room for
any of her clothes as her only suitcase had already been
packed, by Mr. Feeley. The suitcase was at her feet where she
could keep an eye on it, although the chances of anyone
stealing a worn pasteboard box with a rope holding it
together seemed slim.

In a paper sack on her lap was the lovely rayon
housecoat and matching slippers from Myra and four tasty
spiced-ham sandwiches, wrapped in wax paper. Mrs. Feeley
had been too excited to eat a proper breakfast, and there
was no telling when the driver would stop for a snack.
Besides, there was no sense letting good food go to waste.

LITTLE GIRL TELLS

Beth Brant

The first time it happened to her, she didn't tell
Grandmother or Mother. She quietly walked to the stream
that wound its way through the reservation and washed the
sticky mess off her clothes and hands. Mr. Turner, pulling
her ponytail and twisting it in his left hand, unzipping his
pants with his right hand, pushing her head down against
the open zipper, told her she would die if she told.

She stood in the stream, raising handfuls of water to her
face, warblers darting in and out of the dogwood that grew
close to the edge of the water. She wondered if she would
truly die, how such a thing could happen by telling the truth.
She lay down in the sun, feeling the heat caress her, and
thought about her friend Jonelle. Jonelle, who was one year
older and therefore more knowledgeable, said that Mr.
Turner was gross. That he sometimes did nasty things to the
girls and maybe even the boys. She called Mr. Turner a name
Little Girl had never heard: "Pervert." Jonelle said that
because Mr. Turner was white, nobody would believe a
bunch of Indian kids if they told; so they just tried to stay
out of his way. Little Girl decided that she would not tell,
just in case death was waiting behind the maple tree where
Mr. Turner hid. Death might be scarier than Mr. Turner,
might hurt her even more.

Little Girl lay in the sun until her clothes were dry. The sticky places had dried sharp, like pins. Then she went home, where she pretended that she was the same girl who woke that morning and went to school and had a day like all the others. When Grandmother and Mother asked her what she had learned in school, she found it easy to lie, even though lying was something she didn't do in front of these two women who made up her life.

The second time Mr. Turner caught her, she was on her way home from school again, walking the distance between the woods and her home. This time the zipper opened and Mr. Turner wanted her to take his ugly thing in her mouth. It was like a fat worm, and as it crawled into her mouth, she bit and ran. Mr. Turner came after her, but tripped on a tree root, and she ran and ran, heart thumping in her small chest, until she reached the trailer where her family lived.

"I'll kill you if you tell," Mr. Turner's hoarse and angry shouts followed her. But this time she didn't lie. Now she believed that death, like Mr. Turner, was something that would not dare show its face to Mother and Grandmother.

Later that night, she woke from a nightmare, feeling the women's cool hands on her face, drinking the warm herbs and water they held to her lips. "This will heal you." She fell back asleep, listening to Mother's and Grandmother's soft voices whispering in Mohawk. Before she understood what was said, she fell asleep and dreamed of gold-green grass, meadowlarks singing of spring, turtles coming up from the bottom of the stream to sit in the sun.

As the weeks went by, Grandmother took Little Girl to school and picked her up. Little Girl was not allowed to play with friends unless they came to her place. She was never out of the reach of her family. "Don't worry. We are taking care of you."

Miss Evans, who was the neighbor of Mrs. Turner, was told that Mr. Turner awoke one morning with a sore left arm. As the day progressed, a scarlet mark appeared on the arm. Mr. Turner's employees at the gas station remarked that he took to bathing the arm in ice water and rubbing the scarlet mark. "It burns. It burns," he jokingly told his coworkers. Yet, they said, he seemed in pain. That night, a long straight pin worked its way out of his arm. Mrs. Turner was bewildered, but Mr. Turner laughed and said he was damned if he knew how that pin got in him.

The next morning, Miss Evans said, Mr. Turner awoke with an identical pain in his right arm. This time, the scarlet mark didn't appear until he was eating dinner. He cursed, yelled to his wife to fix an ice bag which he wore all that night. Mrs. Turner told Miss Evans that she didn't get a wink of sleep that night, what with changing ice bags and listening to Mr. Turner yell and complain all night. The next morning, the scarlet mark broke open and a small gray worm crawled out of the wound and curled up in Mr. Turner's hand. "He jumped almost ten feet in the air," Mrs. Turner said. Mr. Turner flushed the worm down the toilet and went to work. His employees said that he was pretty quiet that day and kept unpeeling the bandages on his arms as if he were looking for something.

Little Girl didn't hear these stories. She went about her daily routine—school, home, TV, sometimes going to the grocery store with Mother, feeding the chickens, braiding corn with Grandmother. She did notice that more and more of the people came to their home at night. Speaking in Mohawk, whispering among themselves when the children got too close. The children played, but their usual loud laughter and talk was subdued.

Miss Evans said that a few weeks went by before Mr. Turner had another episode. One morning he woke up and both arms and hands were burning and sore. This time, Mrs. Turner got him to go to the doctor. The doctor probed and pinched and gave Mr. Turner a cream. He could give no explanation for the worm or the pin. Mr. Turner rubbed the cream on his hands and arms and stayed home from work that day. Mrs. Turner swore that at one point Mr. Turner was crying from the pain. "But don't tell no one, dear," she told Miss Evans. "You know how men are."

Soon Mr. Turner was blooming with scarlet marks. They dotted his upper arms down to his fingertips. It was said by Miss Evans that she could hear him cursing and moaning from morning till night. He didn't leave the house, just sat in his chair applying the medicine and moaning.

Then one day Miss Evans heard Mrs. Turner screaming. She says she ran next door and there was Mr. Turner, lying on the floor, arms and hands erupting with blood, and in the blood were pins. Short pins, long pins, straight, shining silver pins. Miss Evans said it was a horrible sight. She thinks she screamed, but was busy helping Mrs. Turner clean up the mess.

Mrs. Turner told Miss Evans that after that day, Mr. Turner got religion. He started going to the Calvary Baptist Church. They had never been churchgoers, but Mr. Turner dragged Mrs. Turner to church every Sunday and even on Wednesday nights. She told Miss Evans that she getting sick and tired of it. That Mr. Turner acted like a man possessed by something, and if he didn't stop this nonsense, she was going to do something about it.

Mrs. Turner did do something. Miss Evans said that early Sunday morning she saw Mrs. Turner fill the car with suitcases and drive away. "She didn't even say goodbye," Miss Evans exclaimed.

Stories about what happened next varied, but most people seemed to agree on the fact that Mr. Turner was seen running naked through the street, screaming, his face and body covered with scarlet marks. He ran to the Calvary Baptist Church, where the preacher was said to turn away from the awful sight. He ran to the police station where the officers say he shouted, "I did it. I did it. Tell them to leave me alone. Tell them." As he stood in the doorway of the police station, Mr. Turner's body was raining blood, pins, and worms all over the steps and floor of the station. Some of the officers were made sick by the gore. Some screamed. Some ran away. In the end, a cooler head prevailed and wrapped Mr. Turner in a coat and escorted him to a cell where he poured out tale after tale about young Indian girls from the reservation and what he had done to them, not stopping for breath.

Mr. Turner lived. People were surprised; they couldn't imagine how anyone could lose so much blood, not to mention those disgusting worms and pins being inside his body. Since they were a god-fearing, Christian town, a story began to take form that it was a punishment from God. Imagine, having a child molester right in their own midst. Even if it was those Indian kids he molested, God still didn't think it was right, and anyway, he might have started on their own kids next.

Eventually, the people from the reservation heard the story. As they shopped at the grocery store, or filled their cars with gas, they heard about the wrath of God, the bloody punishment from on high. The people from the reservation shook their heads, "Is that right?" they said.

Little Girl heard the story from Jonelle, who claimed that those people in town were stupid. How could they not know what Mr. Turner was up to? she wanted to know. "Stupid," she proclaimed.

As Little Girl walked home, she walked by the places where Mr. Turner had caught her. She touched the tree root; she waded in the stream that had washed her clean. She heard the warblers as they flew past her, alighting in their dogwood. She wandered home, where Mother and Grandmother were hanging up the wash. They smiled at their beloved girl. "Everything's okay now."

Little Girl lay down in the sun. The hot, yellow globe danced around the sky, drying the sheets and towels, bathing her with heat. She laughed out loud, startling the robin who hunted in the dirt by her feet. She watched him fly away—higher, higher until he was a tiny spot in the sky.

Catacombs

Helena Basket

I ran away after church on a typical Baltimore Sunday in July: the sky was purple-green and sour, the wind filled with fumes from the harbor, Bethlehem Steel, and the Carling Brewery. I didn't have a particular plan, just to be out on my own, practicing to be a grown-up. I walked along, the damp breeze blowing up Charles Street from the harbor at my back, fairly certain my mother would take another route home and not see me here. She was set in her ways, and I had run away before. She knew all she had to do was wait for me in the kitchen, and I would show up sooner or later. I sweated as I walked, day-dreaming about a normal mom.

I glanced over my shoulder at the sound of a car coming up the street. It was someone else's Dodge Dart, not Mom's Plymouth Barracuda. Although I knew it was irrational, I felt sulky that she wouldn't look for me. She knew I could take care of myself, and I knew she enjoyed having more time for her anger to fester. I never stayed long when I took off like this, and it didn't really matter what I did anyway. I might as well take what I needed where I could get it.

At that moment, I knew where I was walking: to the Catacombs, deep inside the Walters Art Gallery a few blocks up Charles. In the cool dusk of the Catacombs, I could visit Joan of Arc and prepare myself for battle with my mother.

Heavy lavender clouds sank through the deep sky above me. A thunderboomer was brewing. The heat envelope from the asphalt began to parch my mouth. I tried to stay in the shade of the buildings. I crossed a bubbling tarmac street near the Gallery, which loomed against the road. The marble museum, taller than the churches and brownstones around it, shimmered opalescent in the eerie storm sky. A long, purple-and-gold banner flapped limply from an upper balcony, proclaiming July "Celebrate Maryland: Official State Sport Jousting" month.

"Dreary day," I muttered to myself. The museum would be refreshing, shadowy, and dry. I rummaged in my pocket as I approached and dug out my student ID. Climbing the steps to the Charles Street entrance, I pulled open the heavy brass door. Inside, the chill, dim passageway was blocked by a small, dark wood ticket box where a black man in a red uniform leaned comfortably on the counter. "Yes, miss?" he asked.

"Student," I said, and showed him my Baltimore County Day School ID.

"Fine school, there, young lady," he commented, and handed me a tin button to clip to my collar. The button was navy blue with a white phoenix printed on it. "Know where you're headed?" asked the guard.

"Yes, sir, the Catacombs," I said respectfully.

"Ah, the Armor Room," he said knowingly, putting his finger beside his shiny brown nose. The only people who ever spent time in the Armor Room were jousting fanatics and Renaissance Festival people, and weirdoes like me. I smiled at the guard and went past him into the marble-floored museum gallery. Along the walls were chambers stocked with jeweled chalices and moth-eaten tapestries, glass cases of ancient coins and signet rings from Alexander's empire. Under the tall, arched windows were squeaky, red leather couches wonderful for studying and napping. A red velvet rope blocked passage through the narrow doorway that led into the depths of the museum. I unhooked its brass clip and slipped through, rehooking it behind me.

A staircase twisted down steeply, the marble risers worn deeply in the middle so that my feet pigeoned as I stepped down. I touched the curving wood railing gently to guide

myself and went down quickly, cautious of lurking
war-spirits. Cast-iron sconces lit the wall with banded,
yellow light. A gentle breeze blew up the staircase, lifting my
hair. I trailed my fingertips along the railing. There was no
sound save my tapping feet and the breeze.

The staircase ended as soon as I rounded the second
revolution, and my imagination soared: the Catacombs, the
Armor Room. The Armor Room was the old stone basement
of a nineteenth-century mansion that had been transformed
into the Walters Art Gallery when its venerable owner died.
Mr. Walters had built his mansion with an eye for the
romantic, and his cellar was a dim, vaulted crypt, a secret
stone dungeon under the depths of Baltimore's finest street.
The cellar was constructed out of dark gray stone. Each
vault in the ceiling arched over a room-sized nook. Ten or
twelve of these nooks stuck out from the central archway,
like the many arms of a Celtic cross. The nooks were lined
from floor to ceiling with glass cases edged in polished
wood, and backed by richly colored velvet. Tiny silver hooks
stuck out from the velvet walls, and from these hooks hung
weapons, shields, and armor.

I turned into the first nook and gazed intoxicated at the
glass case backed with amber velvet. In this nook hung
swords, clubs, bludgeons, cudgels, scimitars, rapiers, sabers,
broadswords, cutlasses, fencing foils, jousting lances, spears,
pikes, maces, and javelins. Among their muted glints, I saw
the bright eyes of soldiers dead in battle, and I imagined
them having died to protect me. I held my hand on the glass
over a ruby-jeweled golden dagger, the kind a besieged
princess would use to disembowel her attackers. A tiny red
light blinked at me from the corner of the case. I trailed my
hand silently along the glass and rested it again at a bayonet
emerging from a carved mahogany walking stick. I imagined
effortless murder, the bayonet slipping through coat and
shirt to slice out Jack the Ripper's kidneys. I saw frothing
hordes of demons and malefactors falling at my feet,
cowering, slain, stilled.

At the edge of the nook, before it emerged into the main
cavern, stood a tarnished suit of armor on a brass-studded
wooden box. I squared my shoulders in front of the dead
soldier. It was not as tall as I. The faceplate was down over

the invisible face, and I peered into the eye-slits hoping for a
glimmer of ghost. The carapace stared back at me, empty
and sullen. I danced my fingers along the rigid forearm,
tapped lightly on the chain mail hanging over its gut, looking
for rusty spots from dried blood. Dust motes sprang from
the tightly woven metal links. I wondered if mail could mute
the force of my mother's fists, or if it would add teeth to the
blows. My mother was the kind of person who would pour
boiling oil on a knight and laugh as the knight's flesh fell off
his bones like barbecue. I imagined what it would feel like to
be stewed alive in a suit of armor while clinging to a castle
wall. I imagined my last anguished moments, the boiling oil
coating my skin inside the armor as I reached up, valiant and
blind, to slit the throat of the murderous defender. I
imagined my mother's soft throat caught on the end of my
spear, dragging her out from her safe spot behind the wall,
flinging her over my head and into the moat where savage
piranhas thrashed in anticipation. In my dying act I would
destroy her, feed her to a thousand tiny mindless jaws.

In the aftermath of murder, I found myself sweaty. The
Catacombs were still. A distant air-conditioning vent
murmured and I heard the words *withdraw, escape, secede,
flee*. I found myself staring at the suit of armor's crotch, a
worn and moth-eaten red velvet codpiece just big enough to
hold an apple. "That's a man," I mumbled, disappointed,
and looked away. As my eyes left the codpiece, I thought I
saw a flicker of movement from the black slits in the helmet.
Maybe a moth, maybe a ghoul. My heart raced and I went
across the hall into another nook. This one was full of piece
armor and shields for people and horses. Here I would find
my equipment. In my mind's eye, Joan of Arc rode toward to
me through screaming clouds of bloody dust, and quickly I
began to pick my weapons so I could mount my warhorse
and join her. First I selected a dull steel faceplate for my fiery
steed. The face plate had steel hoods over the eyes and
nostrils so the horse could see and breathe but be protected
from blows. Then I selected a polished brass bit and fastened
it firmly to a wormy leather bridle. I snatched up a
chain-mail garment for myself, staggering under the load. I
pulled on a helmet covered with jewels and enamel, and

slipped on heavy leather gauntlets. Then I read the tiny
cardboard sign: falconer's gloves.

"Whoops, wrong gloves," I whispered to Joan of Arc.
Behind me her steed stamped impatiently and blew out a
smoky huff in annoyance.

"Make haste, my valiant knight!" shouted Joan. I drew
an embroidered cape over my shoulders, stepped into huge
leather boots with steel plates on the tops, and shouldered
an intricately engraved bronze shield. I turned to face my
leader, waiting for her approval.

I met the eyes of a thin, pale boy a few years younger
than I, wearing a dark, shiny Sunday suit and a clip-on plaid
bow-tie. I let my fierce pose drop slowly, not quite sure if he
was real, not knowing if he had seen me imagining.

"What are you doing?" he asked.

I took a deep breath. "Waiting for my mother to get out
of church," I said defensively.

"Girls aren't supposed to be down here," he said
condescendingly. "This is the Armor Room."

I put my hands on my hips, certain he did not know half
as much about the mysteries of this room as I did.

"Want a Tootsie Roll?" asked the boy suddenly. He
stuck out his hand and offered me one. I realized he was just
bluffing, that I had probably startled him as much as he had
me.

"Sure," I said, reaching out to accept the candy.

"Psych!" he yelled, and scuttled off into another nook. I
stood frozen, embarrassed, angry. How did boys get this
power?

From a distance I heard a woman calling, "Joey, Joey,
where are you?" I heard the boy's shoes scuffing down the
corridor away from me.

"Joey, your mama wants you," I snarled. His footsteps
receded into the depths of the Catacombs. *Good riddance!* I
thought, but then I heard him trotting back. My shoulders
ached, and I tried to ignore him and go back to the
battlefield with Joan. No luck.

The boy whirled into my nook, white-faced. "There's a
ghost back there, in the Japanese warrior section," he
panted, wide-eyed.

"Yeah, right." I snapped. "I been here a million times and I never seen a ghost." Why share my secrets with this jerk? Boys didn't know shit about ghosts.

Joey shrugged, then. "I don't care," he said huffily, then turned his head and paled again. Joey swallowed a wad of mucus and whined, "You don't believe me? Come on, I'll show you!" He stomped off into the back of the Catacombs and turned into the farthest nook where the Japanese warriors stood guard. I was a little afraid of those soldiers, with their huge triangular jaws and fingernails like sabers. Japanese armor looked like demons, designed to horrify. I followed Joey apprehensively. "Come on," he called.

I went into the last, dimly-lit nook, and he caught me sharply by the wrist. "Come on, scaredy-cat!" he hissed. A stiff line of armored specters receded into the nook, holding their weapons upright, ragged pennants hanging limp from the handles.

Joey pushed his hands against my shoulders, and I staggered into the glass case along the far wall. "Hey!" I shouted, wrenching myself away from him. I forced myself not to hit the glass too hard, fearing it would break, and I ended up closer to him than I wanted to be. The blinking red light caught my eye and unnerved me.

"I told you girls aren't supposed to be in here," growled Joey, and then he tried to kiss me, his breath foul with Tootsie Rolls and nerves. Sickened and furious, I shoved him away from me, wishing the samurai would awake and do him violence, but he held onto my shirt and pushed me into the glass case again.

"Quit it, Joey, it's going to break!" I yelled, slapping at him and trying to twist away. In the corner of my eyes, I thought I saw the Japanese warrior's pennant tremble. I heard something scrabbling inside the intricate chain mail, and thought of rabid mice.

Joey put up his elbow and slammed it into my side. I gasped and bent over, and he kneed me in the stomach hard enough to make me groan and double over entirely. The warrior creaked, and its left glove dropped an inch. The air-conditioning vent mumbled and cut off. We froze.

From the distance the woman's voice came again, "Jo-ey, Jo-ey."

I glared up at the boy through my hair and lashed out one foot, catching him on the shin. "Your mother wants you, you little shit," I whispered hoarsely.

Joey stood over me for a moment, clearly wanting to do more damage, but clearly nervous.

"Better go," I whispered again, and then, shamefully, "I won't tell on you." The emperor's guard stood motionless, scornful. I imagined even the mice were disgusted with me. So much for being Joan of Arc's right hand.

Joey spat at me, and his aim was poor. A bubbly wad of spit and Tootsie Roll slapped onto the stone floor near my foot. I didn't flinch, but stared at it as if it were fire. Joey's shiny shoes whirled and he took off running, screaming, "Lesbo, lesbo, dirty lesbo!" all the way out of the dungeon and up the main stairs toward his mother.

I collected myself and fought off tears of shame and anger. No sense losing my composure here, in my safe dungeon. I walked slowly toward the exit and my secret staircase. I glanced sadly at the glass cases filled with weapons and armor, wishing that just once I could shatter the glass and take a spear for my very own, and a small, jeweled dagger to hide in my sleeve. There was much I needed protection from. As I passed each glowing nook, I imagined encouraging whispers saying, *Be brave, valiant knight, be brave.*

I reached the foot of my secret staircase and stopped when I saw that Joey had spat there, too, leaving a shiny splat on the bottom step. I felt defiled. I turned away from the winding stairs and went out the main door, up utilitarian concrete steps and out the side entrance near the museum shop. Joey was standing in the shop near a tall, frail-looking woman. He tugged her sleeve and pointed at me as I passed. I looked hopefully at her, hoping she would smack him, but she made a disgusted face and put her arm around him protectively. I left.

◆

The wind had cooled and thinned, and Charles Street heading back toward the bus stop home was overcast and gloomy. The thunderstorm was near. My hair began to curl.

I hunched inside my shirt and began the long, slow dread of going home, knowing that punishment for my escape would be swift and severe. I snuck into a flyer-pasted doorway to wait for the bus.

Once on the bus, I stared out the greasy window at the heavy Baltimore day. Off to the left spread the long vista of a grand old cemetery, disappearing into the lavender and yellow haze over the harbor, rising to thunderheads scooting up the bay toward the city. I gazed thoughtfully at the rows of gravestones and angel-capped pylons, thinking about death. When would it come? How soon was my relief?

I rested my sweaty forehead on the bus window. The sky was darkening to a rich green-gray. The fresh wind slipped through the bus windows. I was the only passenger left as the bus roared along the road toward my mother's house. The thunder sounded like a troop of roller skaters on a freshly-waxed rink.

It was time for me to pull the greasy cord and tell the driver to let me off. I could have walked to the front of the bus to say thanks and good-bye, but I felt surly and tired, so when he braked to a stop I snuck off the side door. I trotted the short block to my mother's house, hunched against the first drops of cold rain. I wondered what form my punishment would take this time: a simple beating with a hairbrush or ruler, or perhaps her rage would have passed normal levels and she would slap and kick me until I curled up like a hedgehog. Feeling sick, I trudged up to the kitchen door, letting myself get soaked with grimy rain, and opened the screen-door quietly.

My mother stood in the kitchen waiting for me, her face white and her eyes protruding. Her lips were wet. She was gripping the kitchen counter with one hand, and her other hand was clawing at her dress. I wondered how long she had been standing there like that, waiting for me. I knew I was in for it. The thunderboomers rolled closer with a great, cold gust of rainy wind. The screen sucked itself shut with a bang.

"Where did you go?" hissed Mom. She controlled herself with effort, a thick vein in her neck rippling.

Rain slammed against the screen and shattered inside on my neck and arm. I set my bag down carefully on the pale linoleum floor next to me.

"Don't litter the place with your trash!" shrieked my mother, but she did not move to touch me. I stared at her carefully, wanting to foresee. There was a brilliant crash of light, and a thunderhead exploded just overhead.

Mom began to quiver, and tears rose like blisters in her eyes. "Come here, Beatrice," said my mother softly. I knew better than to run. I picked up my bag from the center of the floor and set it down again on the radiator. My hands were shaking. I wanted something to do with them. "Are you sorry for what you've done?" asked Mom softly. I nodded faintly, looking at the radiator. The rain slowed. It didn't matter if I was sorry or not, or even how penitent I looked. She was following an internal script now, one that twisted and turned away from me.

I stepped slowly toward her, not wanting to set her off, not knowing what would. There was always the chance that she would feel guilty or grief-stricken, or maybe even proud of me. I never knew. I looked cautiously into her eyes, hoping she would love me. Suddenly she bellowed, "How can you disrespect me, you demon child!" She flung her pale, strong arm across her chest, and then swung at me back-handed. Her knuckles caught me in the temple, and I fell.

My glasses crashed against the side of my nose and skittered off onto the scuffed linoleum. Pain bloomed in my nose like lightning tendrils. I tried to follow where the glasses went, my dim eyes tracing their wobbly tortoise-shell outline along the floor past Mom's faded Keds, my ears roaring—or perhaps it was the rain—and in that moment of unawareness she hit me again, this time knocking me across the room into the counter. I felt myself disengaging, slipping outside into the cherry tree where I could not feel her. I hit the wood counter hard, and felt my hip bone sharply through the muscles of my hip. I saw her as a black-and-white shadow, an outline of something to be avoided. *Why why why why* raced through my head.

I was moving in slow motion, calculating how much to relax and how much to tense as she swung again. The edge of her hand caught my jaw and I heard a dull painful pop—or maybe it was a lightning strike on the transformer outside. I bit down hard on the edge of my tongue. *It doesn't*

matter, screamed my brain, *I feel nothing, I feel nothing.*
Mom's hand whipped out and the bony knuckles connected
with my lip. I felt a comforting warmness spread down my
chin and touched my lip with my aching tongue. *I'm hungry,*
I'm tired. Outside it poured.

When I tasted my blood, rage boiled up in me. I peeked
through my tears for a knife, an iron skillet. But Mom's
imminence prevented me from killing her. I knew she would
fight me horribly, and the pain would freeze my body. I
knew I would not kill her while I clung to the wall of her
castle and that she would indeed set me afire with oil from a
flaming barrel while she laughed.

"Why can't you be a real daughter to me!" wailed my
mother, and kicked my arms and legs as I writhed away
from her. Inside my head I chanted, *I feel nothing, I am*
dead, I feel nothing, I am not here, it doesn't matter, I am
dead, I feel nothing.

Between her sobs, Mom hummed tunelessly, drumming
her fingertips on the counter, hugging herself with one arm. I
curled up around the cold grate along the bottom of the
"fridge and waited until she left the kitchen. I pressed my
sore mouth against the metal, sucking coolness into my
tongue. Moments moved slowly, steadily, forward. I felt
nothing.

◆

I uncurled cautiously. My back ached and I felt feverish.
My lips were swollen and did not quite come together. I
noticed drool trickling out between them onto my chin.
Without warning, a wave of anger poured over me and I felt
hatred boiling hard enough to melt the flesh off my bones. I
fought it down. No sense causing myself any more harm.

Listening carefully for Mom's footsteps upstairs, I
crawled awkwardly to my feet. Some of my muscles were
seizing up; some were asleep. My skin burned with the prints
of her hands. I could feel the blood punching through the
capillaries in my new bruises. As soon as I could stand
without clutching the "fridge, I began to limp toward the
basement door. I could hear her humming and crying
upstairs, and knew she was off in her own world. I was safe

for the moment, and if I could get to the cellar before she remembered me then I would be safe through the night.

Mom was afraid of the basement and only went there to do laundry on bright, sunny days. I edged carefully through the short hallway to the basement door, pulled the door open cautiously, took off my shoes, and snuck down the wooden stairs, knowing where to avoid creaks in the boards. I grazed my fingertips along the cracked plaster of the stairwell and listened carefully for noises. I heard the muted slap of rain and thunder buried deep above, the quiet scratching of mice in the walls, the wisps of sound from my feet on the stairs. Faint, grainy light flowed up the stairwell from the basement windows, tucked under the rafters and hinged from above so one could crawl in and out if the upstairs doors were locked. My throat hurt with tears. *She does not love me, she does not love me. Nobody loves me,* I moaned inside my head.

When I stepped into the cool, quiet cellar, the floor was slick and dark with seeping water from the rain, and the outer surfaces of the ground-level window panes were splattered with mud. Along the grimy white-washed stone walls hung a rake and a coiled hose, an ax, hedge clippers, and a saw shaped like a one-stringed harp. The rafters were bare and ribbed with nicks from the axes that had formed them. Hooks screwed into the rafters suspended my mother's clotheslines across the basement. A load of damp linens hung limply there, rippling gently in a silent draft, as if someone had just left, but the water on the floor was still.

In the corners of the basement, I saw shadows move, and I reminded myself desperately that I was good at imagining. I stepped slowly through the water, concentrating on the coolness bathing the skin of my feet, willing my heart to slow down. I recognized the feverish sparkle of adrenaline that would keep me awake and sweating long into the night. I needed a warm spot to curl up in, where I could leave my body safely while my mind soared into the night sky with the thunder clouds.

I passed slowly through the alleys of laundry, trailed my fingers through shadowed sheets, towels, and pillow cases. The laundry was a comfort, swaying quietly, enveloping me like fog. I took a handful of linen and pressed it against my face, sucking air through it into my aching mouth. My tears and sweat dissipated into the cool, damp cloth. The towels closed gently around me. I shook with a sudden chill, wanted to sit down but was afraid of the seeping slimy water under my feet. The towels against my bruises were cool, comforting, almost alive in my hands. I felt gentle pressure easing the ache, but nothing reached inside to quell the rippling nausea.

When I was little I used to crouch in the laundry basket, covered with clothes, and she couldn't find me. When I emerged triumphant, she said I was cute and clever and gave me hugs. I remembered those hugs, remembered feeling alarmed as her arms came toward me, flinching away from her, and how her eyes went from crazy sweet to crazy hurt-and-angry in one blink.

Thunder was moving away from the house, leaving the slow simmer of humidity to poach the rain-washed air. Between the slaps of rain on mud, I thought I heard my mother's heavy footsteps on the floor above my head. My heart leaped and my guts twisted, my legs felt bare and vulnerable below the edges of the towels. The towels clung to my skin, and I shut my eyes and sobbed silently. There was a gentle rumble in the far corner as the sump pump measured the water to see if it was time to suck it outside. I didn't hear my mother any more.

There was a toilet-closet in a corner of the basement near the sump pump. I let go of the damp towels and passed through the swaying wall of laundry. The cloth caressed me as I pushed through. I shut the bathroom door behind me and pulled the light cord, amazed that I could still function so well. I squinted at myself in the cracked and blistered mirror above the sink. My face was ugly and blotchy and plums were rising on my mouth, my eyebrow, my nose. I touched my cheeks and looked at myself, hopeless. I was so ugly, so repulsive, no wonder she hated me so. I felt entirely worthless. *Why should someone live like this? What made it worthwhile?* Hot tears of self-pity swelled in my eyes and rolled out onto my damp cheeks. Joan of Arc would never put up with this. I bared my teeth at myself in the mirror. My top front gums were raw where the impact of her hand had smashed the flesh against my teeth. My tongue was raw

where I'd bitten it. My mind leapt ahead to school
tomorrow, and I was overcome with grief and despair. *How
would I explain this?* Crying, I turned on the faucet and
rinsed my mouth with tap water. Outside, the rain rattled
steadily on the garbage can lids and the cement sidewalk.

I rested my hands on the cool porcelain sides of the sink
and stared at the insides of my elbows, where tough, blue
veins emerged from my white, freckled skin. I thought of
taking the rusty packet of razor blades from inside the
medicine chest and slicing through my skin to those firm ripe
veins. I felt so weak already, loss of blood would put me
gently to sleep.

The rainfall became unbearably loud, and thunder
cracked just outside, as if it had speared the old cherry tree
by the back door. In the mirror, I saw the bathroom door
swing open sharply. It slammed against the wall. A sudden
urgent twanging sounded, as if the tines of the rake were
being plucked. I whirled and saw the shadowy laundry
shivering wildly along the clotheslines. The towels and sheets
were swinging, bobbing on their lines, snapping themselves
above the roar of the rain. I felt dead calm inside me. The
sump pump roared to life and bellowed with a hollow metal
voice, *Be brave, valiant knight, be brave!* Fright overcame
me and my guts moved. I tried to kick the bathroom door
shut while leaning over the toilet to vomit, but the door was
immobile and I couldn't throw up. The pillowcases reached
toward me, blowing toward me in a gale wind. The sump
pump crackled and grumbled, whined, moaned at me,
Beatrice! Come here! Come here and climb down into me!
Thunder boomed and lightning flashed in the yard outside. I
felt my blood thinning in terror and collapsed exhausted on
the toilet seat. I knew I would not kill myself.

As if it had never spoken, the sump pump relaxed into
its usual gentle rumble, and I saw slight tremors cross the
black surface of the water as it was drawn into the depths of
the pump. Upstairs I heard Mom's footsteps walking calmly
across the floor toward the kitchen. The towels relaxed,
seemed to beckon to me, damp and soft and protective. The
cord of the bathroom light whipcracked on my neck, and I
leaped forward out the bathroom door into the wet
basement. I saw lightning through the muddy windowpanes

and ran open-armed into the laundry. The towels closed
around me protectively.

The cellar door opened and I heard my mother
whispering, "Beatrice? Are you down there?" She took one
cautious step down the staircase and paused, whispering
hoarsely, "Beatrice?"

I shrugged off the laundry and reached for the ax.

Edna & Carole

Joyce Wagner

Edna could see Carole's manicured toes through the glassy stillness of the bath water. *Pushing sixty and she still paints her toenails like a teenager.* Edna allowed herself a curdle of sentiment toward her perfect sister and then snapped back to the task at hand. The shower curtain was drawn, as if Carole had something to hide after all the years they had lived together. Edna wiped the fog from the mirror over the basin and stared at the pudgy middle-aged woman staring back. Her hair was Clairol "old lady" red, and squarish glasses sat atop a bulbous nose sprinkled with undeserved gin blossoms. It always seemed to Edna a cruel joke that she and Carole looked so different. Same parents, different combinations of genes. She had always felt that Carole, with her slim body, elegant taste, irreproachable nose, and black hair—now graying splendidly—got the better combination. She was sure Carole felt that way, too. Edna peered into a face that easily appeared ten years older than Carole's. No one would guess Edna was the junior of the two.

Edna's eyes fell from her reflection to the face cloth she was wringing over the sink, then to the blow dryer perched precariously close to the edge of the vanity. She had suggested to Carole several times that it might not be good practice to set it so close to the tub, especially when it was still plugged in. Carole agreed, but kept doing it anyway. The very day before, Edna had mentioned to their friend Dorothy how Carole was so tidy about every little thing but that and wasn't it downright dangerous? "Practically suicidal!" Edna had remarked and, of course, Dorothy agreed.

Edna couldn't see her face, but she knew Carole had thin slices of cucumbers covering her eyes. She smiled when she thought of Carole's salt-and-pepper hair curling in the humidity and the white vegetable rounds where eyes should be, like a middle-aged Little Orphan Annie.

Edna opened the door to allow some of the super-heated fog to escape the room. Carole did not stir. The dog next door was barking his Sunday-morning bark as people passed on the way to church. The only sound inside the house was the "boik, boik, boik" of the faucet dripping into the bath water. As Edna leaned over to tighten the knob and stop the leak, one of her enormous breasts brushed against the blow dryer, then pushed it off the vanity. It hit the side of the tub with a crack, bounced up, came down again, sliding down the inside of the tub and into the water. It hissed and it sizzled; then the circuit breaker deep in the corner of the basement broke, and it stopped.

Eyes closed, fingers splayed across the bottom of her face, shoulders hunched, Edna could hear nothing but the dog, the faucet, and her own stunted breathing. She turned toward the tub and pried one hand away from her face to push back the shower curtain. Carole was as considerate in death as she had been in life. After the shock had brought the top half of her body bolt upright, she had the good manners to fall forward, bent from the waist, face down in the water. Edna couldn't see on Carole's face the beginnings of the scream that was cut short by the sudden halting of her heart. In spite of this, in spite of the fact that Carole's death was not nearly as gruesome as Edna had imagined when she had planned it just a week before, and in spite of the fact that it had been much easier to carry out than she had hoped, Edna fainted dead away.

♦

"Such a tragedy. Such a god-awful tragedy." It was
Esther's voice. Edna heard it as if in a tunnel. When she
opened her eyes, she was surrounded by friends—Carole's
friends. All of *their* friends were Carole's friends. Dorothy,
with her bony hands and bad wig, sat on the chair next to
the bed, and Esther and her nincompoop husband Tom
hovered near the door.

"Oh, dear, you're awake." Esther drew nearer. "How do
you feel, dear?"

"Head hurts." Edna lifted a flabby arm and felt for the
pain above her ear.

"Well, you just rest, dear. Doctor said you took a terrible
knock when you fainted," Dorothy told her.

"Yes, you just rest. We'll take care of everything."
Esther's words ended in a whimper, and Edna looked up to
see her press a handkerchief over her lined mouth. "Too
much sun," Carole used to say. "She should wear a hat when
she gardens. She's ruined her skin!" Then Edna realized
Esther had been crying all along. They had all been crying.
Even Esther's nincompoop looked a bit puffy around the
eyes.

"Oh, God! Carole!" Edna's face turned crimson and
squinched, and she shoved her head hard back into the
pillow. "Oh, God! Carole!"

Edna felt the mattress sink and looked up to see Dorothy
sitting sideways on the bed. She caressed the hair from
Edna's forehead and peered with rheumy eyes into Edna's.
"Yes, dear, Carole's dead. It's terrible. Just terrible. Try not
to think about it now. Get some rest, dear."

"Oh, God! I killed her! I killed Carole!"

"It was an accident, dear. Just an accident." Dorothy
continued to stroke Edna's hair.

♦

Edna remembered little of the funeral. After her release
from the hospital, the doctor prescribed heavy sedatives.
Dorothy and Esther had, as they promised, handled all of
the arrangements. The relatives and friends, now gathered
over finger foods in Edna's living room, were convinced that
Edna was blaming herself for a tragedy that had been

waiting to happen. As Edna rested in her bedroom, she could hear Dorothy's quavery old voice push through a mouth full of cheese and crackers.

"You know, you couldn't find two more devoted sisters." She used that exact word: *devoted*. "And now, poor girl," Dorothy's voice dropped to a raspy whisper, "she thinks she's murdered Carole! Imagine it!"

Edna wanted to scream out how she had planned it all along and that she hated—yes, hated!—her sister and wanted her own life once and for all! She must have known back in high school—no, before even—that Carole would always control her life. And now, now that she was unshackled from Carole's control, she was thankful for the narcotic leadenness that kept her from thundering it out to all the kindly funereal folks she also hated.

◆

Carole had been a saint. Everyone thought so. When John and Sophie Kovac had arrived in Chicago from Poland, Carole (then Carol—without the *e*) was ten and Edna was on the way. Because little Carole mastered the difficult new language quickly and because they felt childlike and confused in their adopted country, John and Sophie Kovac attributed to Carole a wisdom beyond theirs and often deferred to her judgment. Carole became a kind of mini-matriarch and presented the family face to the world.

Carole's first sweet taste of directing Edna's life came when Edna was in the first grade and had a friend over to play, a pale child with thick, blonde braids that tapered to nothing at the ends. Carole passed by the yellow, polished oak of Edna's bedroom doorway and stopped to catch the little girl depositing a toy—a tiny plastic charm, one of a boxful Edna had collected—into her pocket. What's more, she watched Edna watch the girl do it. Carole scolded Edna's playmate until she ran out of the house, cheeks wet with guilty tears. Carole forbade Edna ever to play with the girl again. When Carole translated and explained her actions to her parents, they reveled in the maturity and wisdom of their firstborn, as usual.

Carole allowed their acclamation to roll around and warm her soul. When it cooled, she wanted more. Carole eventually eliminated each of Edna's friends, to the nodding approval of her parents, until Edna was totally bereft of playmates.

♦

Edna's dresser became the center of her social life. In the mirror she could conjure wonderful friends. Mickey Rooney would poke his head out, his wide, open, freckled face sporting a huge grin. "Hey, Toots! That's a swell hat you're wearing there!" Judy Garland would lean out and insist in that sugary, curly voice of hers that Edna was perfectly right. "That sweater fits you just fine!" As Edna grew older, her entourage expanded with her exposure to movies, old and new, and then television. Her friends doted on her, always counting on Edna's presence to start the party. When Edna came of the age that was past pretending, her looking-glass friends became more insistently real. Although they never travelled beyond the back edge of her dresser, they became the cheering section she needed, agreeing that Carole should let her go to the sock hop; Carole should let her wear lipstick; Carole should mind her own business!

Carole never thought she was unjust to Edna. Long past the first few tastes of power and praise bestowed by John and Sophie, Carole truly did not believe Edna could manage her own life. She wanted to protect her from the challenges and failures that might have helped her grow and learn. Yes, Carole considered Edna stupid—never allowing that Edna might only be immature, or even just distracted from sensibility by the normal events of youth.

When Carole finished high school, she added the *e* to the end of her name, and Edna developed stomach problems. Carole became more and more sophisticated, while Edna planned every excursion from the house around available bathrooms and her diet so far that day.

There was a brief reprieve for Edna when Carole married a man on the verge of being shipped out to war. When he was among those who didn't return from the police action in Korea, Carole moved back home, relieved that the burden of sex was past and that she wasn't pregnant. She immediately resumed her vigil over her younger sister who was deep in the process of discovering boys. The natural progression of youthful attraction ground to a halt, however, with lectures on the baseness of teenaged boys and threats to send Edna to live with relatives in Poland.

After high school, Edna acquired a job packing cookies in cases and lived a passionless life with Mother, Father, and Carole, until her parents grew old, withered, and died.

♦

Now Carole was dead and Edna could begin her life— if she could dominate the panic borne of guilt and fear of discovery. She was not unprepared. She had observed Carole for years, noting how she paid the bills, handled service people, ordered at restaurants, conversed with friends. Edna had practiced when Carole wasn't home, rehearsing for the time she would be alone. She would share a glass of wine and tinseled conversation with her movie-star friends in the mirror, hold well-modulated discussions with the electric company on the phone, her thumb pressed hard on the receiver button.

Murder had not been Edna's first choice. Her original plan was to save up enough money to move away. Far away. A whole new life. Perhaps up to Michigan. She could open a bed-and-breakfast somewhere—fill her life with gracious food and antiques. Then she realized Carole would never allow it. At the very least, Carole would track Edna down and take over Edna's new life, make it her own. Besides, it would be unfair for Carole to get the family house and money while Edna scraped by in hiding as she began her business.

Beyond the notions of escape, Edna had begun to notice the careless things Carole did. Her lack of caution with the kitchen knives, leaving them helter-skelter in the soapy water of the sink. Driving—backing out of their narrow driveway without first looking. Negligently using electrical equipment—dropping the toaster, leaving her hair dryer too close to the tub. Perhaps Carole was tired of living two lives. Perhaps Carole would continue to live for both of them until

one of them died. Perhaps it was time for Edna to start living
for herself. "Practically suicidal," Edna mused to her friends
in the mirror.

Once the hubbub of the funeral died down, Edna began
to map out her new life. First on her list was a cruise. Edna
had begged and cajoled for years to go on a cruise, but
Carole claimed seasickness. Carole had suggested to Edna,
with that coy sidelong glance of hers, that Edna might think
about going alone. Edna always answered, "Maybe I will!"
They both knew she wouldn't. Until now. And so, against
the rallied protests of Dorothy and Esther, who insisted Edna
wasn't quite herself yet, Edna dialed up Cruises Are Us and
thumbed her nose at the spirit of her older sister.

◆

Pam, a perky, blue-uniformed official from the ship, met
Edna's plane. She corralled Edna and the other vacationers
from her flight into a cohesive little group and herded them
to the friendly yellow-and-chrome bus. A man sat next to
Edna, cradling his potbelly. He introduced himself to
everyone within shouting range—"Third goddam cruise on
this ship and I can personally guarantee you're all gonna
love it!" Edna's embarrassment for the man was eclipsed by
his reassurance that she'd done something right. The man's
outburst had broken the ice and the passengers exchanged
information about their points of origin, their experiences
with previous cruises, what they'd heard about or
experienced with this particular cruise line. Edna listened
with tingly enthusiasm, absorbing the influx of information.
She imagined that one day that she would, herself, as veteran
of several cruises, hold court—perhaps on this very bus.

When Edna stepped down from the filtered ventilation
of the bus, the salty sea air tickled her nose. She crossed the
swing-away bridge into the humming lobby of the ship. The
carpet, the color of persimmons, was soft and bouncy
beneath her feet. Directly in front of her was a staircase
circling a shimmering chandelier dripping prisms as far as
the eye could see. Everywhere was light, bounding and
rebounding, diamonds glinting off chrome and marble.
Another bubbly, shiny-haired official intercepted Edna,

requesting her paperwork while easing it from her hand and directing her down the lush staircase to her deck and stateroom. Edna congratulated herself on her planning and efficiency. The tasks Carole had pretended were such a hardship seemed to be quite easy after all.

Opening the door to her cabin, Edna looked into an opening the width of a large-hipped woman and only as deep as the tiny bathroom with commode and shower and the single bed beyond. On her right stood a vanity sink, a tall closet, and a small chair. There was no porthole. At first Edna thought surely some mistake had been made. Could this possibly be one of the staterooms shown in the brochure? Her luggage had not yet come up from the loading dock, but she knew her two large suitcases would not fit anywhere in this room.

Edna collected fortitude from the sea air and attempted to find her porter. The aisle teemed with passengers searching for their rooms while luggage was hurled about by burly men. Edna was jostled and elbowed with messages of "Oh, sorry!" and "Hi, neighbor!" A pinch-faced, balding man who introduced himself as Martin advised that her porter was probably busy with baggage and that if she sat tight in her stateroom he would, no doubt, catch up with her soon. She caught a peek of Martin's room.

"Oh! Your room is tiny, too!" The words slipped out before Edna could check them for propriety.

"Oh, sure! They're all tiny! The only large staterooms are the real expensive ones up top."

Edna's eyes grew distant and her lips tightened to thin pink lines.

"Hey, you're only gonna sleep there, right?"

"Well, yes, I suppose . . ."

"There you go!"

Edna thanked him, stepped over several suitcases, and reentered her room. Her luggage had still not arrived, so she set about emptying the toiletries from her vinyl carry-on and waited to dress for dinner.

♦

Edna felt herself being swept gracefully into her chair. Her eyes drank deeply from the melange of glass, silver, mirrors, and tiny lights that made up the ship's dining room. A giddy, fairy-tale sensation tickled the inside of her chest from the moment Carlo, the very foreign, very charming *maitre d'*, took her arm and escorted her to the table. Now he stood behind her and she could feel his hands on the back of her chair. The tickle grew more insistent.

"My dear friends, this is Edna Kovac. She is a lovely lady I am entrusting to your care. Please make her feel welcome." Carlo leaned down and whispered in her ear. "You have a wonderful meal, lovely lady. If all is not perfect, you talk to Carlo." The tickle turned to heat and surged to cover her face. She felt a smile play on her mouth, and her hand rose to her lips to subdue it.

A fiftyish lady with blonde hair and softly crinkled eyes sat next to Edna. She turned and held out a hand with long, delicate fingers and neatly manicured nails of pink. "Edna, it's such a pleasure to meet you. I'm Patricia Jensen. Friends call me Trish. I hope you will, too."

Edna's left hand began to rise, realized its mistake, and dropped in deference to the right. Trish's hand felt powdery dry, as opposed to the fresh salmon of a paw Edna presented. She had never shaken hands with a woman before. Edna decided she liked it and would adopt this strong, sophisticated habit for her own.

Trish nodded toward the young black couple seated across the table. "This is Ben Thomas, right? And his wife, Merilee Davis." She leaned in, conspiratorially. "They're married, but she kept her maiden name."

With new reserves of confidence, Edna turned to Ben and Merilee. She could feel the comforting low rumble of the engines, the song of the ship. Her hand released Trish's and moved toward the couple across the table. Edna's eyes locked on Ben's, and an electrical charge in her brain registered the fact that he was black and sent a message to her hand to stop and await further instructions.

Ben's white teeth caught the glint of the candle as he began to rise and extend his own hand toward hers. The charge jumped across the table from her fingertips to his, the friendship fell from his face, and he too stood suspended in time.

Edna was aware that her action, or lack of, was being interpreted as prejudice, yet she couldn't seem to break the moment. She knew she wasn't a bigot, merely sheltered from all her sister found unpleasant. Unfortunately, that had included black people. Edna plain didn't know how to act. And now, in this state of thick, motionless tension, she could hear the tinkling of glasses and silverware and the hum of conversation around her.

Merilee and Trish looked at the frozen tableau with discomfort and pity. What Ben couldn't see through his anger was obvious to them. This middle-aged, middle-class lady, with hide-that-gray red hair and a mother-of-the-bride dress, simply didn't know any better. They swapped the knowledge through their glances as their brains searched for the words to break the tension.

Edna's mind worked in fits and starts. She searched for the right face to put on and the perfect thing to say. Or anything to say. Or any face to wear. Anything but the confused look she was wearing and the painful silence that hung heavily between her Eastern European pallor and his dark, dark African heritage.

Carlo, again standing behind Edna's chair, came to the rescue. "My friends, I want you to meet these two wonderful ladies. This beautiful lady is Kelley, and this lovely young woman is Melissa. And, you, my friend, Ben, are the envy of all the men on the ship. You have all of these beautiful women to entertain you. (Please to sit here, Miss Kelley.) There have been many offers of large money if I can get you to change places with other men, but Carlo is honest and I tell them 'No. You must try to be happy at your own table.' But they all want to sit here with the beautiful women. What can I do? Enjoy your meals, my friends. If all is not perfect, you tell Carlo."

The seating and introductions of the two young women gave Edna time to regroup. She decided that if she had been prejudiced, she would no longer be so, and, by the end of the meal, that nice young colored couple would know she definitely was not.

Edna perused her dinner companions as they made getting-to-know-you small talk. Merilee was an art director with a medium-size advertising agency in New York. Ben was a "rep" for a printing firm. Trish noticed the quizzical look on Edna's face and explained to her that *rep* was the new term for *salesman*. The two girls were administrative assistants at a law firm in Houston. Once the introductions were made, Kelley and Melissa withdrew from the conversation, whispered and giggled between themselves, and blatantly stared at a nearby table of college-aged travelers.

Edna liked Trish. She seemed very outgoing and friendly without being gushy and phony like Carole had been. Trish was leaning close to Edna, confiding what a romantic figure she thought Carlo made, when, with much hoopla, their waiter appeared, passed out menus, and disappeared, allowing the diners to discuss their preferences.

Another dilemma for Edna. Somehow she had thought the menu would arrive and she would automatically pick out the perfect combination of foods. Now, as she looked over the bill of fare, she was overwhelmed by the choices. What if she ate something that disagreed with her? How embarrassing it would be to have to rush away from the table to go to the bathroom. Her eyes left the menu and darted around the huge hall, searching for the tell-tale alcove or three-quarter wall, hiding the facilities from view. There was no bathroom in sight. The ship gave a little lurch, just enough to shimmer the water in the stemmed glasses, and Edna felt a little twinge deep in her bowels. Just a tiny warning cramp that told her anything she ate would now be unwelcome. She wondered what her deceased sister would do in this situation. Then it occurred to her that Miss Perfect Carole would not have had this problem and that the purpose of Carole's demise had been to free Edna to make her own decisions. Edna ordered poppyseed dressing on her salad, pumpkin soup, shrimp scampi, and baked Alaska.

Edna survived her salad and was starting on her soup when she received another message from deep in her digestive tract. It was another little cramp, and a small sound came about five inches up from her seat cushion. *I will not give in to this. This is my first chance to live and I will not give in to my stupid glass stomach.* Her system replied with a little tighter squeeze and a little louder noise. Edna sat with her filled spoon poised above the lovely orange-brown brew. The ship gave another little shiver, and a drop fell from the spoon and made a tiny splash in the bowl. Beads of sweat were forming on her upper lip. Then Carole asked her how she liked the soup. "Fine, thanks." *Wait. Carole was no longer alive.* Edna looked up from her bowl. Trish was smiling with her warm, blue eyes.

"Your soup. How is it? Edna, you're so brave. Pumpkin soup. Sounded too exotic for me. What am I missing?"

"It's good."

It's good? IT'S GOOD? Very sophisticated, Edna. Carole's voice rang through her head, and Edna's eyes filled with tears. She knew now that what she really was and what she thought she would be were light years apart. Then it occurred to her that she had risked far too much for this new life to let a—*what would Carole call it?*—a faux pas—discourage her.

Trish and Ben and Merilee were ooohing and aaahing over the cuisine. Melissa and Kelley were giggling and spearing morsels from each other's plates. A parade of waiters carried a birthday cake to the next table. Edna sat, again frozen in tension, trying one line and then another in her head to find the perfect description for the soup she hadn't really tasted. "It's too spicy!"

Trish's attention snapped from the Thomas/Davis couple to Edna, the warmth in her eyes turning to question. Melissa and Kelley stared at Edna, glanced at each other, rolled their eyes, and snickered behind their hands. Edna looked from face to face at the table. Her fingers tingled and she felt the blood drain from her head. "The—the soup. It—it's too spicy."

All the tinsel and glitter of the room took on a jaundiced and smeary cast through her tears. The waiters' strains of "Happy Birthday" sounded off-key and wilted. A steelworker's fist grabbed and twisted Edna's lower intestine, and, as the gang of revelers at the next table cheered the anniversary of a birth, Edna knocked over her chair and fled the room.

◆

Edna left the claustrophobia of her stateroom early the next morning. As she carefully followed her map through the ship to the Lido deck pool, she made a mental note of all of the doors marked "Ladies" on the way. She pushed through the glass portals of the Caribbean Lounge and out into the bright blue and sun-drenched yellow of the morning and the sweet oniony smells of the breakfast buffet. Already a line had formed to the splashy food tables, and people dressed in shorts, T-shirts, and dresses in the colors of parrots milled about the poolside tables, balancing plates of food and cups of coffee while they jockeyed for places to sit.

Edna inhaled the perfumes of scrambled eggs, raisin toast, and sausages floating on the currents of the brisk sea air. The water and sky were dressed in hues that Edna had only seen in pictures, and there seemed to be stark, sizzling movement everywhere. The ship's gentle pitching and low rumble continued to calm her as it had in her stateroom bed the night before—after she had spent a goodly amount of time in her tiny bathroom. Once she felt in control again, the ship's lullaby had soothed her and she was like the child curled up in the dark back seat of her parents' giant DeSoto on the way home from a wintery Sunday afternoon visit. She had slept the sleep of an infant. This morning, her stomach and disposition were uncharacteristically calm.

As she took her place in line, her platter-brimmed straw hat collided with that of the lady in front of her. When she recoiled, it bumped the striped umbrella over the food tables so that the hat became perched ambivalently over her ear. She loosened one hand from her tray and returned the hat to its original position. She thought of removing it, but her hands would soon be busy with food and coffee. If she kept it on her head, it was sure to bump into the angled umbrellas beyond. If it fell off, there would be no graceful way to retrieve it.

"Hi, Edna!" Trish appeared at her elbow. "How're you feeling this morning?"

Edna's head swiveled. Her hat didn't. She dropped the scrambled-egg spoon into the steam tray and rotated the errant chapeau with her freed hand. "Oh, better. Much better."

"Oh, good. A little seasick, eh? Let you in on a little secret. . . ." Trish put her hand on Edna's shoulder and her voice tickled Edna's ear. "You were not, by any means, alone. A lot of people left the dining room after you did," she moved in closer still and through the side of her mouth, at a lowered pitch, continued, "Never to be seen again."

Edna barked an open-mouthed laugh that startled her in its unfamiliarity. "Really?"

"Really! Listen, I have a table over there." She pointed a pink nail toward the railing. "Come join me, okay?"

"Sure. Okay." Edna's hat bumped into the hair of the lady behind her, leaving a dent in the heavily sprayed bubble of a coiffure. The woman narrowed her eyes at Edna, scowled, and loudly begged her pardon. Edna felt her face flush and stood contrite but unable to express her apology.

"Edna, why don't you let me take your hat?" Trish reached up and caught the offending straw just as it was about to topple off Edna's head. "You don't need it under the umbrellas. I'll just put it on your chair."

"Okay. Thanks, Carole."

"Trish."

"What?"

"Name's Trish. You called me Carole."

"Oh, sorry."

Trish turned and faced the scowling lady with the dented hair. She flashed her warm blue eyes, touched the lady on the forearm, and told her to be sure and have a wonderful day. Then she flounced back to her table by the sea. The lady scowled again, first at Trish, then at Edna. Edna skipped the scrambled eggs and moved up in line.

♦

"Braids? Braids, pretty lady? I make beautiful braids for you!" Edna and Trish pushed through the herd of dark girls—Trish with a resounding "No!" Edna with a timid "I don't think so." Five ships were moored at the docks, spilling out their passengers in unison. Edna and Trish were carried in the wash of tourists swarming toward the huge, tan stucco building that comprised the straw market. Inside were booths upon booths of vendors—more dark girls weaving brilliant raffia designs in prefabricated straw baskets and trays while bellowing accented promises of the best deal on the island. Trish headed for a table of woven bowls. Edna already knew she wanted a straw shopping bag, and she spotted just the very one within three feet of the entrance to the building. Remembering the admonition of the cruise director at the shopper's orientation that morning, "Don't pay the given price," Edna was ready to dicker. "Ten dollah, pretty lady. Ten dollah." Edna guessed the girl couldn't have been more than eleven years old. "You can't get no cheaper!"

Edna picked up the bag, natural straw with raffia flowers splashed over the front. She could see herself, arm through the handles, flower side out, toting it to bingo. "Why, Edna, where did you get such a lovely bag?" "Oh, it's just something I picked up in Nassau." She pictured Carole at flea markets, wearing her this-is-a-disgusting-piece-of-crap look, ready to bargain. Edna held the bag up at eye level by two fingers and assumed her best revolted face. "I'll give you seven for it."

"Seven! Cost me seven! Nine!"

Edna dropped the bag on the table and began to turn away.

"Okay. Okay. Eight! You make me poor!"

Edna wore her tote like a trophy. She spent hours making her way among the tables, discriminately shopping for souvenirs. She picked out a string of pukka beads for Dorothy, a set of straw coasters for Esther and family, and a rose-quartz choker for herself. She deposited her treasures in her new bag, patting the side after each transaction. It was when she purchased a new, small-brimmed sun hat that she noticed the broken handle. One of the woven grips had broken loose from the bag. Edna examined it, figuring she might be able to do a quick repair herself. As she fingered the frayed straw, her what-would-Carole-do processes kicked in. She doused herself with courage and made a beeline back to the vendor near the door.

"It's broken."

"You didn't buy here."

"I certainly did. You sold it to me."

"I no did. Just got here. Late today."

"It was you! I know it was you! I want a new purse or my money back right now." Edna spoke between clenched teeth. Her face was crimson and she could feel her blood pounding in her ears.

"You crazy, lady. I no here. Just got here. My friend tell you." The girl nodded toward the next booth where a native child about the same age stood behind a table of baskets. "She tell you I no here!" The other girl nodded and shrugged.

"It was you. You're both lying. I want my money back!"

"You crazy. You get out. I get police." The girl turned and disappeared into the crowd.

Edna looked again at the frayed end of the handle. *Maybe I can fix it myself.* She knew she could not. The feverish thrill of shopping had dripped away to disappointment, and Edna headed toward the arched opening of the building and the ships beyond. She stopped where the dock met the water and transferred her purchases from the damaged bag to her old string bag.

"Hey, Edna! What'd you buy?" Trish trotted up behind her, wrestling with four large baskets and two hats. Edna held out the bag by its one intact grip. "What happened?"

"It broke."

"Did you take it back?"

"Tried to. She wouldn't take it. Said I bought it somewhere else."

"That's ridiculous." Trish spat out the words, rearranged her cargo, and grabbed the satchel from Edna. She stomped back toward the market. Edna toddled behind.

"What do you mean she didn't buy it here? I saw her buy it here."

"You confused, lady." The girl spread her arms wide, encompassing the surrounding booths. "All look alike!"

"Bullshit!" Edna jumped at Trish's profanity. It was Carole's last-resort swear word, the one whose bite always gave Edna a start. The girl and Trish stood facing each other, Trish looking steadfastly down into the girl's dark eyes. Trish began to speak loudly in staggered, measured words. "Do you mean to say . . . that this lady bought this purse from you . . . it broke before she even left the building . . . and you won't replace it?" A plumpish woman examining a pair of earrings at the next table dropped her hand and turned to listen. Trish continued in a louder voice. "Do you mean to say, young lady, that you won't stand by your merchandise?" The surrounding tables grew quiet as one tourist and vendor after another turned to the promise of a conflagration. The girl looked toward the other native girl who gave her a furtive glance and dropped her eyes to the project in her lap. Edna could hear the humming of the acts of trading going on deeper in the building and the gregarious shouts of the tourists outside, going to and coming from the docks. In the far distance, she could hear the melodic bonks of a steel-drum band. She stood a few feet behind Trish, eyes down, twisting the handle on her string bag. She was fifteen again, listening to Carole heatedly exchanging the oversized sweater that Edna had loved dearly because she had bought it herself.

"You crazy, lady. I get the police." Edna looked up to see the girl turn and take two steps toward a thick, sheltering crowd of tourists. Trish dropped her purchases and caught the girl by a bony shoulder. The girl stopped and swung around. A wide grin spread across Trish's face.

"We'll both get the police. Shall we go together?"

The girl's shoulders dropped in resignation, and she reached out her hand for the bag.

Edna longed for the air-conditioning of her tiny room. She started back to the ship in a lazy, zig-zag lope. Carole strolled along at her elbow, which was a surprise to Edna. She was sure she had just left her at the straw market. She could feel Carole's hot breath in her face, sarcasm dripping from her lips. "Not feeling well, darling? Well, I'll fix you up in no time."

♦

Nora Charles rested a begloved elbow on the bar, balancing a sparkling martini on the ends of her fingers, and leaned out of the mirror. "Edna, dear, there you are! We were beginning to worry about you!"

Nick Charles turned from his conversation and leaned over his wife's shoulder. "Edna, join us, please. We've been waiting for you. Are you all right, dear?"

Edna glanced at her friends, turned and let her eyes wander the room. "Yes . . . yes . . . I'm fine . . . have to dress for dinner."

"Well, by all means, then, dress! We shan't distract you another second. We promise, don't we, dear?" Nora's voice oozed from the mirror, punctuated by her trademark squeak.

"Of course! Edna, why don't you wear that delicious pink frock. It'll look divine with your new rose-quartz choker."

"Yes. Of course. I will." Edna stood, feet apart, fingers of one hand drumming on the vanity, listening for Carole. When the ship lurched slightly in its separation from the dock, Edna lurched with it. She could feel the low rumble of the engines, the growl of the ship.

Edna forced herself to focus on the coming evening— wary against Carole's reappearance. She hadn't heard Carole's nagging voice since climbing the gangplank. Edna laid out her clothes and showered in opposition to the ship's sway. When her thumb pushed through her pantyhose as she put them on, Edna's eyes pooled with tears, but she was able to regroup and blink them back to safety. She applied lipstick—Mary Kay Watermelon. Carole always thought the color looked good with her red hair. Edna slid the gown over her arms, smearing her lips as it passed over her head. But it was fixable. It was when she attempted to fasten the choker around her neck and the resisting pads of flesh forced her to pull a little too tight and the flimsy string snapped, bouncing globes of rose quartz off the vanity, that Carole appeared in the mirror. "Things are not going too well, are they?"

"Go away." Edna turned from the mirror and tried to concentrate on the next task in dressing.

"Tiny room you have here, Edna, but not unsalvageable. I'll bet if we work together this room could be darling. Just darling."

The hall outside of Edna's cabin and the surrounding rooms were empty of passengers—all in the dining room or partying on the upper decks. There was no one to hear the smashing of the mirror.

◆

At 10:30 p.m., Edna heard Carole's voice from the other side of the stateroom door. Edna stood, tentatively reaching for the doorknob, her eyes traveling back and forth between it and the shards of mirror lying face-down on the vanity. She thought she had managed to keep her sister fairly well contained in the tiny pieces of glass, but now Carole was in the hallway outside the stateroom asking if she was all right.

It had been a crapshoot all evening. Edna longed for the company of her friends in the mirror or to try her social skills again in the ship's dining room, but Carole and the Charleses and Fred and Ginger and the rest of her sophisticated comrades were playing a sort of musical chairs in the shards, and Edna could never be sure when she picked one up and turned it over whether it would be friend or foe. She couldn't leave because Carole was in there with them, probably winning them over. Soon they would all be on Carole's side and Edna would be alone. The only solution was to keep Carole busy and that meant doing her bidding. Carole was obsessed with redecorating the room. But now—now—if Carole was on the other side of the door, she would be flesh and blood, and Edna had dealt with that before.

When Edna finally pulled open the stateroom door, Carole's disguise did not fool her for a second. Edna saw past the warm blue eyes, the blonde hair, and the pink nail polish at the tips of the lightly tanned fingers holding out her straw bag.

◆

The porter had first called kindly through the door, and Edna had admonished him to leave her alone and go away. It had been four days, and she had not allowed him in to clean. A stench was emanating from the room, and the passengers on either side of Edna's cabin leaned in their doorways, handkerchiefs guarding their noses. The porter saw his tips draining away swiftly if he didn't get in and clean up whatever was making that smell. With the ship's first mate behind him, he turned the key in the lock. A large obstacle on the other side kept the door from opening more than a few inches. At first the porter thought it was Edna, but after pushing his head through the narrow opening, he could see her sitting in the chair in the shadows at the far end of the cabin. What appeared to be streaks of brown smeared her face, her hands, her slip. The porter felt his Adam's apple bob in an involuntary swallow. He wished he hadn't eaten so much at breakfast.

With the help of the first mate, the porter was able to push the door open enough to squeeze into the room, with his thinner superior right behind him. The officer flipped the switch next to the door, and the scene was exposed in the garish overhead light. The obstacle, Trish, clad in bra and panties, now pushed sideways under the vanity by the door, had been dead for several days. Large bolts of mirror were pushing out of her chest and abdomen, and hundreds of smaller shards had been systematically inserted under the skin of her arms and legs.

Elaborate flowers had been finger-painted on the walls. The petals were painted with blood, the centers a conglomeration of thick wads of lipstick and rose-quartz beads. Strings of straw and colored raffia were draped over the lampshade and strewn about the room. The bed and the chair in which Edna now sat staring at her blood-streaked hands had been reupholstered in strips of Edna's and Trish's clothes, held together by hair pins straightened and woven in and out of holes in the fabric. Not an inch of the room remained unaltered.

When the officer whispered an order to the porter to quietly—*quietly!*—locate the captain and ask him to come right away, Edna seemed to notice their presence in the room for the first time. She looked up from her fingers, her eyebrows pushed together, head tilted slightly. Then the quizzicality left her face and the presence of the two men seemed to soothe her. She caught the eye of the officer, then the porter, and requested that they please see if they could find her sister. She told them that Carole had been there just moments ago. She couldn't imagine where she had gotten to. Could they please find her? She was sure Carole would take care of everything.

"Carole always seems to know just what to do."

NEVER TOO OLD

Toni Brown

I followed my directions to Mount Airy and took a left onto the client's street. There was a parking spot in front of the house and I pulled right in. I sat looking at the large stone house. This was a nice house in what had been, a decade or two ago, a pretty solidly middle-class neighborhood. Now many of the big houses have been divided into apartments, evidenced by multiple mailboxes and doorbells. In a window a sign read, "This is a Town Watch Neighborhood."

I checked to make sure my beeper was on. My identification badge was clipped to my blouse just below the fourth button. I flipped it up and twisted it around. Yeah, it's me. My name, Leslie Hill, is neatly typed beneath my signature. This is under a picture of myself taken five years ago, on my date of hire. My dreadlocks were inch-long twig-like spirals then, held back with a blue-and-green kinte-cloth hairband. At the top of the badge is the name of the corporation, Municipal Elder Services, and my division, PROTECTIVE. At the bottom of the ID, in heavy dark print, INVESTIGATOR.

I looked sweetly businesslike in that picture, the navy dress with the scattered tiny flowers, the little silver hoop earrings, and the tasteful-yet-telling silver labrys on a delicate matching chain. I smiled, remembering my attempt to make a good visual impression. Was that makeup trying to hide the lavender "L" on my forehead?

The picture was taken when I was still a fresh and optimistic social servant, out to save the grandmothers and grandfathers of Philadelphia from the bad things that can happen to frail elderly people. Like what had happened to my grandmother at the hands of my cousin Louis. It still caused involuntary shudders.

My once-short dreadlocks now reach well past my shoulders. At work, I wear my hair pulled back from my face and tied with long strips of African print cloth. I am no longer fresh, I am still somewhat optimistic, the bad things are still out there.

I climbed out of the car and locked the doors. I crossed the street. I rang the doorbell twice. I could hear footsteps approaching.

"Who is it?" a tentative voice asked.

"Elder Protective Services, Leslie Hill."

I heard the sound of locks tumbling. The honey-colored oak door opened. Standing before me in the doorway of the big stone house was a woman in her forties. She was round and wore square glasses. She looked at me, expressionless, and said, "Can I help you?"

"My name is Leslie Hill. I'm with Elder Protective Services," I held up my ID. "My office has received a report that Eugenia Harris might be in need of protective services. Is she here?"

The woman looked surprised. Her eyes were wide and she picked at the top buttons of her blouse.

"Come in," she said, stepping away from the door. "I'm Madeline Gardener. What is this about?"

Madeline Gardener and I stood behind the closed door as I explained to her what the report had alleged. Madeline took my jacket to the closet and then returned to face me, still standing at the door.

"I need to see Eugenia Harris," I said.

"Okay. Come on." She turned toward the stairs.

◆

Madeline opened the door to her aunt's bedroom. It was so quiet, it felt like the room of someone who had died. It smelled faintly of menthol salve and lemon oil. The drawn shades glowed like parchment against the morning sun. Madeline stepped into the room and switched on the light. I was right behind her.

"Aunt Eugenia, I have someone here to see you."

The room was neat and prettily decorated with simple furnishings. A bureau with pictures and personal effects. A bedside table that held reading glasses, a leather-bound Bible, and false teeth in a container of water.

The bed was one of those dark mahogany four-posters with pineapple-shaped finials carved into the wood. Eugenia Harris was a small lump in the bed. Turned toward the wall, she could have been mistaken for a bundle of covers.

"I told you I didn't want to see anyone. Go away." The muffled voice spoke from beneath the blankets.

"Auntie, she's from Protective Services. I think she can help us." Madeline's voice was patient.

"I don't need any help. I said go away, Madeline, and I mean . . ." Mrs. Harris paused, turned, pushed the covers away from her face, "I mean get out of here!" Without teeth the words sounded wet, like she was spitting them at us.

Madeline's aunt glared at us, eyes shifting from Madeline to me then back to Madeline. Her face was tiny and loosely covered with dull, walnut-colored skin. Her toothless mouth was an empty dark cave, but her brown eyes sparkled with life and anger.

Madeline shrugged and motioned for me to go. Once we were in the hall she closed the door softly.

"I'm sorry. She hasn't always been like this."

"It's all right. Actually I kind of like it when they can get it together enough to throw me out. It's like they care enough about their lives to want me out."

Madeline led me down the carpeted stairs to the living room and offered me a seat on the couch. She continued walking through the dining room to a narrow galley kitchen, where she filled a stainless-steel kettle with water and placed it over the blue gas flame.

She sat down beside me on the couch and placed two mugs of steamy tea before us on the coffee table. "How did you hear about this?" she asked.

I took a sip of tea and replied, "Somebody called in the report. I can't say who. They thought your aunt needed help. How long have you lived here with her?"

"Since August, about three months. I moved in when my aunt started going downhill." Madeline glanced up the stairwell and then back at me.

"It started with a car accident, last year. Aunt Eugenia was sued and she lost her job and her driver's license." Madeline picked up a hot mug and blew into it. "I kept thinking she would get better, that she was just depressed after everything that had happened." Madeline sighed. "Then she stopped eating and I started to panic. It got to the point where I had to *make* her leave the house. She finally refused to get out of bed no matter what I did. I called her woman friends from the church. I was going to call Elder Social Services myself. I guess *somebody* beat me to it." Madeline smiled wanly. She took a sip of her tea. "She was an active, vital person until the rug was pulled out from under her."

"Has she seen her doctor since she's been like this?"

"Oh yes, she saw her doctor pretty soon after she lost her license because she was feeling so bad. I drove her there. She belongs to one of those HMO plans where they tell you who to see. She came out with a fistful of prescriptions. Nine different medications, most of them psychotropic. Mood elevators, anti-depressants, sleeping pills, you name it. She came out of there, handed me the 'scripts and said, 'He says I'm depressed. Hell, if I take all these drugs I'll be dead.' We laughed. It was probably the last time we had a really good laugh." Madeline looked into her tea.

"Is she taking the meds?" I asked, but I had already guessed the answer. The lady upstairs did not have the eyes of a person on Haldol.

Madeline shook her head, "No, but she has heart and blood pressure medication she's also not taking."

"Did the doctor schedule a follow-up?" I began to see the reasons for the call to Protective.

Madeline shook her head again. "This guy must have a million clients. He has offices all over the city. If she just quietly took her drugs, he would never see her again. He gave her enough refills, why schedule a follow-up?"

"I'm going to have to go back up there," I said, indicating the stairs with my eyes. "I need to talk to her so I can develop a care plan for her." I didn't say that a psych evaluation would probably be part of that plan.

◆

Being in Mrs. Harris' room without Madeline was like being in an empty room. Eugenia's things were there but not Eugenia's *life*. The elderly woman didn't turn when I gently knocked on the door before stepping inside. She did not respond when I stood beside her bed.

"Mrs. Harris, I'm Leslie Hill, I want to help you. I need to talk to you." There was no response. "Mrs. Harris, I'm from Elder Protective Services and I need to talk to you." Still no response. I took a slow deep breath preparing for what I was about say.

"Mrs. Harris, I am from Protective Services and because I'm from Protective Services I am mandated to investigate the allegations reported to my office. These allegations say you are experiencing serious neglect and the reporter names Madeline as the abuser. If you do not talk to me, two things can happen. The first thing is you can be removed from your home for your own well-being, because, let's face it, you're looking pretty bad. And the second thing is, Madeline can be charged with neglect. It's a felony in this state. In any case, I can't go away unless something happens, the least of which is you talking to me." I'd stretched the truth about Madeline being charged. Mrs. Harris would have to be near death for that to happen. But I hoped it would make my point. And get a rise out of Eugenia Harris.

"Well, that would make two criminals in the same family, wouldn't it?" Mrs. Harris spoke while turning to face me. I didn't find out what she meant by that until later.

Mrs. Harris reluctantly cooperated while I asked her questions designed to reveal evidence of serious emotional and physical abuse, or financial exploitation by a caregiver.

She pulled back the covers and her nightgown to let me look at her body. There were no bruises, scars, or outward indications of physical abuse. She knew what the date was; she knew her mother's maiden name. When I asked her who the President of the United States was, she said, "Oh that young fellah, Clinton." She could not remember who had been president before him. Mrs. Harris was not mentally impaired, but anyone could look at her and see that she was dangerously neglecting herself. Gathering my papers and pencil, I sat back on the bed and looked at the skeletal woman with the blazing eyes.

"What would you like me to do for you, Mrs. Harris?"

"I don't want you to do anything for me, truth be told. I never called you, Madeline never called you. Your getting out of my house with a quickness would be about the only thing you could do for me." She was sitting up in the bed and I could swear that her color was a little better.

"When I asked you about suicidal thoughts, you said you were tired of living. Why? Being unemployed and not having a car is bad, but it isn't something to want to die over." I could see that she was tired from my questions, tired of holding up the shield protecting her pain. She was too tired to muster the anger I'd seen earlier. Tears began to well up in her eyes.

"I don't just not have a car," she began slowly, "I had an accident and they took me to court, charged me like a criminal, and took away my license. I'm not just unemployed. I was driving the agency's van when I had the accident. I was sued, they said I was negligent, and the agency fired me. It wasn't just an accident—there was a child involved. They said I hit her." Tears dropped to her cheeks. "The little girl was really hurt, broken bones, bruises." She covered her face, trying to stop the tidal wave of tears with her hands. She sobbed loudly, her chest heaving as she gasped for air. My own chest tightened as I watched her. I reached out to touch her and she began to flail her arms. She slapped my hand away. She began to yell while crying, "Get out! Get out! Look what you've done. Are you happy now? Get out!"

I picked up my papers and moved toward the door. She was sobbing and repeating, "Get out, get out," as I pulled the door closed behind me.

Madeline was standing near the bottom of the stairs, gazing up at me with concern and disbelief in her eyes.

"What happened up there?" She had been on her way up, already on the third step. When she reached me, I touched her arm. "Wait. I'm sorry I upset her, but what she says about the accident, is it true?"

Madeline pulled away from me. "If she said she was fired and they took away her license, that's true. If she said she was blamed for an accident that involved a child being injured, that's true too. What else do you want to know? I need to go to my aunt." She passed me on the stairs, hurrying toward the sound of Eugenia Harris' sobs.

When Madeline came back downstairs I was sitting on the couch. She sighed and flopped down in a chair. "Is there anything more?" She looked as resigned as her aunt.

I stared at her incredulously. "Yes, there's more. If your aunt is depressed because she hit a child with a company van, then she needs help. A psychiatrist or a companion, *someone* who can help her face what happened and get past it. Was driving part of her job? I mean if she was a Paratransit driver I can see how her agency might feel the need to get her off the road, but if it wasn't her job, they couldn't just fire her without there being some other circumstances, could they? Did she have a lawyer?" I leaned forward, my head tilted at an angle, questioning. I realized my heart was pounding. I was already overinvolved in this case.

"I didn't say she hit anyone. I said she was *blamed* for hitting a child. The family sued the agency. Aunt Eugenia was charged with reckless driving or endangerment, I don't really know, she won't talk about that part."

Madeline told me her aunt had been a senior companion for the Echo Hill Senior Center. She was on her way to see someone. In fact it was right on the street where she was going that the accident happened. Travis Street in South Philly. A man was standing in the middle of the road. She thought it was peculiar that he was there, and she slowed down. He wasn't looking at her; he was facing the curb. His arms were extended like he was reaching for something. She looked to see what he was reaching for, and out from between two parked cars came a little girl. The child looked maybe three or four, but the accident report had said she was five years old.

Eugenia had slammed on her brakes and jumped out of the car. The man was holding the crying child in his arms.

Some woman was up in a window yelling that she'd seen the whole thing. The woman came screaming out of the house, "I saw you. I saw you. You hit her!"

The police came and the woman and the child were taken to the hospital in the back of the police car. Everybody was looking to find fault—the lawyers and insurance companies. The Senior Center suspended her. Then the family filed a civil suit against her, and her insurance was canceled and her driver's license was revoked. Soon after that, the Center let her go.

We sat in silence for a while. Madeline looked at her watch.

"It's lunch time, I'm going to try to get her to drink some tea and maybe eat something. So what do you think? Is there anything you can do?"

Madeline got up from the chair and walked toward the closet.

"I don't know. I've definitely got to do something about her not eating and isolating herself. The stuff about the accident sounds bad, but accidents happen. Maybe if you got her a lawyer . . ."

Madeline got my jacket and showed me to the door.

♦

Safely behind the wheel, I recorded my mileage and checked my watch. It was 2:15. I'd missed lunch and hadn't even noticed.

I drove toward Center City, thinking about the story I'd been told. The sound of a car horn startled me. I must have been driving on automatic pilot. Not a healthy idea on the expressway. I decided to go to South Street. I was hungry; maybe I'd get some chicken wings. I decided to go to

Brother's and Sister's, a soul food restaurant on
Twenty-fourth Street.

The smell of fried chicken wings filled my car as I
continued south. I wasn't fooling anyone; I knew I was
headed down Twenty-third to Travis Street. I drove along,
stopping at every corner stop sign. I could clearly see both
sides of the street. I reminded myself that it was November
and the incident had taken place in February when there
were probably snow piles between the parked cars. As I
approached the 2300 block, I slowed down. This block was
a little run-down but not too bad. Halfway down, I pulled
over and sat in my car. I opened the bag of wings, spread my
napkins, and began to eat and observe.

There wasn't a lot of activity on the street, but what
there was, was consistent. There was some kind of pattern
going between the corner variety store and the apartment
building at 2304. People would go into the corner store, buy
something, come out of the store with a brown paper bag,
and then go into the apartment building. They weren't in
there long before they trotted out and on their merry way
sans the bag. I wished that I had one of those time-lapse
cameras; I was sure it would show a steady ant-like stream
of people coursing between the two points. After I'd finished
the wings, I realized that I wanted something to drink. I
looked down at the corner store and had what I thought was
a brilliant idea.

Armed with a bottle safely tucked into a brown paper
bag, I intended to go into building 2304 and see what I
could see. I came out of the store and walked toward the
gray cement steps. The outside door was unlocked, as was
the inside door. I walked into the dimly lit hall. I was
surprised to see a little girl sitting at the bottom of the stairs.
I said hello and she ignored me.

The child looked about five years old. She eyed my paper
bag suspiciously. She said, "I don't have to talk to you,
you're a piper!"

Her laugh tinkled through the stale air. I pulled the bottle
of iced tea out of the bag and made a show of opening it,
showing her that not all brown paper bags were used to
conceal crack cocaine. I took a sip.

"Do you know of a little girl who was hit by a car last winter? She was really hurt bad. She went to the hospital." The little girl began to shake her head "no" furiously. She had stopped smiling and her lips were pushed tightly closed. She looked up the stairs.

"Kenyatta, who are you talking to down there? I told you about talking to those pipers. Get outside or come in the house to stay!" The girl ran quickly out the door. Replacing the cap on the bottle and sliding it back into the bag, I started up the stairs toward the voice.

I called out, "I'm Leslie Hill from Elder Protective Services." On my way up, I begin to formulate a story about how I was researching Mrs. Harris' accident. Maybe this woman could tell me something.

She was standing in the doorway, and before I could fix my lips to say anything, she said, "Protective Services again." She spoke loudly into the hall landing, "I don't know *who* keeps calling Protective Services down here, but they better mind they business and act like they know!" She focused on me and the ID badge I held up.

"I'm Leslie Hill," I held out my hand to her. She ignored it.

The woman standing before me was almost as thin as Eugenia Harris. Her brown skin was dull-looking and sprinkled with dark freckle-like marks. She was nearly as tall as I, and would have been taller if she had had better posture. She was dressed in slacks with a long African-print caftan over them. She wore plastic sandals with gold-colored straps, her toenails painted blue. She looked me up and down, evaluating me with expressionless eyes.

"My name is Pearl Sidney, as if you didn't know." She backed into her apartment and pointed down the hall to the last door. "She's back here, probably asleep. Ain't nobody doin' nothin' to that old lady. I know who called you. You don't have to tell me, *I know*."

Pearl opened the door to my second darkened room of the day. "Mama, they called Protective again." Pearl didn't turn on the light. When my eyes became accustomed to the darkness, I saw a woman sitting hunched in a wheelchair by a dusty window. Pearl pulled a kitchen chair out of the darkness, set it across from the woman, and offered it to me. I sat down. I did not take off my jacket.

"Could we have a little light in here?" I asked.

"Light hurts Mama's eyes, don't it, Mama?" Pearl stood behind me, her hand resting on the back of my chair.

"It's all right, Pearl," the woman said, "Turn on the light."

I could feel Pearl tighten her grip on my chair and her knuckles graze my back. When the lights came on, across from me, in a wheelchair, sat a wizened old woman with tobacco-colored skin. Her hair was pulled up into a tiny rubber-banded bun on top of her head. She wore a filthy house dress covered with an even filthier apron. Both of her legs had been amputated at the knee. Out of the corner of my eye I saw dark spots running along the floor toward the shadows under the bed and bureau; they ran on unseen highways up and down the wall.

Pearl said, "See, she's fine."

I looked into the face of the woman in the chair and introduced myself. Her eyelids were droopy. I held out my hand and she brushed my fingertips with hers—at least an attempt, I thought. "What's your name?" I asked.

Pearl answered the question for her. "Her name is Hattie Jackson. She's my husband's grandmother—we like to call her Mama." Pearl sat on Mrs. Jackson's bed. The sheets were dingy and stained and looked as if they hadn't been changed in months. On the bureau among Hattie Jackson's toiletries was a photograph of her with a little girl on her lap. It was the little girl I'd seen earlier on the steps. They were both smiling.

I asked Mrs. Jackson if she could tell me today's date. Pearl answered in a sing-song voice, "It's Wednesday, isn't it, Mama?"

Ignoring Pearl, I asked Mrs. Jackson if she could tell me her birth date.

"Mama was born February the fifth, 1919."

I told Mrs. Jackson and Pearl that this was a preliminary interview, that I would be back to conduct a formal and *confidential*—I looked at Pearl—interview in a few days. Pearl's expression told me that she was not happy about that. Mrs. Jackson turned her face toward the window.

As Pearl led me down the hall, she muttered, "Last time they was accusing me and my husband of taking her money. We don't need her little bit of money. Look, I want to get this over with. Nobody's doin' nothin' to that old lady." Pearl walked me to the door and nearly slammed the door in my face.

I couldn't wait to get back to my office. I bent over the computer keyboard and typed in the name Hattie Jackson. Surprisingly, luckily, there was only one entry. She was in the computer because she was known to Protective Services. Nearly a year had passed since the case had been closed. The case was coded unsubstantiated. But an unsubstantiated case should have been shredded by now. I keyed in the code, and the name of the investigator who had this case previously glowed on the screen.

♦

It took some prodding, but Dee began to remember Mrs. Jackson. She had gotten the case just after the client's second amputation. A visiting nurse who was treating Mrs. Jackson and thought that her living conditions were abysmal had called Protective. The nurse also thought that the client was supporting the household with her Social Security checks.

Dee wheeled around in her chair to face me. "That was a sad one. They were taking her money, kept her all doped up in the back room. I was going to set her up with direct deposit and a nice savings account. I found her a boarding home that was wheelchair-accessible. But she told me that unless she could take her great-grandchild with her, she wasn't going anywhere. She said that Pearl and her grandson were taking good care of her and she paid them for that care. Paid them her whole check, I guess. Well, that kid is probably a check to them too." Dee paused for a moment, then said angrily, "I hate junkies. I was about two steps away from calling DHS on them."

"So why didn't you involuntarily remove her from the home?" I asked.

Dee sighed, "The lady had the capacity to make decisions. She said she was making a *bad* decision to stay in that household and give them her money. She was really afraid that if she left the home she'd never see her great-grandchild again. She didn't trust that I could hook it up so they could stay together—she really loved that little girl. I did refer her for a senior companion though, and placed her on the waiting list." Dee turned back toward her computer. "Did she ever get one?" She began to type.

I sat staring at Dee. I couldn't believe what she'd just said.

Could Eugenia Harris have been the senior companion assigned to Hattie Jackson? I looked at the screen that revealed any services Hattie had been referred for. There was only one: senior companion through Echo Hill Senior Center. I looked up and whispered a thank you to the Goddess. This link between Hattie Jackson and Madeline Harris legitimized my involvement on Travis Street. I called Echo Hill Senior Center and asked for the coordinator of the Senior Companion Program. I asked about Eugenia Harris' employment as a senior companion and the client most recently assigned to her. I was told that the identity of Mrs. Harris' client was confidential and that Mrs. Harris had resigned. When I asked for information regarding her reasons for resignation, the coordinator became flustered and told me that all personnel information was confidential and if I insisted, I could speak with the lawyer for the Center, attorney William Harter. I thanked her and hung up.

I called the attorney and told him that the Senior Companion Program Coordinator was requesting clarification regarding the status of the Center and the Eugenia Harris accident. He asked careful questions about my identity and what information I wanted. I told him I was an investigator, but not for whom. I came away with the impression that Echo Hill Senior Center had avoided litigation by separating itself from Eugenia and paying a lump sum settlement to the family of the child.

I called Evelyn McQuery, a lawyer friend of mine, and asked how I could find out about the lawsuit between the Center and the child's family. She said the information was a matter of public record that could be found in court documents.

I pulled out a travel sheet and dated it for Tuesday morning. I would be going to the county courthouse first thing. By the time I'd finished writing the progress notes for Eugenia Harris' case, it was a quarter to five. I began clearing my desk to go home.

♦

Wearing my best job interview suit and with a leather attaché under my arm, I stood before a clerk in the court records office. The office was busy and I stood five deep in a line of others requesting court information. I filled out requests for records regarding civil action against Echo Hill Senior Center and/or Eugenia Harris taking place this year. Where the form asked for my signature and affiliation, I scrawled illegibly. The harried clerk took my requests and using the form like a map she searched the long stacks of record books.

I took a seat at a table near a window and opened a thin folder for the case between Echo Hill Senior Center and Pearl and Joseph Sidney for the minor child, Kenyatta Sidney. The lawyer representing Kenyatta was Brian Howe. I recognized his name immediately from his firm's television and radio ad, "If you or your loved ones have suffered from wrongful injury or malpractice, call Brian Howe at the law offices of . . ." But this little case didn't seem worth the time of this sleazy lawyer with a reputation for high settlements.

I closed the folder; there was still something missing. Returning to the front desk, I requested information regarding civil actions initiated by Brian Howe for the Sidney family.

I now had three very thick folders to carry back to my table. There was the case between Eugenia Harris and the Sidney family: pending. Then a case between Echo Hill Senior Center and the Sidney family: closed. Finally, there was a pending case between the Sidney family and Benjamin Franklin Hospital. *Bingo.* The malpractice suit against Benjamin Franklin Hospital was for negligence. The plaintiff alleged that Kenyatta was ignored in the emergency room despite the seriousness of her injuries. She was described as being made to wait in a crowded ER until her mother, responding to the child's discomfort, took her home, where she suffered needlessly. The damages asked for in this suit was $2.5 million. Included as part of the complaint was a photograph of a child so battered, bruised, and lacerated that it was painful to look at her. The label on the photograph read, *Kenyatta Sidney, age five years.* She looked like the same child I'd seen in the hallway on Travis Street, but I couldn't be sure, her features were so distorted by her injuries.

As I drove from the courthouse to my office, I tried to understand what was going on. Whatever it was, it seemed far less about getting satisfaction for an injured child than about money. When all of this was over, the Sidneys would be millionaires—or in any case there would be a large settlement, even if the hospital settled out of court. It seemed too big a coincidence that Kenyatta Sidney and Hattie Jackson lived in the same house.

I stopped in the office long enough to pick up an investigation packet and to sign out for 2304 Travis Street.

Pearl answered the door and reluctantly let me in. A man sat hunched over the kitchen table; he looked up at me but quickly returned to his breakfast. Pearl pointed down the hall, indicating Hattie's room and started in that direction. I told her that I had to speak with Mrs. Jackson alone. I could feel Pearl's eyes as I walked toward the back room. She muttered loud enough for me to hear, "This is *my* house and I can go in any room I please."

There was more light in the room. Hattie Jackson was sitting in the same position near the window as when I had seen her last. Her head lolled, chin against chest. Her breathing sounded like she was asleep.

"Mrs. Jackson? Mrs. Jackson, it's Leslie Hill again." I leaned forward and gently shook her arm. Hattie's eyes opened with effort; her mouth seemed sealed with sleep-induced saliva. She smiled faintly.

"Miss Hattie, can you hear me?" I shook her arm again, put my hand to her cheek. *What* was going on with this woman?

Hattie nodded sleepily but didn't speak. I went to the doorway and called out to Pearl, "What's wrong with her?"

Pearl yelled back without emotion, "Nothing. After she's had her meds, she's sleepy like that all day."

I turned back to Hattie. She rippled her lids but did not raise them—did not seem to be *able* to raise them. Her hands were fists in her lap, and I wondered if she might be holding something.

I stepped forward and shook the old woman's shoulder. Hattie startled awake, then smiled, then relaxed into a nod. I pulled the kitchen chair close to her. I leaned toward the dozing woman's ear and whispered, "I've been to the courthouse and I know about the lawsuits." Her eyes opened a slit.

"I can understand that they're doing this for the money. But what do you have to do with it? I can't believe that you are involved, not if you want to keep your great-grandchild. If they get caught, everybody's going to jail and that little girl's going to foster care."

Hattie Jackson, her eyes still closed, whispered back to me, "They ain't gonna get caught. I listen and they say the case is almost over. They say they gonna be rich. Then they'll pick up and move again. It'll be the last time. No more roach houses and Kenyatta can have things she's s'posed to have."

"And what about you?" I asked, my hand lightly resting on her balled-up fist.

Hattie's eyes never opened as she told me, "I'm an old lady. I don't take up much room. I keep my mouth shut. As long as Kenyatta gets taken care of, what happens to me don't matter. I don't know why you waste your time coming in here anyway. You young social workers come in and stir up a whole lot of stuff that I have to live with after you leave. You can't do anything about what's going on here, and I ain't leaving without my little baby girl. Why don't you go on back to your nice office downtown. Like I said, what happens to a little old doped-up lady doesn't matter."

Then Hattie Jackson looked up with eyes as clear as the sunny November day. She opened her hand to reveal four yellow, oval pills in her palm. She never raised her voice above a whisper.

I frowned at her. Her complacency had made me angry. "It *does* matter—do you think they will take you with them, do you think they care about dragging a little girl and an old lady along with them after they get all that money?" I thought back to the picture of the badly injured Kenyatta

Sydney. "Do you think anyone who would do what they did to that little girl to get the money would want her around to share it?"

Hattie was silent. I got up from the chair and pushed it back to its spot beside the bed. I pulled out my wallet and dropped one of my cards into her lap.

"Think about what I said, Mrs. Jackson, and give me a call."

As I walked toward the door, Hattie hissed at me, "If there *was* a phone, how do you suppose I'd get out to it? My chair doesn't fit through the doorway."

I turned to find her looking at me with her head sarcastically tipped to the side. Then she closed her eyes and let her head gently drop chin-to-chest, as when I had entered the room.

I lambasted Pearl about the overmedication of her grandmother-in-law and the dangerousness of her virtual imprisonment in that back bedroom. Pearl sucked her teeth; it was obvious that she couldn't have cared less. Kenyatta sat silently at the kitchen table, pretending not to listen.

♦

I drove directly to Eugenia Harris's house from Mrs. Jackson's.

Madeline had barely opened the door when I began to tell her about everything I had found out. I needed to talk to her aunt one more time.

I let myself into her room and got right up to the edge of Eugenia's bed. "Mrs. Harris, I need to know more details about the accident. I've been to Travis Street and to the county courthouse. The little girl you were supposed to have hit lives in the same apartment as the woman you were going to companion for. This is all too coincidental. I've got to know more about what happened on the day of the accident."

Mrs. Harris's first concern was for Kenyatta. She had seen the picture included in the court record and had been devastated. I assured her that aside from being a little obnoxious, Kenyatta was fine now. Madeline got her aunt a cup of coffee, and Eugenia began to tell her story.

Eugenia detailed how slowly she had been driving—
because she was very close to the house she was going
to—when she saw the man standing in the street. She stood
shakily and demonstrated how the man had been standing,
and both Madeline and I felt he had been holding out his
arms, beckoning the child. Eugenia said Kenyatta wasn't
wearing a coat, even though it was February. After the
accident and once the police had arrived, the man carried the
little girl in his arms and handed her to the woman who had
been in the window. Eugenia had never seen the child lying
on the ground. The woman had opened the back door of the
police car and climbed in with the child, demanding to be
taken to the hospital. The scene was chaotic as the cop took
Eugenia's name, license number, and van registration. By the
time the policeman drove away, the child was no longer
crying. Eugenia said the child's clothes weren't torn or
noticeably dirty. Eugenia had then returned to the agency
and filled out an accident report. The Echo Hill Center had
asked Eugenia not to drive the van until the case was cleared
up. She was asked to take an unpaid leave and shortly
received a letter advising her to resign. Soon after that she
was summoned to court about her driving.

"I felt so bad, I didn't show for the hearing and they
suspended my license. For weeks I'd kept saying, 'don't you
think I would know if I rolled over something as big as a
child?' But no one listened. Everyone assumed because I'm
old, I must have been distracted or blinded by the snow.
They assumed I didn't know what I was talking about. They
assumed I hit the child." Eugenia grew quiet for a moment,
then continued. "After that, some awful lawyer came over
and showed me the pictures of the little girl. He said the
bruises came out later and that she was hurt so badly she
had to be hospitalized. That took the last bit of fight right
out of me. After they took my license away, I felt so bad, like
no one could help me. I didn't bother to get a lawyer; it
seemed useless."

When Eugenia had finished her account of what
happened, I didn't believe that she had hit the little girl—I
believed that Pearl and Joe Sydney had hit the girl, and not
with a car. I believed that they had planned to sue the senior

center for the staged hit, but whatever happened at the hospital had changed everything.

Eugenia glowed with excitement while telling her story; by the time she had finished, she had drunk two cups of coffee and eaten three slices of toast. Eugenia wiped crumbs away from the corners of her mouth. "You say the little girl is all right?"

I nodded, but wondered how long she would remain all right.

"What are you going to do?" Eugenia asked.

"Call the cops, get your license back, close the case." I answered flippantly.

"What's going to happen to Mrs. Jackson and the little girl?" Eugenia pulled herself up in bed and arranged the covers neatly around her waist.

I had to answer, "I don't know."

I went back to my office to write progress notes and decide who to call about this. I was just about to go to my supervisor's office when my telephone rang. It was Eugenia Harris. "I want to go with you to Hattie Jackson's," she said. "I was her senior companion once—it seems like she *really* needs one now."

♦

Eugenia was very thin but not as weak as I had thought she would be. She made her way up the dim stairway to the Sidneys' apartment. I knocked; there was no answer. Just as we prepared to leave, the door opened a crack and Kenyatta's face appeared behind it. Eugenia smiled at her.

It took some convincing, but Kenyatta let us in. It was Eugenia's gentle manner that won her over. Eugenia and I made our way to the back room where Hattie sat in her chair. She was more awake than I had seen her. After introductions, Eugenia and Hattie fell into talking, little Kenyatta leaning against Hattie's chair, taking in every word. I sat back in silence, careful not to lean against the wall, remembering the roaches.

In the car on the way back, Eugenia told me that Hattie had told her everything. Pearl and Joe had staged the car accident to get rid of Eugenia and make some bucks in the process. Kenyatta hadn't been hurt, unless you counted the numerous bruises she had from the frequent hits she took from Pearl. They went to the emergency room and were checked in. Maybe because the ER was very crowded and because Kenyatta didn't seem seriously hurt, time passed and they hadn't been seen. Hattie wondered if maybe Pearl had planned to leave all along. But Pearl and Kenyatta left the ER and came home in a taxi. That night Joe and Pearl argued. Their fight spilled over onto Kenyatta. They beat her until she couldn't cry any more. Hattie couldn't get out of the room to help the child—all she could do was scream. The next day Kenyatta was covered with bruises. Pearl had remarked sarcastically, "You look like you've been in an accident now." That must have been when she got the idea to try to sue the hospital, as well as Eugenia.

Hattie told Eugenia she had overheard Pearl and Joe plan what they would do when they got the money from the claim against the hospital. They were planning to leave as soon as the money came. Pearl was giving her more pills, and Hattie was growing more and more afraid that she would be left behind, alone in that room or dead. Eugenia had promised to keep visiting until they thought of what to do. I agreed to wait a reasonable amount of time before I blew the whistle on everyone, but I was worried about both of them.

♦

Almost a week passed before I heard from Eugenia again. She left a message on my voicemail. "Madeline has been driving me back and forth to Hattie's. Pearl acts like she's never seen me before and often leaves us alone in the house with Kenyatta. She underestimates the power of an old woman." Eugenia took a deep breath and said, "Hattie and I have decided she's leaving the apartment the next time Pearl leaves us alone, and we're taking Kenyatta with us."

Thursday morning there was another message from Eugenia in my voicemail, "Hattie says the hospital settled out of court. Pearl and Joe are going down to the lawyer's office to get a check this morning. I'm calling from a public telephone at the corner store. Hattie and I are leaving today. Madeline is driving us."

I called the lawyer for the hospital and told him what I knew; then I called the police. I got into my car and drove across town to Hattie's apartment. I thought better of parking on Travis Street and parked the car around the corner on Twenty-third.

I took the steps two at a time and pushed open the apartment door after a cursory knock. Hattie and Eugenia screamed as I came in. They were crowded down at the end of the hall. Hattie was transferring from her wheelchair to the kitchen chair. The plan was to fold the wheelchair and push it to the other side of the door jamb, then Hattie would transfer back into it. Eugenia would roll Hattie out the back door in case Pearl and Joe came up the front. I wondered how Hattie was going to make it down the steep back stairs.

I went to the kitchen window and looked down into the street. The hospital lawyer would call Brian Howe, the lawyer for Pearl and Joe, and stop payment on the check. If they hadn't gotten the check by the time the call came, they wouldn't be getting it. They would, in any case, be racing back here. I went out to the back hall to check the progress of Hattie, Madeline, and Eugenia. Hattie was bumping slowly down the filthy steps on her bottom. Behind the back door was a five-gallon kerosene can. I kicked it; it sounded full. I went back into the apartment and heard Pearl and Joe noisily making their way into the front of the building. I sprinted to the back stairs and glanced down. Hattie, Eugenia, and Madeline were nearly at the bottom, but where was Kenyatta?

"Where's Kenyatta?" I asked. The expressions on the faces looking up told me all I needed to know. I turned and headed back to the apartment and met Kenyatta coming out the back door. She was carrying a little tin box.

"Come on, honey." I picked her up and nearly fell down the steps on fear-weakened legs. I could hear Pearl swearing at the top of her lungs as I made my way to the bottom of the stairs. Eugenia was pushing Hattie in her wheelchair along the narrow brick-paved alleyway that led behind the houses to the end of the block. I put Kenyatta down and helped Eugenia push. Pearl's screams seemed to open out

and blend in with the whooping police siren's as we rounded
the corner.

I drove past the front of the house as the police were
taking Pearl and Joe out. Hattie, Kenyatta, Eugenia, and
Madeline were speeding safely away toward Mont Airy in
Madeline's car.

♦

When we were all back at Eugenia's house and settled in
around the dining-room table, Kenyatta opened the tin box.
It had chocolates in it.

"My G.G. gave it to me and Mama took it away."
Kenyatta called her great-grandmother G.G.

Hattie smiled gently at her and said, "Baby, I gave those
to you last year. That candy is not good any more. Let G.G.
take it." Hattie took the chocolates and wrinkled her nose at
the first one she picked out. It smelled rancid and stale. She
was bouncing the tin up and down on her palm considering
its weight, when Kenyatta snatched it out of her hand,
declaring, "No, G.G., it's mine!" The little girl, standing on
her chair, pulled the tin out of Hattie's hand. The momentum
of the snatch threw Kenyatta backward out of the chair to
the floor. The contents of the tin, old chocolates and swirling
dollar bills, followed her.

Pearl had kept her ill-gotten gains in this box. When we
had finished counting, there were two layers, five across, of
ten one-hundred dollar bills. Ten thousand dollars—not a
fortune, but enough.

Eugenia asked Hattie and Kenyatta to stay and live with
her, and with very little persuasion, they accepted. Madeline
happily planned to move back to her apartment in Center
City.

Later that afternoon, Madeline went to Pearl and Joe's
house for Kenyatta's belongings. The apartment door was
open; there was very little left.

I went back to my office and worked on closing the
Eugenia Harris case. I wondered how much of what
happened would end up recorded in the file. My
concentration was broken when a fat manila folder was
dropped on my desk by an office clerk.

I opened the folder and began to read the allegations. This case was about a seventy-two-year-old man, about to be evicted because he had too many cats. I opened my lower drawer, pulled out a spray can of flea repellent, and set it on the desk. I turned to face the computer monitor and began to key in the new client's name.

GRANDFATHER IN A BOX

Joanne Dahme

I realize now that living in a classic suburban development like Meadowbrook is not a talisman against evil, but when Mark and I first married, it was partially that belief that brought us here. Our development is at least an hour's drive from the nearest city. The events broadcast on the nightly news all seem so urban—a world away from Meadowbrook. The stone and masonry three- and four-bedroom homes that typify our community, laid out in cookie-cutter perfection, may not be top-of-the-line, but they're comfortably placed on wide, curbless streets that curve and wind to accommodate the big, leafy oak and maple trees that dominate them.

Our neighbors are friendly and caring—not the type to stop by every day to borrow a cup of sugar, but they do invite one another to backyard barbecues, lend their leaf blowers, and even go so far as to shovel the snow from the driveway of a senior resident without being asked. Meadowbrook is a decent community, one populated, I still believe, by people who certainly don't have it all, but most of whom have enough sense to be sincerely thankful. After four years here, I couldn't imagine it being any other way—until Cindy and Tom Parks moved in.

At first, although I wouldn't go so far as to say their arrival was just what the doctor had ordered for me, I did greet the event as something hopeful. As a writer who works at home, juggling my time between nurturing my three-year-old daughter and nurturing ideas for my work, I had recently felt kind of stale, particularly with regard to an article I was writing for a national family magazine. The article, a cover story tentatively titled "Family Dynamics in the 90s," seemed dull and overdone. But the deadline was fast approaching. I greeted Cindy's arrival as an opportunity for some new insights. Nothing like new blood in the neighborhood.

Cindy, her husband Tom, their three-year-old son Todd, and Tom's elderly father moved into the house next door to ours two months ago. The house had been vacant over the summer, so I was glad to see new neighbors move in. I had been sitting at the dining-room table, struggling to put some thoughts for my article down on paper, when I saw them pull into the driveway. Tom was at the wheel of a new white Lincoln Continental, with Cindy sitting primly by his side. Todd was strapped into his car seat in the back, the top of his head barely visible. An enormous moving van was right behind them. Tom immediately positioned himself on the front lawn, orchestrating the unloading of the furniture. Cindy took to the house, periodically reappearing, it seemed, to inventory what remained in the van.

They looked and dressed like the wholesome young couples featured in the Lands' End and J. Crew catalogs. Cindy was a thin, stunning blonde, with model-delicate features, cool and composed. Tom was thin too, but buff, like he worked hard to maintain his physique. Their son Todd was running circles around them, positively exuberant over this new adventure. I didn't see the grandfather that day. I guess he arrived later.

Well, they say appearances can be deceiving. Cindy hadn't been our neighbor for a week yet, really hadn't even spoken to me at that point, beyond a waved hello from the mailbox at the end of her driveway, when she showed up at my front door. It was a Sunday night, and I was just cleaning up after dinner, when she rang the doorbell. No, no, she didn't have time to come in, she said. She was strictly

business. She had enrolled Todd at the same daycare center
my three-year-old daughter Sarah attended. A member of the
daycare staff had suggested to Cindy that we carpool.

Cindy thought this was a wonderful idea and had come
by to suggest it to me. Except she wanted me to do all the
driving. Since I was a writer, naturally I didn't have a real
schedule to live by. And she needed to be home on a
constant basis to care for her very sick father-in-law who
lived with them. I was making the trip back and forth now
every day anyway, right? So of course I wouldn't mind,
would I?

She *was* my new neighbor, and I couldn't argue with her
logic. I *was* making the trip every day, so it wouldn't affect
my schedule—or lack of one, as she implied—particularly
now, since the cover story was finished and so, apparently,
were my new ideas. Still, I was silently peeved.

But Todd's wonderful effect on Sarah was one of the
reasons that my initial resentment of Cindy, and my own
displeasure at myself for not being able to say no to her
request, eventually dissipated. Sarah had hated
daycare—had screamed and cried every morning I dragged
her out to the car. Some days I was so sure that I was
permanently damaging her psyche that I was ready to give
up writing altogether. Until that first morning I took Todd to
daycare and braced myself for the fight of my life—two
miserable children instead of one. But when Sarah met Todd,
it was love at first sight. Sarah was quiet and cheerful. And I
was left to drive to daycare in peace for the first time.

◆

It was on our way to daycare one especially gray
December morning that Todd first talked about his
grandfather. It all sounded innocent enough at first,
especially coming from a child, when Todd said, in that
exuberant, news-breaking tone that three-year-olds use, that
his grandfather was in a box now. Sarah stared at him, rapt.

"What's that, Todd?" I asked, barely listening at first. I
was already mentally editing the long list of things I needed
to do that day. But the oddness of the announcement had
caught my ear. I looked at Todd's reflection in my rearview

mirror to make sure that I understood him correctly. He sat, or maybe more accurately, was crammed, in his car seat, which he was fast outgrowing. Although I had remembered to unzip his winter coat, I felt a twinge of guilt thinking about the difficulty he might be having breathing. Sarah, who sat in her own seat elbow to elbow with Todd, looked tiny to me in comparison.

Todd gazed right back at me, his big brown eyes emphasizing that total innocence of children. Todd is a beautiful, dark-haired child, who almost always wears a naturally mischievous grin on his face, making him all the more irresistible.

"My grandfather is in a box now," he announced more loudly—as if I hadn't heard him the first time. Sarah didn't say a word. Her blue eyes were fixed on Todd in total admiration. Sarah and Todd are opposites in appearance and personality. Sarah is petite, even for a three-year-old, with baby-fine curls of pale blonde hair and two wonderful dimples that only a select few have been lucky enough to see. She smiles constantly for Todd, which is nice, but at the same time a shame, as I feel it's a spendthrift use of a limited resource. I continually reassure myself that Sarah is simply going through a grumpy stage—grumpy with everyone but Todd, that is. And now she was transfixed by Todd's announcement of his grandfather being in a box. The thought process that would somehow shape this idea in Todd's head fascinated me. What could he possibly be talking about?

"Well, how *is* your granddad doing, Todd? Your mommy told me he's very sick."

"Unhuh," Todd said, nodding in agreement. "But he's in the box now."

In the box now, I repeated to myself. Maybe it was because all my ideas for any new articles were bottoming out that the notion of Todd's grandfather being in a box jolted me so. This kid had a lot more imagination than I did.

"Okay, we're here guys," I announced in my overly cheerful voice that I couldn't shake as a result of those earlier, Todd-less days with Sarah. Todd immediately took to the task of struggling to undo his seatbelt.

But even after I had them safely in daycare, I couldn't shake Todd's weird announcement about his grandfather. Could he mean that his grandfather had actually died and Todd had seen him in a coffin? I hadn't seen an obituary in our local paper. Would it scare Todd, or confuse him, if I just came right out and asked him if his grandfather had died? But why wouldn't Cindy have said something to me since I see her practically every day? Maybe she didn't want me to know that she had lost her excuse not to share the carpooling. I immediately felt ashamed of that nasty thought.

I tried to picture Todd's grandfather during my short trip home, but all I could envision were TV images of sickly old men. I thought it strange that in the daily relationship I maintained with Todd's family I had never actually seen the grandfather. I remembered that on our first trip to daycare together, the trees that encircled the modest homes in our development still had plenty of leaves. Now the trees were starkly bare. Yet in all this time I had never even glimpsed Todd's grandfather. Was that as odd as it now seemed? Or was he really just as sick as Cindy claimed?

One of my neighbors, Mrs. McNally, who lives across the street from us, had actually seen him once. She had been so proud of herself at the sighting, too. She makes it a point to know what's going on in our neighborhood, as she's retired and a widow and remembers reading somewhere that it's senior citizens who make most of the crime-prevention calls to local town watches and police. From the day we had moved to Meadowbrook, Mrs. McNally had been a beloved though slightly eccentric figure in our lives. When she learned that both Mark's and my parents lived in other states, she gently yet firmly assumed the role of surrogate parent to both of us. And when Sarah was born, her joy could not have been more genuine. She was a surrogate grandparent now, too.

I think it was because Mrs. McNally had become a part of *our* lives so seamlessly that she was hurt when Cindy had ignored her overtures of welcome. I can still picture the tin of cookies and bouquet of cut flowers that Mrs. McNally left at Cindy's doorstep, because Cindy refused to answer her door. Mrs. McNally later told me that she *knew* Cindy was home. So, as if to spite Cindy, Mrs. McNally made it her goal to spot Cindy's father-in-law.

Mrs. McNally saw him being helped—practically carried, she corrected herself—from a black limousine early one evening. It was dusk, but Mrs. McNally could still make out the grandfather's stooped figure. She said he was wearing a black overcoat obviously several sizes too big for him. He had no hat, so Mrs. McNally could see that the few tufts of white fuzz left on his head did nothing to soften the sharp outline of his skull.

Mrs. McNally didn't let her triumph end with this data alone. After the limo driver assisted Todd's grandfather into the house, Mrs. McNally scurried out of her own house to talk to the limo driver. She was able to elicit some key facts. Yes, he was sickly, maybe a little senile even. In his mid-seventies. But the best tidbit of all was that he was rich—very rich. The limo driver didn't know how rich, as Mrs. McNally pointedly asked, but did know that a substantial trust fund had been set up for his son and grandson. Apparently Tom worked in some management capacity for his father's company, but his father hadn't given up his hold of the company's finances. Not yet, anyway.

How did the limo driver know all that, I had asked Mrs. McNally. Oh, *he knew*, she replied, knowingly. He said he'd been the grandfather's driver for years. Mrs. McNally had gotten the impression that the driver did not approve of Tom or Cindy, she added, shaking her head.

Maybe I need to go over and meet the grandfather myself, I thought, reminded of Todd's bizarre declaration. But the better part of me realized that I was acting just as nosy as Mrs. McNally. I mean, what would I say to Cindy? "Hi. Just wondering how Todd's granddad is doing. Here's some soup." Just the thought of how ridiculous I knew Cindy would make me feel stopped me cold—until I picked Todd and Sarah up later that afternoon. Todd was still fixated on his grandfather.

"How was your day, guys? Did you have fun making Christmas decorations?"

"Grandfather's sleeping in the box now," he told me this time, holding his drawing of something red and green and rectangular close to his lap. Sarah was proudly holding up her version of a tree. Some vivid green lines and swirls.

"Wow, that's beautiful, honey. We'll tape it up in the kitchen as soon as we get home." I was ashamed at how quickly I dismissed Sarah because I wanted to get back to Todd, and what was more information—or so I thought— than his earlier revelation.

"What did you draw, Todd?"

Todd kept his drawing in his lap while he explained it to me. "I made some Christmas decorations for Grandfather. See, I put them around his box." I turned to look. Todd's description matched his three-year-old's art.

Now I was getting nervous.

"Todd, what do you mean about your grandfather? What box?"

"My box," Todd said, pointing to himself. "My box downstairs."

"You mean your toy box, where you put all your toys?"

"Yeah," Todd nodded enthusiastically, apparently thrilled at my breakthrough. "And Grandfather will have decorations now," he added quickly.

"Very nice," I murmured, trying to picture the size of Todd's toy box. And wondering if it now held more than toys.

◆

After we put Sarah to bed that night, I told Mark about my weird conversation with Todd. We both acknowledged a three-year-old's propensity to say all kinds of things. But Mark also agreed that Todd's sudden, untypical obsession with his grandfather was strange, as I had never heard Todd speak about his grandfather before.

"Well, Gina, why don't you make a point of visiting Cindy tomorrow," Mark said, "so we know for sure. Otherwise, you'll keep worrying about Todd. You can say that Todd told you that his grandfather is really sick. And you just wanted to see if everything was all right. That can be your excuse."

I nodded my head thoughtfully. I'm someone who always likes to have an excuse when I'm doing something I

feel uncomfortable about. But really, the way Todd was
talking, I didn't *need* an excuse, I told myself. And Mark
seemed to agree.

The next day I waited until I dropped the kids off at
daycare and came home to have a cup of coffee. Todd hadn't
mentioned his grandfather, and I hadn't wanted to prod or
upset him. So a little self-doubt had set in. What was I
looking to find anyway? That Todd's granddad was indeed
alive and that everything seemed normal over there? Was it
as simple as that? Whatever it was, I had to go over just so
that I could get on with my life.

I was just putting on my coat when the doorbell rang.
When I opened the door to find Cindy standing on my
doorstep, I nearly yelled her name.

"Cindy! Why, what a surprise. I was just thinking about
stopping over to see you. Please, come in." I hoped she
didn't notice how red my face had turned.

"No, I can't, Gina. Actually, I'm here to ask you a
favor." Cindy paused, waiting for a gust of wind to pass. She
stood there, in the icy cold, her jacket unbuttoned, her long,
dark hair blown away from her face. Her expression was
stern; her eyes held no warmth. The ice-lady cometh, I
thought, a little crazily.

"Sure," I heard myself say, "What can I do?"

"I need to stop by Tom's office. Something came up.
Could you stay at my house, for about an hour, just in case
Tom's father needs anything?"

"Well, yes, let me get my bag. I'd be glad to." This was
too weird, I thought to myself. Like she could read minds or
something.

As Cindy opened her front door, I realized I had never
actually been in her house. She always had Todd ready to go
and simply passed him and his carseat to me out the front
door. We reversed the process when we came home. As I
took off my coat, I was relieved that the place at least *looked*
normal. Expensive furniture, tastefully arranged, as if to
show it off. The home's layout was just like ours—all the
homes in our development were a standard design. But
Cindy's house was less homey than those of our neighbors,
like Mrs. McNally. Cindy's house was somewhat stark, the
furniture sleek, all leather and chrome. Nothing appeared

out of place. Not a toy in sight. I remarked on how
child-free the house appeared, trying to sound envious.

"Oh, Todd's toys are downstairs," she answered, giving
me an odd look. "I've got to get going now. Tom's father is
upstairs napping in the middle bedroom. I gave him his
medication and a sedative, so he shouldn't be calling or
needing you. Please make yourself comfortable down here.
The powder-room is down the hall, and there's coffee in the
kitchen," she added, speaking slowly as if I might not
understand.

I don't know what it was she said exactly, but Cindy had
given me the creeps. After I heard her car pulling out of the
driveway, all I could do at first was sit there, perched on the
edge of the white leather couch in the living room, and try to
ease my wariness. The house was oddly quiet. It didn't
sound as if anyone else were there—no creaking bed sounds,
no snoring or even breathing sounds. Maybe Cindy had
closed the door to her father-in-law's room.

I roused myself to get a cup of coffee. I couldn't help but
be impressed that the kitchen was immaculate, too. Clean,
white porcelain counters lined three walls of the kitchen,
which was big enough to fit a beautiful oak table and four
chairs comfortably. A high-chair was pushed into the corner
behind the table. Sliding glass doors opened onto the back
yard, just like ours. The day was overcast, and the view of
the woods behind Meadowbrook looked lonely and
foreboding. As I poured some coffee, a sudden movement
outside near the trees caught my eye. I stood against the
door to get a better look. A deer maybe. At this time of year,
they seemed to be everywhere.

Seeing nothing more but the trees, I sat down at the table
and pulled out my notebook. For a few minutes, I doodled. I
looked at my watch, surprised that only twenty minutes had
passed since Cindy had left. It seemed like an hour. I tried to
ignore the closed basement door opposite me, newly painted,
I guessed, from the whiteness of it. Of course, I couldn't
concentrate at all on writing. All I could think about was the
image Todd had left me with—that his grandfather was in
his toy box. In the basement.

The door was like a magnet. I knew I wanted to go
down and look for Todd's toy box, if just to satisfy my

morbid curiosity. I *should* go down, I told myself, simply to be done with it and convince myself that Cindy might be a little strange and cold, but was otherwise normal. I certainly would *not* find Todd's grandfather stuffed into a toy box.

At first I simply stood before the door. I actually touched it, brushing my finger against it to see if it were as clean as it looked. Not a speck of grime or dust. I noticed that the floor had been recently mopped too. This place was too clean for my taste. As if no one really lived here. As if—

When I opened the door, I don't know what I expected to hear. A feeble cry for help? A frightening moan? But it was quiet and dark. I flicked on the light and peered down the stairway. The walls were painted white downstairs too. I could see white tile flooring and some scattered toys.

Looks normal, I said to myself. But I still needed to go down there. I had to see the box.

I crept down slowly as if each step were mined. Halfway down, I actually bent over to look below the stairwell opening, just in case. *Just in case of what?* I asked myself, trying to calm my prickly nerves.

When I got to the bottom of the landing, I was relieved to see how normal the room looked, exactly like a child's playroom should look—scattered toys, blocks, cars, books piled on shelves. There was a child's table with two chairs in one corner and a blackboard easel in another. An entertainment center, with a large television, was placed against the wall exactly in the center. I inhaled quickly when I spotted the long, pine toy box against the far wall. The weak light shining through the two basement windows along the ceiling above the toy box cast an eerie light in the room. Suddenly, the daylight was momentarily blocked as if a cloud passed over the sun. But that couldn't be. It was a cloudy day. Now I was really spooked.

I forced myself to walk over to the toy box, silently scolding myself for paying attention to my own overactive imagination. *Open the box,* I instructed myself.

I actually counted to three before I lifted the smooth, thin lid. I must have closed my eyes when I did, because I remember being surprised and relieved when I opened them that the box was empty. My first thought was, *no grandfather?* My second, *no toys?* I opened the lid as far as it would go, and then crouched beside it to examine it under the daylight from the window.

There was something smeared on the floor of the box. The stain spread in a network of capillaries from the center, as if the grain of the wood had absorbed something wet. I rubbed my fingers across the stain. It was dry now. I looked at my fingertips to make sure that nothing had rubbed off on them. I suddenly felt a little sick. The stain looked dark red, the earthy red color that blood assumes in clothes—and furniture—after it has had time to dry.

"Looking for something, Gina?" My heart fell to my feet when I heard Cindy's snide voice. I stood up and turned around, feeling ashamed, as if I'd been caught snooping in her bureau drawers. A torrent of misgivings washed over me, along with a deep blush. What if I had been wrong about my suspicions? What if I were just a fifth-rate writer starved for some adventure and excitement? How could Todd be such a wonderful and generous child if his parents were really so awful?

I looked at Cindy. She seemed as if she were barely in control of a volcanic rage, her eyes bright and intense, her mouth set in a hard smile. Her expression was so frightful that I initially couldn't stop staring at her. It took me a minute to notice the gun in her right hand, a tiny silver piece, cold and stylish, like her furniture.

"Cindy," I blurted out in a panic, "I'm sorry, I was just looking around Todd's playroom. It's a wonderful playroom, so bright, so . . ."

"Shut up, Gina. Todd told me what he said to you. I didn't know he had gotten into the playroom that night. I thought I had locked the damn door." She flipped her hair back over her shoulder with her left hand in a gesture of annoyance. "At first, I didn't think anything of it. After all, he's practically a baby. Who would listen to the babbling of a child? But then I realized you might, you're such an idiot."

"Wait a minute. I listen to Todd because I care about him." Despite my fear, she was making me angry. Her two months of taking advantage of my better nature had taken its toll. If she thought I was such an idiot, then I might as well play her game.

"Listen, Cindy. It's ridiculous that you're threatening to *shoot* me just because I'm in your basement, for God's sake. I wanted to see Todd's playroom, because, yes—he did tell me about his playroom. But that's *all* he told me. I don't know what else you're talking about." How could she shoot the nice neighbor who loved her son enough to take him to daycare every day?

"Nice try, Gina. Now get into the box." She walked a few menacing steps toward me, waving her gun. My heart was pounding so furiously I was surprised that the sound of it didn't fill the room. She intended to shoot me and put *me* in the box, now. Todd would be making Christmas decorations for Granddad *and* me. I needed to buy some time. But how. Talk about the kids?

"But Cindy, what about Todd? I have to pick up Todd and Sarah in less than an hour. Please, calm down. We can work this out."

Her nostrils flared this time. "Don't you worry about Todd, Gina. Good old granddaddy rewrote his will so that everything would go to my darling little baby. Todd will be well provided for. Now get in the goddamn box, Gina, before I blow your head off." *She's crazy*, I thought, the realization making me cold and shaky.

"What? Why?! I don't understand." I tried to focus on what I could do to get away from her and the little silver pistol.

"Because I don't want your blood all over the place after I shoot you." She laughed as if my stupidity surprised her. "That's where I put good old granddaddy." The horror I felt must have been apparent in my face, for then she spewed the whole, incredible story. As I slowly straddled the side of that cursed box, she spoke with cool aplomb about how she didn't feel like waiting for poor old grandfather to die on his own.

Grandfather had been thinking about changing his will, she said. He had never *liked* Cindy, and he liked her even less since he had begun living with her and Tom. "And after all the loving daughterly care I provided him," she pouted, mockingly. "He even threatened to write us *all* completely out of the will, unless Tom divorced me. Divorce!" she thundered. "Can you believe it?"

Cindy was spouting her incredible story with the passion of a woman wronged by a lover. But it was apparent that the love interest of this story was money—Todd's grandfather's money. And I knew that Cindy wasn't the type of person to let something promised be taken back so easily—certainly not without a good fight.

I noticed how comfortably Cindy pointed that pistol at me. I did my best not to squirm. I wanted to appear keenly interested in *her* side of the story. She was more than happy to continue her tale for her captive audience.

"That stupid old fool," she laughed derisively. "Before he decided that writing Tom out of his will was the most *prudent* thing he could do . . . ," Cindy let the sentence dangle, obviously relishing the element of suspense she thought she was injecting. I already knew the ending, I realized bitterly. But Cindy was going to finish it for me anyway.

"I certainly didn't want to stay in this sorry development forever," she explained. "Tom didn't either. So I convinced Tom that *Father's* death would actually be in the best interest of us all. And besides, what kind of life did *Father* possibly enjoy now?

Cindy said that it was Tom's idea to slowly increase the medications old Mr. Parks was on—there were so many. Medicine for his heart, for his ulcers, for practically every ailment imaginable. All Tom asked was that he not be at home the day Cindy decided to double them all. But Cindy got more than she had bargained for. She grimaced in disgust as she described how the drugs had made the old man hemorrhage. But before they did, thank God, Cindy had the foresight to invite him down into the playroom to get comfortable and watch some TV. She would be damned if she was going to let him bleed on her nice new carpets or expensive, terrazzo-tiled bathrooms, she added.

"But where is he now?" I was morbidly fascinated enough to ask.

She laughed, with sickening satisfaction. "Properly buried, of course," she said. When he had finished bleeding, Cindy had actually carried his wasted body back to his bed and called the family doctor, who was only too happy to oblige in signing the certificate during this time of sorrow.

"We wanted a very private service. That's what he would have wanted," she added demurely. "He was self-conscious about his appearance. He wanted his friends and employees to remember him as a strong and healthy man—as the leader in business he once was." Cindy rolled her eyes mockingly.

Dear God, I prayed, as I stood—both feet now—in the box. There was no way that I was going to let this sorry excuse for a woman take me out, too. I thought of Mark and Sarah and angrily stepped out of the box.

"I'll shoot you," Cindy screamed. She yelled something else, but it was lost in the sound of splintering wood from upstairs. She turned instinctively toward the sound, and when she did, I lunged at her with all my might, tackling her so that she landed against the staircase. The impact sent the gun flying from her hand.

"Gina, dear. Are you all right?" I heard dear old Mrs. McNally yell down from the kitchen as I wrestled with Cindy, both of us struggling to gain possession of the gun. "The police are here," Mrs. McNally added brightly.

It was over as quickly as it had begun. A swarm of cops descended on us. Thank God for a sleepy little, boring town, I thought. After the police handcuffed Cindy and hauled her away, I told them everything Cindy had told me. Mrs. McNally added her own little insights too, including how she had watched Cindy come over to my house and then leave me at hers, only to be seen an hour later creeping around her own yard by Mrs. McNally. I swore I'd never call Mrs. McNally nosy again. She was a surrogate parent after all, and her maternal concern for me had saved my life.

At the end of it all, I was only fifteen minutes late to pick up the kids. But this time, it was me, not Sarah, who broke down as soon as I looked into Todd's sweet face. The other parents picking up their kids gave me plenty of space.

♦

Todd was sent to live with Cindy's mother who, according to the police, is a good woman who had lost contact with her greedy daughter years ago. She didn't even know she had a grandson.

I still think of Todd often. Shortly after Cindy and Tom's arrest, I wrote a short story. It was a story about a little boy who had an incredible imagination that often got his doting parents in trouble. At the end of the story, everyone realized that it was all a terrible mistake. The grandfather was alive and well—in Florida—actually, with some old cronies. The parents were reunited with their mischievous child.

At least in fiction, I could give Todd a happy ending.

Thin Ice

Meredith Suzanne Baird

It was the second week of December. I'd brought my family up to our vacation home in the mountain community of Lakeside for a pre-Christmas skiing holiday. I stood in front of the tall windows of our A-frame—looking out over the snowy, winter-barren hillside and frozen lake. It was only three o'clock in the afternoon but seemed later, the remaining light being devoured by an increasingly heavy cloud cover. A storm had been predicted for the evening, and we were looking forward to fresh snow for the morning's ski run. The comfortable cedar-paneled living room behind me was washed in the glow from the fire blazing in the huge stone fireplace and reflected in the glass.

I hated to leave that warm room, but we needed more wood for the fire. I pulled on my down parka and went outside. The wind was picking up, and I had to struggle with the tarp covering the woodpile. Beth and our three-year-old daughter, Amelia, followed me out and began playing next to the pine trees behind the cabin. The tree boughs were frosted with a light accumulation of snow from a brief squall we'd had the night before. I watched for a minute as Beth and Amelia knelt in the thin layer of snow. There wasn't enough for a snowman, but it was perfect for the lopsided circle of cones they molded from Amelia's summer sand bucket.

˙ The temperature dropped swiftly as the cold front moved in. Amelia—bundled into a bright yellow, hooded snowsuit—looked like a small, fat chick waddling across the snow to retrieve some pine needles to decorate their sculptures. I wondered how she managed to move so swiftly with that much clothing layered over her tiny body.

An icy gust of wind caught the tarp I was holding and yanked me back toward the woodpile. The savage blast lifted the cover, wrenching the coarse fabric from my grasp. The canvas ripped apart, screaming as if alive. I fought for control.

I yelled for help and Beth appeared almost immediately. She threw herself on top of the wildly bucking sail as I struggled to tack down the corners. It took what seemed like forever to secure the tarp against the wind. Finally, exhausted with effort, laughing at the caprices of weather, we turned away from the woodpile.

Our laughter choked off. Hung there in the air in front of us. Amelia was gone.

We didn't take time to think. We just moved. Beth split off toward the cabin. Her voice broke with fear as she screamed Amelia's name. I raced to the pine trees where they had modeled their ragged ring of castings. Nothing. The miniature Stonehenge guarded its secrets.

Then I saw them.

Footprints. Tiny footprints. They threaded between the trees—dainty in the undisturbed snow. I followed them to the top of the small hill that sloped down toward the water.

Amelia stood near the edge of the lake. A brilliant dash of color against the white expanse. To my relief, she was standing next to the boulder we'd designated as her boundary. She knew she was forbidden to go closer to the water without one of us. I called out to her, but the wind hurled my voice back. She couldn't hear me. She was looking out over the lake. A small animal—a squirrel—had wandered out onto the frozen surface. It skittered toward a darkened patch of ice near the shoreline. A stream emptied into the lake at that point, and the ice was always thinner there.

Keeping an eye on Amelia, I shouted back to Beth and started running down the hill. I kept calling, but the wind tore the words from my mouth. Amelia's yellow hood—tied securely around her face—must have blocked out whatever sound the wind might have let through.

Halfway down the slope, my boot caught on a root hidden under the snow. I pitched forward, arms flailing like a drowning swimmer. The wind was knocked out of me as my abdomen slammed into a cluster of rocks.

Stunned by the blow, I couldn't breathe. I sat up painfully—cautiously—fighting for air. Seconds later, Beth was leaning over me—pulling my arm and screaming the baby's name. Still gasping, I shook my head to clear it and pointed to the shore where Amelia was standing. Where Amelia had been standing. It was empty. Nothing but the footprints. Those heartbreaking footprints. I knew where they were going.

Everything shifted into slow motion. Somehow, I got up and began to run along the edge. Beth was behind me, but we could both see what was ahead. Amelia. Her bright snowsuit shimmered against the dark spread of the ice in front of her. We were almost there. She didn't turn when we called out. Her hands were stretched toward the lake. I saw a flicker of movement on the ice. A twisted shadow.

That's all it took. Amelia headed out onto the ice. A light dusting of snow on the surface gave her some traction. It was amazing how far out she got without the ice giving way under her.

I shouted to her. If I could get her attention. Get her to come back. The ice would bear her delicate weight. If she'd only turn. I shouted again. She never hesitated. Just kept moving forward. Laughing. Reaching. Falling.

The sharp crack of the ice shattering tore through my body. The entire lake seemed to shudder. Splintered rays of broken ice spidered out from the jagged hole where Amelia had disappeared.

I shouted at Beth to get help and threw myself flat across the fragile surface. The ice protested but held. There was no movement in the gap. The water was calm. Only the current from the stream gently lapped at the edges of the break. I plunged my hands into the saw-toothed gash. The freezing water numbed my arms as I frantically searched for my daughter. I thrashed the icy opening, praying for a bit of cloth or flesh to come to hand. It was useless. Amelia had slipped under without a sound. Without a struggle.

Desperate—shaking with cold and fear—I turned my head and looked back to the shoreline. Beth was still there—pacing the edge of the lake. Crying. Calling Amelia's name. I realized she hadn't gone for help.

"Beth," I shouted. "Go back to the cabin and call the police."

She stopped short. Her hands pulled and tugged at the front of her jacket.

"I won't go," she said. "I can't leave you and the baby. I'll come out with you. Maybe I can reach her."

She moved toward the ice.

"No," I shouted. "Stay away from the ice. It won't hold both of us." I shifted slightly to face her. The ice groaned a warning. "For God's sake, go call for help. I'll stay here and keep looking."

She hesitated for a moment—swayed toward me—and then turned and ran back toward the house.

Knowing the futility of my actions—knowing that I had no choice—I thrust my arms back into the freezing hole where my daughter had vanished.

The police came out right away. Said and did everything they could. The rescue teams searched for days. Beth and I walked and scanned the perimeter of the lake as long as the effort continued. Finally, the treacherous ice and a blinding snowstorm forced them to quit. They never found Amelia's body.

The police quickly determined that Amelia had drowned by accident. Beth and I didn't bother to pack. We left Lakeside immediately. I never wanted to see the place again.

♦

I don't remember much about the memorial service. I didn't know what to do—how to do it. Beth looked at me blankly when I asked for help—an opinion—solace. There was no one to turn to. I signed papers. Wrote checks.

Family and friends pressed into the chapel that morning to pay respects. The room was wall-to-wall with grief—subdued floral arrangements—tasteful low music. Somber dark clothing—wet with the snow that always seemed to be falling now—gave off a dank humidity in the overheated chapel. I sat in the front pew and clung to Beth's unresponsive hand. Staring straight ahead, she pulled her hand from mine and shifted away. The pain closed in on me—over me—down on me—as I listened to the chaplain mouth meaningless words of comfort for my loss.

Finally it was over. We were alone. Beth went straight up to the bedroom. I put the kettle on and roamed through the downstairs while I waited for the water to heat. The rooms felt odd and the furnishings disproportionate without Amelia's toys strewn about. The clean lines of the expensive modern furniture stamped the house barren—sterile. The tree we'd decorated the weekend before Amelia's death stood propped in the corner of the living room like an unwelcome and overdressed party guest.

The kettle began to shriek. I went into the kitchen and made us each a cup of tea. I called Beth and, when she didn't answer me, carried our tea up the stairs into the bedroom.

Her black dress lay crumpled on the bed where she'd flung it. For a split second, I thought it was Beth. Then, I heard her rummaging in the closet.

"Beth?" I called. "I have some tea for you."

Silence.

A nameless anxiety wreathed around my neck.

"Beth? Did you hear me?"

It was an effort to keep my voice even.

"Put it on the dresser," she replied. Her voice was strange. Muffled and distant.

I set the cup down. Beth emerged from the closet a moment later. She had changed into a pair of jeans and a white wool cable-knit sweater. Her dark hair was drawn back from her face and fastened into an untidy knot with a barrette.

She was carrying a suitcase in her right hand and had a department store shopping bag and a pile of sweaters draped over her left arm. She threw it all on top of the bedspread and then began to stuff the sweaters into the suitcase. The

shopping bag had tipped over. I caught a glimpse of a
Christmas package we'd wrapped for Amelia. A doll.

My mouth went dry.

"What are you doing?" I managed.

"I'm going back to the cabin," she said. She turned to
the dresser and jerked open a drawer. The tea spilled over
the edge of the cup, making a dark river on the blond wood.

Reality was slipping out of the room.

"There's nothing there that we need," I said. "I can get
someone to go up and get anything you want."

Beth grabbed a handful of underwear and crammed it
into the suitcase. Turned again. Slammed the drawer shut.
Pulled open another. She hurled fistfuls of socks into the case.

"Beth? Did you hear me?"

She finally turned to face me. Her eyes burned out of a
face bruised with grief.

"I have to go back to get Amelia. We forgot Amelia."

I eluded the paralyzing terror closing in on me. Tried to
grasp what reason might still exist before Beth—before both
of us—surrendered our sanity.

"We buried her today," I said. "An hour ago. Don't you
remember?"

She continued to stare at me.

"No," she said. Her contorted features negated her
patient tone. "We didn't bury her. There was no body. She
just got lost. She's still up there. She's scared and she needs
her mother."

"Beth. Please. She isn't up there."

She turned back to the bed and snapped the locks on the
suitcase.

"I'm going."

She pulled both bags off the bed and headed for the
door. Her movements were jerky—forceful.

Stark fear grabbed me—pulled me under. I didn't know
what to do. She was leaving. I didn't know how to stop her. I
couldn't think. I hadn't been able to think since Amelia's
death.

"Wait," I said.

She hesitated for a moment.

"Can I come with you?"

"Of course," she said calmly. "She'll be expecting both of us."

◆

I hate the Friday afternoon drive to Lakeside. I hate everything about it. The two hours of turns and curves that used to add up to a welcome retreat from the reality of my weekly routine are pure torture now. The road still drops me off at the departure of reality. Beth's reality. She's lived up here for three and a half months now. Ever vigilant for Amelia's return.

Beth has her routine. Almost never stops moving. Locks and unlocks the door and windows. Checks each one three or four times before she allows herself to leave the house. Then she takes the path. Carefully recreating each step we all took that afternoon. Anxiously searching the landscape— next to the house—behind the trees. The final trek down to the lake and along the shoreline. To the place where it happened. She stands there for a while. Scanning the lake. Waiting. I don't know what tells her this isn't the time, but she'll suddenly turn and flee, back to the house. Sometimes she'll sit down in her rocker and rock furiously as she watches out the window, but never for too long. Soon, she's up again to check all the windows and doors. An eerie dance—repeated over and over in slow motion.

I haven't given up hope that she'll stop this—that she'll come back to me. I can't bear the thought of losing them both, but it's getting harder to resolve each week. Beth has armored herself against the intrusion of reason. She tolerates my presence on the weekends—includes me on the barest periphery of her activities. I feel that if I tapped the hard casing surrounding her she'd give back a metallic ring. Sometimes, I want to strike her—just to see.

I swung the Jeep into the driveway and parked. Beth was here. I could see her car through the windows in the garage.

I walked around to the back of the cabin. The sky was leaden behind the trees and houses that rimmed the opposite side of the lake. Most of the houses looked empty. A late-season storm was supposed to lock in the mountains for the weekend. Skiing would be impossible. I guessed that most of our Lakeside neighbors wouldn't bother to come up. It didn't matter. The neighbors had stopped dropping by our cabin. Just an embarrassed nod or frank stare in the local grocery store. Everyone knew why Beth was living up here. We'd become a horrifying curiosity.

I looked down at the frozen water. The hill sloping down to the lake was scarred only by the trail Beth had carved into the snow—like a wound that would never heal. The ice was thinning again where the stream emptied into the lake—where Amelia had drowned. The darker patch of ice spread like an evil stain on the surface.

The familiar pain gripped my chest as I stared at the spot where my daughter had died. I averted my eyes. Looked up to the house. Beth was sitting in the window. Rocking. Watching. Waiting.

I waved to her. I didn't expect her to acknowledge—or even to see me. Suddenly, she lifted her hand and beckoned to me. My hopes lifted. Maybe something had happened this week. Maybe Beth was coming back to her senses—back to our life. I hurried up to the house.

The living room was gloomy—the stone fireplace empty. There were no lamps on. Fading afternoon light filtered through the windows. Layers of shadows filled the room and spilled over the dusty pile of unopened Christmas gifts in the corner.

Beth had gotten out of the rocker. She was standing next to the window—straining to look out over the lake.

"Did you see her?" she asked.

My heart sank. It was the same opening line. Nothing had changed. She hadn't even bothered to turn around. I walked over to stand next to her.

"See who?" I asked with a sigh.

I already knew the answer. I reached out to touch Beth's shoulder. I could feel the fragile bones beneath the rough wool sweater she wore. She shifted away from me.

"Amelia," she said.

Beth looked up. I hardly recognized her these days. Her dark hair was pulled back in a sloppy ponytail. Her features, always so quick to break into a smile or laugh, were drawn with intense concentration. Her eyes shifted from the window—to the door—to the window again. A nervous excitement gripped her.

"Amelia is dead, Beth," I said carefully. "She died in December. Over three months ago."

Beth moved back from the window. She sat down in the rocker again and pulled me into the chair next to her. She leaned over to me.

"I have something to tell you," she said. "Something wonderful."

She grasped my hand and looked into my eyes. She was smiling. I almost saw the old Beth. My heart turned over. Maybe it was going to be all right. I caressed her fingers and smiled back at her—waited for the words that would deliver me from the nightmare our lives had become.

"Amelia's come back," she said. "She was here last night."

It wasn't going to be all right. It was never going to be all right.

"She woke me up," Beth continued. "Calling. Crying. I ran to her but she was gone before I could reach her."

Beth put her hand on my forearm. Her sharp fingers dug into me. She was still smiling—almost laughing. "I looked for her all day, but I think she was waiting for you to get here. We can go out now together to find her. Bring her home with us."

My blood turned to ice. This time she had "heard" Amelia. I wanted to shake her hand off—run out the door. Something had finally pushed her over the edge.

"Beth," I began, "listen to me."

"No, you listen to me," Beth interrupted impatiently. "She called to me. Begged me to let her in."

"Beth," I said. But there was no stopping her. She went on and on. Amelia had called to her through the windows—the doors. Stumbling—half asleep—Beth had run to each in turn. The child's voice—pleading—crying—had always moved on before she could get there. Finally, Beth had run outside—calling and searching in the dark—but she knew it was too late. She'd missed her chance.

I put my hand over hers. Tried to pull her bruising fingers away from my arm.

"Beth," I began, "you had a dream. Amelia's gone. She isn't coming back. No dream can make that happen."

A rapid change came over her. Like a veil being ripped away. Her features sharpened. Eyes focused.

"You think I'm crazy, don't you?" she said. Her hoarse voice trembled. She stood up—livid energy pouring out of her. "Do you think I want to live like this? All I want is to find my baby and for all of us to go home and be together again. Last night was no dream. She's out there. She's come back to us. Why don't you understand? How can you throw all this away? What kind of fool are you?"

I grasped her shoulders—beyond caring if I hurt her.

"Amelia is dead," I shouted. "She's never coming back." I began to shake her.

♦

I found myself speeding down the road. Running away. I could barely see through the falling snow. The hairpin turns rushed at me as the Jeep leaped forward.

The fight had been horrific. I had to get out of there. Had to call for help. Maybe the police—or medics of some sort—would know what to do about Beth. I couldn't handle what had happened to her. She needed help.

I skidded into the parking lot at the grocery and slammed into the store. The owner dialed the police and shoved the phone across the counter at me when I told him it was an emergency. He knew who I was. Knew about Amelia. Everyone knew about Amelia. And Beth.

I spoke to a dispatcher. Told them about Beth. What had happened. All the police and rescue personnel were tied up at a huge traffic accident in town, but the dispatcher promised to get a car out to my cabin as soon as possible. I said I'd meet them there and hung up.

I handed the phone back the store owner and thanked him. He shook his head sympathetically as he watched me go back out into the storm.

♦

I'd only been gone about twenty minutes. The house was quiet. Empty. I walked around the outside of the cabin and stopped for a moment to listen to the snow whispering down around me. I called but—like Beth—I knew when it was too late.

I went back into the house and sat in Beth's rocking chair. The light was fading, but still good. The view was perfect. I could see past the pine trees to the edge of the frozen water where the stream fed into the lake. I could see the footprints and then skid marks in the snow covering the good ice. I could see the ragged hole in the bad ice—larger this time. All those marks—all that evidence—would be covered up by the new snow in a short while. But right now, I could see it all from where I sat—and rocked—and waited for help.

♦

They never found Beth's body. The investigation was short—almost nonexistent. The evidence of Beth's madness had been building all those months she'd lived up there searching for our daughter. Her death was ruled a suicide.

They can believe what they will. I'm the only one who really knows what happened that day.

I saw the fresh tracks outside the cabin after I'd returned from calling the police. The footprints came up from the shoreline. Tiny ones. They circled the house—went up to each window. The prints under the windows were deeper at the top of the footmark, as if a child—a very small child—was standing on tiptoe to peer in. I followed them to the door. The footprints turned around here—joined by a larger set—and headed back to the lake. I had called, but it was no use. I must have missed them by minutes.

I live up at the cabin now. I check all the windows—test the doors. I walk the path—the exact path—Beth and Amelia took. I'm not going to follow them. I'm afraid I'll get lost. Lose them. I can wait. I know they'll be back for me.

THE VISIT

J. D. Shaw

The water shimmered, sending darts of light into my
eyes. The sky was a deep, serious blue. A few white clouds
appeared pasted there for contrast.

I dipped my toes into the water as I sat on the dock. The
water was tepid, almost warm. The summer had been
extraordinarily hot. Still, it felt refreshing after my five-hour
drive from Chicago. I wasn't real sure what I was doing here.

Had it been simply impulse or the fact that the city was
steaming and I was so tired of dashing from
over-refrigeration into boiler-room heat and back into
over-refrigeration? Or had it been the oddity of the letter?

I hadn't really kept in touch with Rusty Spranger, a close
friend from my college days. Except for our brief notes on
Christmas cards, we had not communicated in three years.
Then suddenly—out of nowhere—a two-page letter? She
begged me to come and visit her. No sentence or word
actually asked for help, but somehow the sense of
desperation was clear. I changed my plans for Labor Day
weekend, took a half-day on Friday, and here I was sitting
on her dock and questioning myself. Her greeting had been
warm and friendly. Had I just imagined trouble?

Rusty looked the same: a little thin, a little distracted, her
red hair still long but somehow fading a bit. She had hugged

me and showed me around her beautiful house, curved and
split-leveled so that every room had a lake view. It was
furnished with good, old pieces that smelled of lemon oil
and looked comfortable and fit into the modern house by
way of new, pastel chintzes. She had ended our tour at the
well-appointed guest room and had told me to change into
some shorts and she'd see me on the dock. She had to tend
to Jennifer, her four-month-old baby.

The day was so perfect. What sort of menace had I
possibly envisioned? A picture-book lake, a beautiful house,
a new baby. Rusty had hit the jackpot. I laughed to myself.
And I had thought she was the one giving up.

We had shared an apartment in New York our first year
out of college. We both had low-level, low-paying jobs and
were working our tails off. We lived in a fifth-floor walk-up
closet. We couldn't afford to do anything, nor could any of
our friends. It was a frustrating, boring year. I was a gofer on
a magazine with big literary ideals, few subscribers, and a
noticeable lack of advertisers. Rusty was working at an
advertising firm, basically as a secretary. She kept coming
home in tears. They were a nasty bunch.

When our lease came up for renewal she announced that
she was going back to Wisconsin to marry her high-school
sweetheart. She had never mentioned him once in the year
we lived together or the years I knew her in college. That
struck me as strange. I had felt we were close; we had often
talked all night. And Rusty had always seemed so open and
uncomplicated. Not one to hide things, keep secrets. But I
had wished her well, and soon I too left New York, for a job
in Chicago at a local TV station. I had been grateful that
Rusty hadn't asked me to be in her wedding. The last
expense I needed was a stupid bridesmaid's dress. But she
hadn't even invited me. It had just been a small family affair,
she said. So I hadn't seen Rusty since she had walked out of
the apartment in New York, more than three years ago.

A canoe glided peacefully by. There were sounds in the
background—children laughing, a motor boat
somewhere—but they were a distance away, unobtrusive. I
felt myself relax, become tranquil, then drowsy. I had set my
alarm for six-thirty that morning to pack before working my
half-day and had been on the road a long time. My eyes

were closing in spite of my attempts to keep them open. I
was leaning against a mooring post—not the most
comfortable arrangement. There was a deck chair just a yard
away, but I couldn't seem to manage the energy to move into
it. Even turning my head was an effort, when I heard
footsteps on the wooden planking. Rusty was walking
toward me, her arms cradling a bundle of pink.

She sat down beside me and held out the baby. The baby
certainly was cute. She was wearing a pink sunsuit and a
pink bonnet and smelled of talcum powder. Her face was
dominated by huge blue eyes.

"She's beautiful," I said. I always feel inadequate around
babies. There have never been any in my life. I had been the
baby of a big bunch of cousins; I had no younger siblings. So
I was not comfortable about it, but Rusty held the baby
toward me. I reached out and took her, holding on too
tightly, afraid of dropping her. This wasn't a good idea, so
near the water.

"She really is beautiful," I repeated. I guess you can
never say enough to a parent looking at you like Rusty was
looking at me. The language doesn't hold big enough
adjectives to meet that expression of pure parental pride.

"She really is, isn't she," Rusty agreed, smiling at the
baby. Then she paused and looked at me as though about to
say something.

The sound of more footsteps tapped behind us, and I
turned and watched the man coming out on the dock, still in
his business suit. He was male-model handsome, with thick
black hair, black eyes, a strong chin, and noticeably perfect
teeth that were grinning in a friendly smile. I handed the
baby back to Rusty and stood up to be greeted with a firm
handshake.

"Paul Marshall," Rusty's husband introduced himself
needlessly. "We're so glad you could make it, Carol. Rusty
has really been excited about you coming. And of course I
was anxious to meet you. Quite the TV newswoman, we
hear." His voice was deep and rich and couldn't have been
more friendly. So why did I end the handshake a moment
too soon? And why did I look at him and think first cat,
then fox? I am not into animal analogies. But there was
something almost feral about this man.

I mumbled a few words about not yet being any threat to Diane Sawyer. There was polite laughter. Rusty should have been making the situation easier, but she stayed silent. They hadn't greeted each other, even with a look, nor had he so much as glanced at the baby.

Finally Paul excused himself to get into some comfortable clothes and walked back up the dock and across the lawn toward the house. I felt a sense of relief. Perhaps it was just the too-good looks of the man. He hadn't done anything wrong—exactly.

I turned back to Rusty. She was watching me intently, watching me watch her husband walk away. Watching for some reaction? Was I supposed to comment on the beauty of her husband as I had on the beauty of her baby?

She gave a little laugh and began a jumble of small talk. Most of it concerned the baby, and I was not required to contribute more than an occasional *oh* or *ah*. I took it that the timing of the first tooth indicated an extraordinary precariousness. She talked about how wonderful finding the lake house had been.

"Paul and I were very close then. We did the decorating together and everything. That was before the baby came, of course. Now it's rather lonely. I . . . " and then she suddenly stopped talking. She looked up at the house. Paul had disappeared. Again she gave me this intent look.

"I'm so glad you came, Carol. I really appreciate it, I can't tell you how much." Again, innocent words, as in her letter, but somehow desperation underscored her tone.

"Is something the matter?" I asked.

"Carol," she said, grabbing my arm suddenly. "You do investigative reporting. You know how to investigate things." Her eyes were large. I could suddenly see the resemblance between mother and child.

"I'm low-man on the totem pole," I explained. "I *am* learning, but no one's asked me to write an exposé suitable for a Pulitzer." I wasn't just trying to sound modest.

"I've got to tell you something. It's not easy to say. I don't know how to begin . . . ," her voice trailed off. She looked miserable. I reached out and took her hand. I waited.

But she was looking up at the house again. Paul was on his way back down clad in shorts and polo shirt, drink tray

in hand. He had made margaritas. I wished he'd asked. I
don't particularly like margaritas, but I took mine with a
smile and tried to sip beyond the salt.

He sat down in the deck chair, leaned back, his legs
stretched out in front of him and sipped his drink. The man
even had great legs. I couldn't imagine why Rusty hadn't
shown us pictures of this hunk. I didn't know what was
going on here. Back in college, a picture of Paul Marshall in
her dorm room would have been impressive indeed. We did
tend to brag of past conquests. And Paul certainly seemed to
be one.

As soon as he joined us, he took over the conversation.
Whatever Rusty had been trying to say would have to wait.
Paul was in charge now. We were going to grill steaks that
night and he had a special way of doing it that he explained
in detail. He also told us how he made his
margaritas—again, special, different. It required a
compliment, as would the steaks when they arrived.

We took another drink aboard their pontoon boat and
cruised around the lake. I was surprised that Rusty took the
baby out on the boat and told her so.

"I never leave her," she said. "Not with anyone." She
looked at her husband, but he wasn't paying attention. She
seemed so intense. I thought it was odd, but what did I
know about babies?

Later we cooked the steaks and watched the sun go
down. It was a beautiful night. The dying sun sent out a
glow that turned the now-still water into an orange sheet of
glass. Then the moon rose over the lake and its reflective
beam seemed to aim directly toward our dock. It was very
peaceful, incredibly lovely.

"You two are so terribly fortunate," I said. "What a
wonderful place. What a wonderful life."

Paul agreed.

"I thought it was exactly what I wanted," said Rusty.
"After New York, I didn't know what else . . ." Her voice
drifted off into silence.

I was grateful she hadn't finished her thought. I glanced
quickly at Paul, almost fearful of his reaction. But he seemed
not to be paying attention. And the night was too beautiful
to have anything said that might be uncomfortable.

◆

I went to bed in my pretty room and slept well. I only vaguely heard the baby cry once in the night.

I was very anxious to talk to Rusty. By noon the next day, I realized it wasn't going to be easy. Paul was always there, always on stage, spotlight on him. We listened to his ideas, his politics, his peeves, his opinions. He had planned the day. He would have made a good camp director. In the morning we swam and went canoeing. The baby, snug in her little carrier, stayed on the dock with Rusty. I would have been happy to have stayed there with them.

Still, for all his bossiness, he seemed determined that I have a good time. He was trying to make a good impression on me. Trying hard. I wished he'd just relax.

After lunch we took the speed boat out to go water skiing. We brought the baby, which again made me nervous. But not as nervous as the skiing. It was something I hadn't done in years and didn't want to do. But it was easier to agree than to argue with Paul. It took me three tries and a great deal of water in my mouth before I got up and did the required laps around the lake.

After I had taken my turn skiing, Paul decided to show me how to do it right. Rusty drove the boat and Paul cut through the wake, back and forth, with effortless grace. We applauded with gestures. The noise of the engine was loud. We had a chance to talk at last.

"Tell me quickly," I said into her ear, trying not to shout, although it would have been impossible for him to hear. "What's going on?"

"Oh, Carol. You're going to think I'm crazy. But I'm not, I'm really not," she said. Her voice sounded strained. That same underlying desperation of the letter, and yesterday, was there in her voice.

"Of course you're not," I told her.

"I've been told by the best doctors—Paul always insists on the best—that it's just postpartum depression. But it isn't, Carol. It really isn't."

"I believe you. Just tell me." We didn't have much time. I wanted her to hurry.

"It's the baby. There's something wrong," she said. We both looked at Jennifer, snug in her carrier on the seat beside her, bundled in a miniature life jacket. The motor noise or the motion had sent her instantly to sleep.

"Wrong? She's perfect," I protested.

"Oh yes, oh yes, she is. But don't you see, there should have been two. Where is the other one?" She gave a frightened look back at her husband, who was gliding over the waves like some mythical god of the lake. She put her hand over her mouth as though afraid of her own speech.

I had my first doubt. Postpartum depression? What did I know. A severe chill went down my back. It had nothing to do with the bright, sun-drenched day.

"It's a long story," she continued, her words spilling out quickly now, between hurried looks backward at her husband. We both waved periodically and smiled and clapped. The gestures contrasted eerily with the tale she was telling.

It seemed Paul hadn't really wanted a baby. He kept saying later, later. But Rusty got pregnant and was delighted. She went to the doctor and had it confirmed—and still didn't tell Paul. When the doctor told her she thought she heard two heart beats, Rusty had been so excited that she had rushed home to Paul with the news. His reaction had been strange. He was very calm and focused instantly on the fact of twins. He seemed more concerned with that than the pregnancy itself. He seemed suspicious, rather than happy. He would say the same things over and over to her. There weren't any twins in his family, he told her. And there weren't any in hers. Had she taken fertility pills even when he told her he wasn't ready for a baby?

She hadn't. She really hadn't. And finally she felt she had convinced him. Still, he gnawed at the fact of twins. It bothered him. At one point he made reference to her "litter." None of his initial response was positive. In fact, Paul seemed almost repulsed, Rusty said, her eyes glinting tears.

But, as usual, he took over. He had never heard of her doctor and insisted she change, go to one he recommended. He went with her each visit. He turned almost overnight into a man totally involved in the pregnancy. The new doctor was a rather severe man, almost abrupt, impressively dressed in custom suits and ensconced in his plush office. Rusty had felt no rapport with him. He dampened her enthusiasm. She yearned for the young woman doctor who had seemed to share her joy in her first pregnancy. But that was a small matter. At least Paul had accepted the situation.

This new doctor scoffed at the idea of two heart beats. And it was early on. She could accept a mistake. There was a little disappointment. It would have been fun. But one baby, *her* baby, would be just fine.

She grew very large, and she didn't cheat on her strict diet. She was expecting a big baby. That's what the doctor told her. But when her little girl was born she weighed only four and a half pounds. She was beautiful, healthy, born a little early, which might have explained the low weight. Rusty had wanted to be awake; she had taken all the classes and had been looking forward to it. The labor had been uncomfortable, but nothing she couldn't handle. Then someone had given her a shot and when she woke up it was all over. She felt cheated. She also felt that something was very wrong and had felt that way ever since. It was a feeling so deep and so intuitive that she couldn't get past it.

At this point, I must have made some gesture of withdrawal. Rusty stopped her tale.

"You have to believe me," she said. "It wasn't just feelings. Things were strange. When I went to the doctor, it was always after Paul got off work and he'd meet me. There was never anyone else in the office. And I didn't go to a hospital. We went to a private clinic near here, a birthing center, which was fine with me because they promised to do it all naturally. Afterward they said the shot had been necessary, not for me but for the baby. Something about her breathing, her heart rate. *Everything* had an explanation." She looked at me with that same frightened expression. It begged me to believe her.

There was a shout from behind us. Paul was waving us in. We were passing the dock and he made a gesture and let go of the rope and glided right up to the dock before he sank gracefully into the water. Rusty cut the motor and steered the boat to the dock. Our discussion was over for the time being.

After I had changed out of my swim suit, Rusty managed to slip me the name of the doctor and asked me to check him out. I could do that easily. And I would, if only to help her get well. My old friend Rusty seemed part of the past. The new Rusty had begun giving me the creeps.

I went outside and used my car phone to call a friend at my station. I gave him the name of the doctor. I said I'd call back in a little while. I stayed outside in the warm sunny air for some time after the call. I didn't really want to go back inside.

When I finally dragged myself back to the house Paul was getting ready to go scuba diving. Alone. Rusty said she'd better go with him. I had done enough activities. Especially with Paul. I begged a nap. Jennifer was asleep, but I promised Rusty I would check on her. She put the baby monitor in my room so I could listen for her. I hoped they'd be back before she woke. I've never been comfortable with babies, and I really wasn't comfortable with this one.

Before they left, I overheard a small altercation. The first since I arrived. Rusty was telling Paul that his scuba equipment was long overdue for inspection. "You told me you would have it checked," she said, worry in her voice. As he had all weekend, Paul dismissed her concern.

Rusty said something else—something about the worn O-ring his friend had warned him about. She said he really shouldn't dive if it hadn't been replaced.

I watched from the stairs as Paul looked at her and a bit of temper I hadn't seen before surfaced. "Don't worry about it," he said slowing, softly. The tone of his voice did not brook further discussion. What's more, I saw him look at her as I must have yesterday—as if she were a little crazy, needing humoring.

The baby and I both slept until cocktail time. Rusty and Paul had returned, and this time the drinks were Long Island ice teas, another special recipe made, of course, a special way. I would have preferred a beer, but again I wasn't asked. Paul wasn't that kind of host. I began to see how everything always had to be his way.

As we sat by the lake, Rusty gave Paul another warning, this one about drinking after diving. Paul raised his glass to his lips and looked at her. She said no more.

I managed to excuse myself briefly. But instead of going back to the house I went out to my car and called my friend. He had done a computer check of Wisconsin medical licenses. The name I had given him came up empty, no license to practice in the state had ever been issued. Now it wasn't Rusty who was giving me the creeps.

As I helped her make a salad for dinner, I told her about the computer check. She nodded, giving me only a quick glance, and then stood looking out the window, withdrawn into some little world of her own. It was not the reaction I had expected. I said I would check out the birth certificates on Tuesday. She nodded again, distractedly.

"They sell babies, you know. Sometimes they sell them for organs. I read about that happening down in some South American country." She spoke in a monotone, without emotion, chopping the carrots very fine.

"Oh no," I assured her. "That was all just big, overblown rumors. There was no truth in that."

"They sell babies," she insisted. "People who want babies will pay a lot of money for them," she said.

I tried reassuring her, saying how loved such a baby would be. I didn't know what else to say. This was all just too weird. I wished I'd never come.

"There's no way to prove anything. There's no way I could ever really know. It's hard, not knowing," she said in that same monotone, the knife pressed hard against the cutting board.

"I'm sure there's an explanation," I said rather desperately. "And people don't get away with things like that." I told her. But I knew, even as I said it, they *do*. I remembered other stories—*not* in South America.

Dinner was ready to be served. Rusty was busy putting dishes on the table. Jennifer, who had been quite content in her little swing, now began to cry. Paul walked into the room. Rusty, seeing him, put the plates down and quickly picked up the baby and handed her to me. He had not been going to tend the baby. He never seemed to pay any attention to the baby. He had been heading on a straight course for the bar where he made himself another drink. Jennifer cradled her little head against my shoulder and her cry turned into a whimper. I heard myself humming to her, some tune I couldn't have named. She quieted down. It was a nice feeling.

We ate; we talked a bit—or I should say Paul talked, we listened. Rusty ate with one hand and gave the baby a bottle with the other. The skills of new mothers amaze me. Paul seemed annoyed. I told them I'd be leaving the next day because I wanted to avoid the traffic. Neither protested.

The next morning I got up early and packed. I could hear the baby in her room, still in her crib, making small cooing sounds. I went in, leaned over, and kissed her on her soft cheek. Downstairs I saw Paul on the verandah and said goodbye. He was planning another dive. I looked all over the house for Rusty and finally found her in the breezeway bending over Paul's tank. There was a quick glint of some object in her hand. I startled her when I spoke, so much so that she jumped back.

"Oh, Carol, it's you," she said, her face flushing to a sudden red. She hugged me goodbye, but she still seemed distracted. I reassured her I would check out everything and let her know. She hardly seemed to be listening.

I did not sense anything unusual in that last little scene. Not then. Only later, in hindsight, when I saw the short news item about the diving accident. Something about a faulty O-ring. Something about loss of pressure. He shouldn't have been diving alone. He shouldn't have died.

When I called Rusty to offer my condolences, she said it was typical Paul. As Rusty said, he had to do it his way, no matter what other people said or thought. It gave me pause, mostly because Rusty didn't sound distracted anymore. She sounded more like her old self. And something else—she didn't mention that other baby, not then, not ever again.

Nothing could be proved, not about the baby, not about Paul, and I didn't pursue it. Proving one might implicate the other. I simply didn't know, and I felt a guilt of my own. Because when Rusty came with the baby to visit me after the funeral, it seemed very clear. There was such a sense of relief now that Paul Marshall was no longer there. Relief for Rusty, relief for me. Jennifer didn't seem to miss the father who never touched or held her. I finally understood why Rusty had never mentioned Paul back in college. Some men you just don't talk about.

CABALLITO DEL DIABLO

Terri de la Peña

Midnight fog encircles the cruising BMW like the encompassing desire smoldering within. Black-gloved hands at the wheel, she silently maneuvers my car beyond the fringes of Marina del Rey. The mist dampening the windows prevents me from pinpointing our exact location. Somewhere west of Lincoln Boulevard—I know that much because I smell the ocean. Ahead I see vague outlines of several multi-level apartment buildings. She lives in one of them.

Except for the tip of my cigarette, the car's interior is unlit. Even so, her passionate eyes sear me. The promise of sex tinges her throaty voice. "We're almost there."

Lustful heat consumes me. With one crimson fingernail, I brush her right leather glove. "Can't wait. I want you *now*."

She clasps my hand. In a swift motion that excites me even more, she brings it to her mouth. She lets my fingers wander inside. Her tongue teases me. She glides it over my fingers and nibbles them.

My breathing becomes panting. I imagine her next to me, bronze skin a definite contrast to mine. I see her licking me, her hot tongue gliding over my nakedness. Grinding out my cigarette, I lean closer. I want to pull her face to mine, bite her sassy mouth, kiss her till our lips are bruised.

With a quick toss of her moussed head, she eludes me.
"Outside."

"On the beach?" My eyes devour her exotic profile, her
strangely hooded eyes.

"No. A better place."

"There's a blanket in the trunk."

The infrequent street lights cast a dull glow in the fog.
She halts the BMW in what appears to be a cul-de-sac near a
Marina bridge. I can barely distinguish its curved shape. To
keep her in the car, I make a strategic move, but she is too
fast. The sudden motion makes me dizzy. All those glasses of
wine tonight.

Already, she is opening the trunk. With the rolled-up
wool under her arm, she gestures to me to follow.

On the uneven pavement, my high heels are wobbly. She
steadies me by clutching my bare arm above the elbow. The
touch of the glove's soft hide against my skin increases my
desire. I want to peel away her form-fitting leather clothes,
feel the heat of her luscious flesh. The vaporous fog
disorients me. I recognize nothing as she guides me along
graveled ground. I shiver in my skimpy cocktail dress. When
the path becomes rougher, I almost stumble.

"You scared?" she whispers.

"No."

"Not even fear of the unknown?"

"I'll know you soon enough."

She grins suddenly. "Bet you've never done it here."

"I'd do it anywhere."

Past a concrete bank, I hear the slow ripple of water. She
pulls me along, and I marvel at her surefootedness. Despite
the lack of illumination, the swirling fog, she knows the area
well, never misses a step.

She slows her pace, loosening her grip on me. A
chain-link fence looms ahead. With her free hand, she
searches its crosshatched metal surface.

"Duck through the gap."

For a second, I hesitate. "*Where* are we?"

"Private property. A turn-on, huh? Big-time attorney
sneaks in here to fuck."

Her audaciousness amuses me. "Rules are made to be
broken."

"Right." She gives me a nudge through the hole in the
fence.

♦

Far from any streetlights, we become submerged in the
gray mist. Shadowy bushes and low-lying branches convince
me of our eastward destination, away from the ocean. My
heels catch on thick vegetation growing beneath us. Tonight
will not be the first time I have impulsively ruined expensive
Italian footwear. She stays behind me, guiding me by keeping
one hand at my waist. For the time being, I let her take
control. The narrow path meanders, broken only by
sheltering thickets, muddy sections, sporadic pools.

She answers my unspoken question. "La Ballona
Wetlands. About 180 acres. Was owned by—"

"—Howard Hughes' Summa Corporation," I finish.
"One of the last undeveloped tracts of land on the Westside."

She takes a different route. "In the 1800s, this was a
Mexican land grant. Almost 14,000 acres."

"Nowadays the property's slated for massive
development." I frown. "How do *you* know about—"

"I specialize in local history," she says with that I
suppose is a smirk. "Out-of-the-way places, secret
hideaways—you name it."

Her cool attitude appeals to me. No doubt she envisions
herself as a lean, leather-clad butch on the prowl. At least
that is the image she projected earlier in the haziness of the
club. I noticed her at once. Swagger with a hint of mystery.
Her ancestry could range from Mediterranean to Central or
South American, even American Indian. Her bronze skin,
inky moussed hair, those compelling eyes, continue to arouse
me. Before the night is over, I will make her lose
some—maybe even all—control. She might be nonchalant
now, but not for long. She thinks she is seducing *me*. She will
learn otherwise.

Leaning against her leather-clad arm, I murmur,
"Speaking of out-of-the-way places, I really *like* doing it au
naturel. Naked in the bushes or in the back seat on
Mulholland—the thrill of exposure, of being caught."

"You like taking risks."

"You do, too," I whisper against her. "And, afterward, I like to sit up in the car and press my tits against the window. Hot and cold simultaneously. I feel that right now. Can't you tell? Hot for you, cold in the fog. Too bad there's low visibility. I like to flash in the moonlight."

"Ain't no moon tonight," she drawls. "Open air—foggy atmosphere—*is* downright sexy." Next to my left ear, her voice is tantalizing. "No choice but to use your imagination."

♦

She stops within an overgrown thicket, a natural shelter. Small trees and many bushes form its semicircular borders. Releasing me, she spreads the blanket on the spongy vegetation. I watch her smooth movements, the gracefulness of her gloved hands, the curve of her thigh as she leans forward. Shivering again, aroused yet chilled, I wonder about her background. She said "ain't." Despite her sleekness, she is probably a working-class homegirl after white sex. A perverse thrill surges through me. Tonight she will find out who is boss.

Laying the blanket flat, she turns in my direction. "They say Howard Hughes used to stroll across the wetlands and hide in these thickets."

"And do what?" I scoff. "Piss?"

She shakes her head. "More like jerking off. There were riding stables near the bluffs. He'd stand and watch teenaged girls gallop by."

I laugh at that bit of Westside lore. "And who are 'they'?"

"Old timers."

"I see. You're a history buff, after all."

Nodding, she moves panther-like toward me. One gloved hand clamps itself on my shoulder, the other slips behind my back. I feel unevaporated mist from the leather dampen my satin dress. My panties are already soaked from my own moist cravings.

"I ain't like that rich dude," she tells me. "Don't have to hide in any damn bushes. I want to see *you* in the buff. Now. Take it all off."

"Are you tough enough to make me?" I tease, gazing into her unfathomable eyes.

One hand pressing my shoulder, she does not break her fixed stare. She swings her other hand into a jacket pocket. I hear a familiar clink. She dangles a shiny pair of handcuffs.

I pretend to struggle. Thrusting my breasts forward, I push into her. She meets my aggressiveness with her own. Her hand on my shoulder is implacable. She is much stronger, much younger. She curls a leg behind my left calf, forces me off balance. Heady from the wine and the anticipation of sex, I know where she wants me to fall. Letting myself go limp, I sink to the blanket. In the process, I lose one of my shoes. She grabs for the other, hurls it aside. Seconds ago, I could have stomped her with a stiletto heel, but not before getting what *I* want. She has enough raw sexuality, enough outlaw mystique to keep me playing this game.

The spongy undergrowth is like a natural mattress. I lie supine, satin dress revealing my thighs, panting from the combined phony struggle and growing sexual hunger. She straddles me, loops the metal cuff to my wrist. She fastens its opposite end to a sturdy branch of the small tree behind us. The tension stretches my arm back. My eyes never leaving her, I lick my lips slowly, temptingly. The weight of her, those black leather pants brushing my bare legs, makes me moan.

She sinks forward on her knees to stare deeper into my face. I catch a glimpse of something shiny around her neck. She reaches behind me to untie the dress's halter. With my free hand, I attempt to touch her, to grab her face, bring her mouth to mine. She nudges me away and leans on her haunches again.

From another jacket pocket, she removes a small bundle. She tosses it at me. "Put these on."

I smile at seeing the scanty crotchless panties, the tiny bra. She slides off me, positioning herself at the far end of the blanket to witness my actions.

Shaking my shoulders, I let the skimpy satin dress slide off. That leaves me semi-nude, my nipples taut in the mist. Limited by the handcuff, I half-sit to remove the dress over my hips. The crotch of my panties is drenched. I want her to see how much I want her. When the dress is off, I squat and face her. My blatant desire has no perceivable effect on her. She is aloof, her narrowed eyes surveying me.

Leaning forward, I reach for the costume she has brought.

Her voice is abrupt. "Look familiar?"

"What?"

She gestures to the bra and panties. "They belonged to someone a lot smaller than you. Don't know if they'll fit."

"An ex-lover's?"

Her eyes become frigid. "*Yours.*"

I frown. "How could someone like *you* know one of *my* ex-lovers?"

She disregards my question and enunciates each word. "Susanna Machado. Remember *her*? She was Mexican—like me."

I crush the panties between my fingers. "She *wasn't* my lover."

"Didn't think you'd recall her that way, Ms. Margot Smythe, attorney-at-law." Her sensual lips become a sneer. "How about this description: Susanna was the legal secretary you threatened to fire unless she became your sex slave. She was the woman you gloated on humiliating in front of your office staff and whoever else happened to be around. She was the woman you made into your whore, the woman whose spirit you broke and—"

"Bullshit," I spit back at her. "She was no innocent. I'll admit it took a while for her to make up her mind—typical wishy-washy Hispanic behavior. What the hell do *you* know? She was a consenting adult. She—"

"Shut the fuck up!" she snarls. "Put on those damn panties—now!"

For the first time, the intensity of her gaze unnerves me. In the club, she called herself "Dragonfly." For all I know, that might be a gang moniker, not a sexy alias. What else does she have in her jacket pockets? A weapon? Or is her threatening behavior part of her sexual charade?

Awkwardly, I slip the panties over each ankle and pull them up. Susanna was small-boned yet voluptuous. Her panties are tight over my hips, the elastic digging into my flesh. As long as Dragonfly keeps her distance, I am powerless to try to escape. The cuff holds me fast. What did I get myself into tonight? Who *is* this leather dyke?

Dragonfly is relentless. "When you got tired of Susanna, Ms. Margot Smythe, you fired her anyway. She somehow had enough self-respect left to accuse you of sexual harassment. Very bad move. In this fucking town, *you're* Ms. Big-Shot Feminist Attorney. No one believed Susanna."

"Stupid slut." My voice fills with disdain. "She never should've tried to ruin *me*. She didn't have the smarts to survive in L.A."

In a split-second, she is at me, gloved hand at my neck, hurling me off balance. The suddenness of her assault causes me to bang my head against the tree trunk. Before I can regain my senses, she has cuffed my other hand to an opposite branch. Coils of rope surround each of my ankles when I open my eyes. She has squashed my tits into the little strapless bra. At her mercy, I am half-naked, spread-eagled.

She reads my thoughts. "Ain't going to kill you, Ms. Margot Smythe. Won't stoop to *your* level."

"I *didn't* murder Susanna. *She* killed herself." With a mixture of undiminished passion and dread, I watch her. Legs apart, she stands over me like a ruthless dominatrix—the role *I* prefer. "Do you honestly think *you* can get away with this? Obviously, you stalked me and premeditated this scenario. Turn me loose, Dragonfly. We'll pick up where we left off at the club. Let's go to your apartment and forget about Susanna. I'll prove to you that I never hurt her. I'll show *you* what I taught her."

"Don't want to learn a damn thing from you. Know more than enough already," she mutters. "I'll teach *you* about the woman you destroyed."

"Who wants to hear about that loser? I came here for sex, nothing else. You're boring me."

She smirks. "Don't forget I'm in charge." Her gaze sweeps over me. "Know why I call myself 'Dragonfly'?" Her voice quivers for a second before she regains composure. "Because in Susanna's suicide note she wrote that she wished to be one—to be beautiful and elusive. She wanted people to admire her, but at the same time she wanted them to be too afraid to come close. Ms. Margot Smythe, you destroyed whatever hope she had of trusting again, of loving and being loved. Susanna *knew* what you'd done to her. That's why she chose to die. She flew right out her window, into the sky like the dragonfly she wanted to be."

Her remarks do not faze me. For all I know, she is making up everything, suicide note and all. Susanna Machado had wanted *me* to romance her. Her Latin beauty had not delivered on its gorgeous promise. She lacked sophistication, style. She had developed no desire for dangerous sex. I dismissed her because *she* had bored me, too.

My neck begins to ache as I study Dragonfly. "She was a neurotic little wimp. You have backbone. Why waste your time avenging someone who could never be your equal?"

She unzips the leather jacket. At first, I flinch, expecting her to draw out a knife or gun. Instead, she fingers a silver chain around her neck. A vertical charm dangles from it.

"Know any Spanish, Ms. Margot Smythe?"

I shake my head.

"Figures. You live in L.A.—the most multicultural city in the world—but you're too damn arrogant to learn its most predominant second language." Coldly, she stares at me. "In English—in fairy tales—dragonflies are spectacular, magical. In Spanish, *dragonfly* translates to *caballito del diablo*—'little horse of the devil.'"

"Has a kinky ring to it," I joke.

She ignores my comment. "Because of the way you mistreated her, Susanna considered herself to be your little horse, whipped and beaten. She believed *you* are the devil." Squatting beside me, she reveals what she wears around her neck. A genuine-looking silver dragonfly hangs from the chain. "Only another caballito del diablo can avenge Susanna."

As she drops to her knees, I cringe, half-expecting her to pummel me into senselessness. When she does not, I feel somewhat relieved. From another pocket, she pulls out several packets of moistened tissues, the kind included with take-out food. Careful not to leave fingerprints, she does not remove her gloves as she tries to open a packet. At last she rips it apart. She takes the wet tissue and smears it over my face. I turn my head as far away as I can, but she has the upper hand. At first, I think she wants to cram the tissue into my mouth to gag me. Seconds later, I realize she is smearing my make-up, smudging my lipstick, converting my matte-finish face into an indiscriminate palette of colors.

"When you're found, Ms. Margot Smythe, I want you to look as old and ugly as you really are. I want them to see how blotchy your skin is without cosmetics. Booze and cigarettes have done that to you. You really belt down those drinks. I want them to smell the stench of your cigarette breath. Why do you think I kept pushing away from you tonight? You stink."

"You can't talk to me this way. I won't tolerate—"

"Shut your dirty mouth," she hisses before continuing. "I want whoever finds you to see how you can't even fit into those so-called sexy panties you made Susanna wear. I want them to see your sagging boobs, your gray pussy. Sure doesn't match your phony blonde hair. When you're found, I want you to be as humiliated as you made Susanna feel. I want you to be exposed—wide open—for all the world to see what a rotten bitch you are."

"You're not really going to leave me here?" Flat on my back, arms and legs stretched wide, I begin to panic. "I'll freeze."

"Not as cold as Susanna is in her grave." Rising, she tosses the soiled tissues on my stomach. "By the way, you can use these for toilet paper. Who knows how long you'll hang out? Snakes, frogs, and lizards might get curious about you. They might slither all over you. They're not used to seeing humans in the wetlands at night. Won't matter to them if you consent or not."

"How dare you abandon me like this!" In desperation, I struggle against the bonds. "What do you want, Dragonfly? Name your price."

She grins at my entreaties. "Naturalists and birdwatchers come through all the time. It might take a couple of days, but someone'll show up. If you manage to break free—which I doubt—your car keys are locked in the trunk." She zips her jacket.

I endeavor to stay calm. "You told me you live close by. That's obvious because you know this place inside out. You won't get away with this."

She winks. "Next time you go after hot Latina pussy, Ms. Margot Smythe—think twice. Ain't always what we seem."

With a laugh, she backs out of the thicket.

"Dragonfly—come back. Don't go—please!"

Her boots crunch rocks and twigs strewn across the path. Then, I hear nothing. Except for unknown rustlings in the bushes, silence reigns over the wetlands.

◆

The rental car is where I left it near Vista del Mar. Hovering fog has provided sufficient cover for me to return unnoticed. In the car, I pull off the boots and leather outfit. I stuff both into a plastic shopping bag. The gloves remain because my hands would be cold otherwise. Damp from the fog, my hair has regained its curl despite being drenched in mousse. I rub it vigorously, restoring it to its previous softness. In ribbed leggings and a scoop-necked tunic, I slip my feet into flat-heeled shoes. Fingering el caballito del diablo, I begin driving along Culver Boulevard to the motel.

Fog obscures the road opposite La Ballona Wetlands. Without even turning my head, I flash the high beams and head east, away from cherished memories of that childhood adventure zone, its current vengeful reality. Mischievous girls, Susanna and I would chase ephemeral dragonflies through blooming acres of wetlands, stopping only to marvel at the flocks of great blue herons and snowy egrets. We had always dreamed of spending the night in our sleeping bags amidst that natural habitat, but our conservative parents had never allowed us that pleasure.

Ironically, the deceitful creature I deem responsible for my younger sister's death lies there now, hidden and captive in a remote thicket. Margot Smythe—renowned civil rights attorney, darling of feminists—deprived me of my only surviving family. At this moment, I do not care whether Smythe lives or dies.

In the motel room, I take the plastic bag into the bathroom. Carefully, I remove dirt and mud from the soles of the boots and flush the residue down the toilet. I check

the leather outfit for any suspicious traces. When I find
none, I fold and return it to the plastic bag.

Stripping, I step into the shower. After being in Smythe's
company for most of the night, I reek of her cigarette smoke,
alcoholic breath, and the heady Opium perfume she douses
herself with. Vigorously, I soap myself, ridding myself of her
contamination. Tears of relief mix with cascading water.
Until this moment, I never believed I could carry through my
deception.

I had taken a cab to the trendy lesbian club Margot
Smythe frequented. In that crowded atmosphere, amid the
pulsating musical beat, it had been relatively easy to attract
her. Months ago, Susanna had written that Smythe had a
penchant for "dark, exotic types." To her, I was a brand-new
body, a potential conquest—a Latina she had never
encountered. I relied on college acting classes to portray
Dragonfly, a butch dyke, effectively. To my amazement,
Smythe took me at face value. All my plans fell into place.

Scrubbing myself in the shower, I ponder my lack of
remorse over handcuffing Smythe, leaving her defenseless in
the nocturnal desolation of the wetlands. Does my sudden
insensitivity equate with her deliberate seduction and
abandonment of Susanna? Not a chance, I convince myself.
My younger sister was no match for Smythe's twisted wiles.

For once, my sleep is uninterrupted by nightmares about
Susanna. Saturday dawns sunny. No trace of heavy fog is
evident. In the thicket, Smythe will hardly become
sunburned. She may be somewhat dehydrated and hungry
when she is found—but she is unlikely to die. More than
anything, she will crave cigarettes. That thought alone makes
me smile.

While dressing, I turn on the TV. Local news does not
verify Smythe's disappearance. Too early yet.

Fluffing my hair, I glance into the mirror. Dragonfly has
vanished; only the namesake pendant—Susanna's gift to
me—remains. Curly hair frames my face. The business suit is
crisply tailored, slim skirt, black pumps low-heeled, efficient.
I am ready for the flight home.

◆

In the middle of a phone call, the thrift shop clerk waves as I leave the plastic bag on the counter. He gestures toward a receipt book. I point to my watch and hurry out.

On my way to Los Angeles International Airport, I drive past Holy Cross Cemetery. Not even time for a quick visit.

"I did it, hermanita. For you." In the direction of the cemetery gates, I blow her a kiss. "Duermate en paz, Susanna."

After returning the rental car, I sit in one of the airport's lounges. TV offers no news of La Ballona. A reassuring calm fills me. I rise in response to the announcement for the Mexico City flight.

In my window seat, I gaze at the runway, half-expecting to be yanked off the plane by a uniformed officer. Next to me a voice suddenly gushes.

"What a beautiful pendant. Can I see it?"

I face a wide-eyed blonde, bubbly and eager for conversation before take-off.

"Of course," I murmur.

"Oh, it's a dragonfly. Let me—" She giggles. "Gosh, I've been studying Spanish for months so I won't sound like an idiot in Mexico. I *know* the word. *Don't* tell me." For a long moment, she seems mesmerized by my silver dragonfly. "Caballito del diablo," she finally says in triumph. "Such a weird name for a dragonfly."

As the plane becomes airborne, I offer my smiling reply, "I disagree. I think 'caballito del diablo' is actually quite fitting."

METAMORPHOSIS

Judith Katz

"I had hoped, by means of the bouquet of flowers, to appease my love for her a little, it was quite useless. It is possible only through literature or through sleeping together. I write this not because I did not know it, but rather because it is perhaps well to write down warning frequently." —Franz Kafka, Diary, 1911, about the actress, Mrs. Tschissik

I don't live in Cambridge. I was visiting Lillian and our sweet friend Max. I was carrying a bouquet of flowers over my shoulder and toting a bag full of fish back from the health-food grocery store, carefully planning the spectacular dinner I was about to cook, when I ran into my first lover.

It is a miracle I ran into anyone at all. This fish-and-flower extravaganza was designed not only to thank my host, dearest Lily, best loved of my invented family, but was also functioning as a seduce-a-girl dinner with Max in mind.

Max was not yet my lover, but I wanted her to be. I had a theory that Max and I were Franz Kafka and Milena Jesenska in a past life. It so easily explained my star-crossed and prolific passion for her. I live in the iceberg land of Minnesota, far from lustful imaginings of Prague, although not far from lustful imaginings of Max, who lives most of her life in Tel Aviv. I am nearing forty. A filmmaker. A romantic.

I first met Max in the early '80s in Lily's attic apartment. Lily, most beautiful of all my friends, drew Max to her from Israel, and introduced us in that attic apartment over *shabbat* dinner.

To be honest, I felt the possibility of a life between us even at that first meeting. I filed it away because it seemed so impossible. Max was with another lover; she lived thousands and thousands of miles away. I was some hack Jewish lesbian videographer in the habit of writing Max letters—obsessive, minutely detailed, cherishing, hopeful. Imaginative—the letters visual like my work; romantic, like my heart. Slowly I saw our connections to Kafka; clearly I felt who each of us might have been in Prague and Vienna sixty years ago. Of course, to this day I have never revealed my theory to Max. But it was there, in my letters—like the letters between Kafka and Milena.

As I tell this now it's so obvious that *I* was Kafka and *Max* was Milena, although at other times in our long relationship I am Milena and Max is Franz. Of course, at other times I wonder that I am not Beethoven reincarnated or Mary Shelley or Moses Mimonadies. Maybe I was all of them. But in relation to Max, Kafka it is.

I don't for one minute think I have Kafka's genius, only his genius for falling for unavailable women. But my eyes are dark like Kafka's and I sometimes take to brooding and worrying about every ill. Yet Kafka would not be caught dead living in Minneapolis if he were alive today, nor would he be making videos about lesbian lives. I don't think so anyway. Kafka's vision telescoped in; mine periscopes out into the world. Maybe I *was* Milena then. But if I was Milena, then so was Max. Brilliant Max whose black-and-white films thrill me. Beloved Max who can break my heart with a tender hand to my cheek.

It's rather something the way she pronounces my name. Not bland, flat Robin Zelkind; skinny, sallow, too serious Robin Zelkind. Max gives a deep, guttural *R* for Robin, *Chrobin*. Full of that choke Israelis give their *R*'s, which renders me fat, healthy, and fully absolutely Jewish. *Chrobin*

Zhelkind. Kafka in my last life, Jewish dyke in this life, happy at last in the life to come.

♦

What began as a walk in the rain in Cambridge with groceries and thoughts of red snapper pan-fried to perfection, followed perhaps by a kiss in the kitchen, leads now to thoughts of Max and me as we must have been once, trudging up Austrian mountains, me breathing freely for the first time in my life, she encouraging, coaxing, urging me to become healthy and whole. As full as her voice saying my name makes me feel. My Max, my Milena.

My boots made a satisfying clop-clop on the cobblestone sidewalks just blocks from Harvard. One thought led to another and I was convinced that it must be true—I was absolutely Kafka reincarnated as a Jewish dyke in 1990, and, Milena or not, Max was part of the picture (Felice, or Mrs. Tschissik, or even Kafka's sister Ottla)—and I was duty-bound to convince her of this without seeming insane because it was vital, not only to my own romantic life, but to the history of art, and the Jewish women's movement. The romantic and historical connection excited me. The Jewish connection excited me. Of course, I couldn't tell the whole lesbian community, but I had to confess this theory to Max sooner or later. Besides, the fact of her handing me Kafka's diaries settled it. Somewhere, deep inside, Max knew who we were to each other, too.

I was by now some distance from where this trope had started in my mind with an exquisite *shabbat* dinner for my friends. I was all the way to the end of my desire for Max, holding her in my arms, finally revealing my startling theory; how thrilled she would be to know I saw it too; how she covered me with kisses at this moment of recognition—when I distinctly heard somebody call my name.

"Robin Zelkind? Is that you?"

I looked up from my fish, flower, and Kafka reverie to see Laurel, who looked exactly as she had twenty years before. Same blue-flannel shirt, same jeans torn in the knees, same scuffed-up old work boots, taped glasses, long hair

stringy and tied back. Standing on a porch. As if twenty
years hadn't passed.

"Laurel?"

"My god, I thought that was you." She jumped down
three steps and met me on the sidewalk. "Then I thought,
what would you be doing in Cambridge? I thought you were
stuck permanently someplace in the Midwest. Indianapolis
wasn't it?"

"Minneapolis. I still live there."

"Let me get a good look at you."

Only one thing was different about Laurel now. She
spoke in full sentences. She did not jump on me squealing
like a puppydog. She articulated like an adult now. "What
brings you to Boston?"

I eyed her suspiciously. When you haven't seen a woman
for years and the next-to-the-last time you saw her she had
her whole right hand up inside you and you were begging
for more, and then the next time you saw her you were too
embarrassed to give her the time of day, what did you tell
her? *Oh, I'm here trying to convince my friend, Max, that
we are historically famous lovers and she really ought to fall
in love with me.* Did I admit that twenty years later I was
still having limited luck in love?

Or could I say only, "Visiting," which I did, and "You?"

"I live here," she said, "right here in that house. With
my lover, Kit and her two daughters. We've been together for
five years."

I nodded. I was in shock a little, for two reasons. The
first, as I said, because when I knew Laurel in college, she
was virtually mute. And now here she was, talking in novels
about her new life. Second, I never would have pegged
Laurel for the wife, two kids, and house-near-Harvard type.
But then, I have lots of old lovers I couldn't imagine as
married yet who are.

"Do you want to come in?"

I didn't. I held tight to the flowers, gestured to my bag of
fish. Did I mention it was raining?

"At least come onto the porch. What have you been up
to all these years? When was the last time I saw you—'75?"

I followed her slowly up three steps. "That time you told
me you were going back to school—"

"Yeah, oh yeah. That'd put it at '78—I went back and got another bachelor's degree—in, what was it that time?—oh yeah, that's when I got one in animal science. Really, Robin, you look great. Come on in, just for a minute."

I looked forlornly at my flowers.

"Just for a minute—I'll make some tea."

This couldn't be the same Laurel. Was I the same Robin? I dragged my feet over the threshold into a living room strewn with girl toys and boy toys, Barbie dolls mingled with electric racing cars, Crayola crayons, pop beads, and candy wrappers. The rug smelled like children and cat piss.

"Sit down!"

I looked at the couch, which was covered with animal hair; I perched on the edge, held my flowers up so they didn't come in contact.

"What have you been up to? Still making movies?"

This was my sore spot, my source of great shame. Whenever I run into anyone I knew more than five years ago, the first thing they ask me is, "Are you still making movies?" Which I construe to mean, "Because I still haven't seen any of them in a theater, so what are you, *dead*?"

"Yeah, I'm still doing it. I won an award at a national women's film festival last year."

"Far out," squealed Laurel, who slapped me hard on the back, and I knew now it was indeed the same Laurel. "Gosh, I admire you. Plugging away at it all these years . . ." She stared hard and straight into my eyes through her cracked glasses. I wriggled uncomfortably.

"Where's your wife and kids?"

She looked at me as if I were speaking Latin.

"Kit and her kids—"

"Shopping for school clothes, I think. I just got home from work a few minutes ago. Want tea or coffee?"

"No."

We sat quietly for a minute. Me on the hairy couch, Laurel in a chair strewn with doll clothes and crayon shards.

I couldn't think of one polite thing to ask her. Finally I said, "Have you lived in this house long?"

She shrugged. "About four years. Kit teaches at Radcliffe. Romance languages. I'm a faculty wife."

I shrugged next. "Sounds good." Laurel? It didn't seem
real.

Laurel squealed. "It's great. Don't you think it's *too
funny*? Lesbian faculty at *Radcliffe*? I think it's a scream. Are
you sure you don't want some tea?"

I looked at Laurel amongst the doll clothes and I
couldn't quite figure it. I thought for sure people who taught
at Radcliffe had cases for their doll clothes, money for
cleaning people, glasses that weren't cracked and taped. I
looked at my flowers. I was starting to worry that they'd die
before I got to present them majestically to Max. *Milena*. I
really didn't want to be sitting here in Laurel's living room.
Kafka would not have been seen here. I had absolutely
nothing to say. "Can I use your bathroom?"

"Sure, it's right down the hall. First door on the left."

I gathered my groceries and flowers to me. "You can
leave those out here," Laurel offered.

"It's okay," I said, and headed off down the hall, which
started off wide and regular, then suddenly became dark and
narrow. I wasn't sure there was a bathroom down this too
dark and narrow hall at all. I thought maybe I should go
back to Laurel, but I really didn't want to. I asked for a
bathroom because I wanted to get away from her. It was too
strange to be sitting in her domesticated living room listening
about lesbians at Radcliffe. It was way too strange to be
anywhere near Laurel, who I had hardly thought about in
the past twenty years, except to remember her tripping on
LSD under a pile of leaves on the University of
Massachusetts campus the fall her brother died. Except to
remember that she was the first woman I ever held naked in
my arms, touched with my tongue, got fired from my job as
dorm counselor for.

♦

The hall was getting darker, narrower. Photographs lined
the walls but I couldn't make them out. There wasn't a
doorway on the right or on the left. I began to think I was
done for, doomed to go back the way I had come, doomed
to another twenty minutes of conversation with Laurel
before I could go cook my fish—

"Find it okay?"

"Couldn't find it at all."

Pause.

"Sure you won't have some tea now?"

"I've got to get going."

"Call me the next time you get into Boston, we can have lunch."

"Sure, I'd love to meet Kim."

"Kit, Robin."

"Kit."

—sure that by the time I emerged from the hallway back onto Harvard Street the fish would have rotted and the flowers would be dead.

And then, just as I was becoming absolutely certain that there was no alternative but to turn back and face the Laurel music, a line of light appeared at the end of the hallway. It bordered a doorway that was definitely not on the left, but it was the first doorway I had seen since I rounded the corner and I knocked on it lightly. It opened a bit.

"Who is it?"

The voice was vaguely familiar but I couldn't place it. "I'm a friend of Laurel's," I said, peeking into the room, which was not a bathroom at all, but a study or an office of some kind, books on three walls, plants and papers everywhere.

"Who the hell is Laurel? Jesus Christ, Robin, what are you doing here?"

There behind the fattest manuscript I had ever seen in my life was Remi, my smartest lover, with a blue pencil in one hand and a cup of coffee in the other. My heart absolutely skipped a beat. "Remi?" I started giggling like a maniac, I couldn't help it. "I didn't know *you* lived here *too*."

"What are you talking about Robin? I live alone. How did you get in here anyway?"

"Laurel invited me."

"I don't know any Laurel, I don't know what you're talking about. Can't you see I'm working?"

I pushed my way into the little study. "Remi, I was just in the living room visiting with my first lover, Laurel, and I had to go to the bathroom—I didn't really have to go to the bathroom, I had to get out of the living room. I was choking

on cat hair, so I asked where the bathroom was, and Laurel
sent me down the hall to the first door on the left only there
wasn't any door until I got here and then it's not even the
bathroom, it's your room."

"Who is Laurel? God, Robin are you high? I heard you
quit smoking pot. What is with you? Of course you're in my
room—this is my house—did you call and say you were
coming and I forgot?" Sarcastic.

"Remi, I didn't know I was coming until I got here."

Remi flipped another page of her manuscript. "I am
really busy, Robin." Irritated.

"I can see that." I sat down on a stack of books by the
doorway. "Only I haven't seen you for about five years. You
think that since I happen to be here you could spare a couple
of minutes?"

Remi made a few wild slash marks. Muttered.

"What are you working on anyway?"

She put down her papers with an exasperated sigh and
pulled her glasses off. Then, as if I were an idiot, "My
thesis." Moron implied.

I burst out laughing. "Is this the same thesis, or are you
getting a new Ph.D.?"

Remi looked at me with the vicious daggers I
remembered well. I sat back and studied her. She had
changed a little. She looked like pictures I'd seen of her
recently in *off our backs* and *GCN*. Her work shirt and
overalls were replaced by a flowing rose-colored jersey and
baggy cotton pants, her face was fuller, and she was rounder
all over. I got that same feeling I used to get every time I saw
her, like I wanted to jump into bed with her and I'd been
called into the principal's office all at once.

"Of course it's the same thesis, Robin. Don't you get it?
The field keeps changing, I have to keep up with it. Anyway,
you should talk. I haven't seen anything new from you in
years. Those flowers aren't for me, are they? I hate roses."

I looked at the flowers to make sure they hadn't wilted
under Remi's ice-box stare. They were fresh as ever. "No,
but if you want the fish I'm sure I could work out a creative
way to let you have it."

"What?" I could tell she was getting distracted. She
fingered her glasses and started chewing on her blue pencil.

I yelled, "*DO YOU WANT SOME FISH?*"

"What is that, one of your bizarre come-ons?"

"No, it was a bad joke. What else are you doing besides your thesis? Did you ever find your keys?"

"Yes, they were in my coat pocket the whole ti—" She looked at me like she wanted to punch me in the face but it was strictly against her feminist precepts. "Listen, Robin, I don't know who you think you are, bursting in on me while I'm working and then insulting me on top of everything else—keys, fish—"

"Remi, really, I had absolutely no idea you were here. I was honestly looking for Laurel's bathroom."

"It's just off the kitchen. Use it and get out of here. I'm giving a talk about post-modern lesbian-feminist concepts of peace tomorrow and I really do not have time for old times—"

I settled in further on the book pile. "We haven't seen each other for six years. Don't you ever think of me. . . . I mean with romance in your heart?"

Remi rolled her eyes and tapped the manuscript with her blue pencil. "I've had three lovers since we broke up. I dare say you've had twice that many—"

I did a quick tally in my head. "Counting Jana or not?"

"You're not still fucking *Jana*?"

"Once a year we do it. Then we get mad at each other because we have no self-control and it takes a year of letter writing and tenuous phone calls to get to a place where we can agree to see each other again. But only if we don't sleep together. So I take a plane to Manhattan or she makes an epic drive to the Cities, we meet for dinner in some little romantic out-of-the-way place, we have a great meal, the candlelight is lovely, we start holding hands under the table, then we feed each other dessert, and before we know it, we're in one or the other of our apartments and then within fifteen minutes we're kissing, and then before either of us can do anything about it, we're in bed together, and the whole cycle starts over again."

Remi got that glazed look she often got when anyone started talking about sex. Her chest heaved slightly. Then she caught herself. "*That is sick.*" Irritated again.

"Yes it is, but it's consistent. Anyway, counting Jana it's roughly three times as many."

"Roughly?" Sarcastic still.

"Yeah, not counting making out with some women or dancing real close—"

"You're insatiable."

"I'm joking, Remi. I've only had about five lovers since we were together."

"Counting Jana?"

"No, Jana is in a class by herself. But I haven't spoken to her in about three months."

I was expecting Remi to push her glasses back onto her face and wave me out of the room, but instead, for possibly the first time since I happened on to her, she was absolutely attentive. "Who's your lover now?" Her eyes darted from side to side.

"I don't have one."

"Who are the flowers for?" She held her glasses. They quivered like antennae.

"Max."

"A guy?" she choked.

I rolled my eyes. "Remi, who was your first serious woman lover?"

"You were."

"Do you think now, ten years later I'd be hot for some *guy*?"

"These are tenuous times, Robin. All kinds of queer people are going back to the opposite sex."

"Yourself included?"

"Oh sure. Like I have a choice. So what does she do?"

Was there some real interest in Remi's voice, or was she just humoring me so I would hurry up and get out? "She does what I do."

"Makes movies that never get shown?"

Another old familiar feeling was coursing through my body. I wanted to slug Remi now. "She's a filmmaker, if that's what you mean. I like her very much. I'm going slow. We have a special connection."

"Who is she, Kafka or Milena?" Sarcasm.

I was jolted to my feet. "What do you mean?"

"When we were going together I was Kafka and you
were Milena and then I was Milena and you were Kafka."

If this was true, I had totally forgotten it. "Who's idea
was it?"

"It was a joint fantasy."

"You're kidding me."

"Don't tell me you've forgotten. All those days plowing
through the Czech dictionary together in bed—"

"Come on, Remi, you're making this up—"

"I'm not making it up—I've got that damn dictionary
here someplace—" She began to shuffle through the stacks
on her desk.

"They wrote to each other in German. Milena translated
his work into Czech—"

"Neither one of us knew that ten years ago—"

I was devastated. "You're absolutely positive?"

Remi looked at me with mind-fuck in her eyes. "No, I'm
just trying to drive you crazy." A huge cockroach scuttled
across her desk. She dropped the Czech dictionary on it,
then brushed the flattened remains into her wastebasket.

"You're sure I didn't think you were Felice?"

"Kafka loved Felice because she was efficient. That ain't
me, babe."

"You're right about that." If I ever got out of this house
I was going to have to reevaluate my entire relationship to
Max. I began to hyperventilate. I thought it best to change
the subject. "Lily said you were living with someone."

"Yes, and *she* thinks I was Kafka too."

I felt my fist ball up involuntarily.

Remi stood up and stretched. "You know, you really
don't look bad." Her eyes moved from my face down to my
breasts. I felt them stay there.

"What are you staring at?"

"I was just letting my mind wander." She laughed lightly.
I was suddenly worried that my fish smelled.

"Listen, Remi, I've got to split—"

Remi plopped down in her chair and let out an
exasperated sigh. "This is so typical of you, Robin
Zelkind—"

"Ditto," I said, holding my roses to me, "—but before I go, Remi, I would like to know why you never answer my letters."

She picked up her blue pencil and jammed her glasses on. If she were a smoker, now would have been the time for a blue cloud to fill the space between her and me. Instead there was an ice wall three feet thick and she was buried in her thesis again. "I really have a lot to do, Robin. If you want to use the bathroom go ahead; otherwise, there's the door." She pointed with her coffee cup and didn't look up. "Besides, at a certain point you know Kafka stopped writing to Milena entirely."

"*You* aren't Kafka—"

She looked up from her manuscript. "But *you* are?"

"No, I'm Robin Zelkind—" I wanted to ask again about her long silence but thought better of it. "Where does this door go?"

Remi flipped pages, "Out into the hallway you came from."

"I came from Laurel's living room." I was really confused now. "I'm not even sure what city we're in."

"Boston, Robin. The T stop is half a block from this building. Go back to your Czech honey and make hay, just don't bug me."

"She's Israeli."

"I'm busy, Robin—"

"I'm leaving," I said.

♦

I closed the door and threw my back against it. I looked desperately for a padlock, a barricade of any kind. I wanted nothing more than to lock Remi in. I listened at the door. I heard her blue pencil skritch-skritching against her manuscript. I clutched my packages to me and tiptoed down the hall.

What did it mean that I thought Remi was Kafka once? More to the point, what did it mean that I totally spaced it out? Did that invalidate my so-sure feelings for Max? Was I deluded when I was so sure about Remi? Was I suffering from double delusion now? Was the only part of me that was Kafka the delusional part?

The floor underneath my feet was linoleum now, dirty gray and black squares. More photographs lined the walls. They looked vaguely familiar. Just ahead of me was a staircase, and coming up from the stairs I heard music and laughter. I couldn't go back through Remi's door; I had almost forgotten about Laurel. I forged ahead and took the stairs one ginger step at a time. My groceries and roses were heavy in my hands, but I had stopped worrying about them. I was a million miles away from that sexy dinner now. I was walking down a set of strange stairs to an unlocked door.

My knock was met by women's laughter. Then the door opened and—why was I surprised?—there stood Jana, absolutely naked with a champagne glass bubbling over in her hand.

She opened her arms to me. "Robin, we've been expecting you!"

I wasn't sure if I should run into those familiar outstretched arms or run back to—where?

"We?" I bussed Jana's cheek and looked over her broad shoulders to the brass bed that filled the room. Didn't fill it exactly, for there were candles burning everywhere, ferns and ostrich feathers in vases, and jars atop old-fashioned tables. Two women who looked a little bit like I might have known them were lounging naked on the bed, and another woman I thought I knew was languishing on a divan along one wall. The curtains were pulled, but a fire burning in a cheery little fireplace gave the room a mellow, delicious light.

"Yes, *we*, you sweet silly thing." Jana swept the packages out of my arms and deposited them on a chair. "We're having a party and you're the guest of honor."

"Take your clothes off and join the fun," invited one of the women in the bed. The other started laughing her head off. I dropped my leather jacket onto the floor and slipped by boots off, then my socks. I unbuttoned the first couple of buttons on my shirt, but I stopped there. I sat down on the bed. "Do I know you girls?"

The laugher kept on laughing. Jana sat down behind me and rubbed my shoulders. She was pouting a little, the way

she did. "Listen to that. She can't remember us now that
she's won that big award."

I kissed Jana on the mouth. "I remember you," I said,
still kissing.

"But what about these, your old friends—" Jana
gestured to the other women. "Your penal colony."

All three waved. The laugher began to giggle.

"I don't know who they are."

Jana offered me her champagne glass. I shook my head.
"Oh, you don't do that anymore. I keep forgetting. Well, let
me re-introduce you, Robin Zelkind, since you have the bad
manners to forget." She pointed to the laugher, who was a
very sweet-looking blonde woman with pale green eyes. I
hate to say cherubic but that's exactly how her body was,
every part of her was rosy and glowing. "This is Dinah. You
two had a one-night stand in 1973."

Dinah giggled.

"How do you do?"

She giggled again. The woman beside her in bed, who
was darker and older, started kissing her neck.

"That's Evie."

Evie stopped kissing Dinah long enough to say hello.

"When did we uh—"

"You were nuts about me for about three months in
1979." I could see how that was possible. This Evie had one
of those raw silk voices and knotty carpenter hands. "Then
as soon as I got interested," she tossed back her graying hair,
"you dropped me for some intellectual snob who kept losing
her keys. Frankly I couldn't see the attraction, but you had
some weird idea that she was Franz Kafka and you had to be
with her."

I gulped. "Remi—was that her name?"

"Beats me. I forgot all about you and got over it." She
nibbled on Dinah's ear. Dinah didn't giggle; she moaned.
Pretty soon their faces were covering each other. I turned my
attention to the woman on the divan who was flipping
through a magazine. Her hair was jet black and absolutely
straight. Lying there on the couch she looked exactly like a
Goya odalisque. She stared up at me with burning black eyes
but said nothing.

"Who's that?" I whispered to Jana.

"That's Mara," she whispered back. "You proposed to her in 1982 in Taos; then as soon as she accepted, you headed back to Cambridge and never answered any of her letters."

"I've got a perfectly good girlfriend now," said Mara, "but I've never forgiven you." She went back to her magazine. She looked dangerous.

Jana took my face in her hands and began kissing me. "I've never forgiven you either," she said, sliding the shirt off my shoulders. "Fortunately, I don't have to." She was sucking my breasts now and unbuttoning my jeans, and I was enjoying it. I felt her fingers play across my pubic hair. I was melting into Jana when I sat up suddenly.

"I've got to get to Lily's to make dinner." And Max. Would I ever get back to her?

Jana kept kissing me and pretended she didn't hear. I moved her hands. "Honest, Jana, this is real nice—unexpected surprise and all that—but I really have got to go. I promised these friends of mine I was going to make dinner—there it is on the chair over there. I have to go."

Jana kept kissing and started talking. "Why don't you make dinner for us?"

"Because," I said, holding my breath, peeling her hand off my breast, "I offered to make Lily and Max dinner—I am a guest in their house."

Jana pushed me away and sat on the bed sulkily. "I've just about had it with you, Robin. I mean, here we are, three former lovers and me, your current roller-coaster ride, we're here, we're eager—"

"I'm not eager," Mara whispered hoarsely into her magazine.

"Available, anyway, and you're out the door to cook dinner. Give me those roses; I'll put them in water. There are plenty of vases around. And let me take this fish—" She grabbed at my fish. I pulled the bag away from her, setting it out of her reach next to me.

I sat on her bed and buttoned my shirt. "I can't do this!"

"Why not?"

Indeed. Why not? I looked around me at those four beautiful women and I pulled on my socks. I leaned my head against Jana's shoulder. She pulled away.

"That's one reason," I said. "If I ever need anything real from you, you disappear quicker than Houdini."

"You're the one walking out the door to make dinner."

"Just now, this minute, I wanted some human contact—my head on your shoulder."

"Yeah, well somehow I'm not in the mood."

I pushed my feet into my boots one at a time. "I just ran into Remi, you know, upstairs. It blew me away. She was just as mean to me as ever—and I was mean to her right back. Then I come down here, and there you are, and three other women who I was not exactly great to, and not only that, but I'd forgotten them."

"It's no big deal," giggled Dinah, "I forgot about you too."

Evie laughed a little and kissed Dinah again. "Really, you're not the beginning and the end of the world, you know."

"I know," I said, "I get that part. What I don't get is why you've all popped into my life now when I'm on my way to make dinner for Max and Lily—"

Jana looked wounded. "I never popped in. I've been here all the time."

"Yeah, but so has everybody else."

"Please," said Mara, who dropped her magazine, wrapped a blue silk kimono around her, and walked out the door.

"Where did she go?"

"The bathroom—how should I know?"

I put on my jacket. "Jana, I'm sorry. I've got to figure this out myself."

"That's what you say, but you're going to meet your Jewish girl friends now—so you won't be alone."

"No, maybe not." I took up the flowers and inspected them. They looked all right. I'd given up worrying about the fish. What I really hoped was that I'd be able to find my way back to Lily's apartment. "Listen," I turned back to Jana. I was going to tell her how sorry I was that things weren't working out, but when I looked over at the bed, she was entangled with Evie and Dinah. There was no way for me to tap on her shoulder and apologize without totally humiliating myself. Just as I touched the doorknob, Mara came back into the room. She was beautiful in her blue kimono. She lit a cigarette and sat back on the divan.

"I'm very sorry I hurt you," I said.

She didn't say anything right away, but she looked at me carefully. Finally she said, "I hated what happened between us, Robin. You got me to open up and then you vanished into thin air. I wanted to be your lover, Robin. More than a lover, I wanted to be yours and yours only. Once I made that known it was the beginning of the end."

I sat next to her on the edge of the divan. I juggled my packages so I had one free arm, which I put around her shoulders. "I'm not particularly proud of the way I treated you then, but I can't erase it either."

"It doesn't matter. I'm with a lover now who cares about me more than I ever expected to be cared for."

I fought back envy and the very beginnings of old-lover desire. I remembered Mara, now, perfectly. Long sleepy days in her sunny New Mexico room. Our love-making was deep and silent. I did ask her to marry me, but I never meant it.

"I wish you the same sometime."

"That's very generous."

"Yes it is," smiled Mara. "Take care, Robin." The smile had a malevolent twist.

I nodded and walked toward the door. Just before I opened it I looked back. Jana, Dinah, and Evie were in a fleshy knot on the bed, but Mara stood still, watching me, her robe half-opened. I could see what looked like the silver handle of a revolver. "You'd really better go now, Robin. I don't think there's anymore for you here right now."

Her face remained stern, serious. I opened the door and walked into the hall.

I had no idea where I was going. Photographs lined the walls. I thought I saw one of Remi and one of Jana. A large roach ambled along a baseboard. I was turning this journey over in my head like India clubs. First Laurel, then Remi, then Jana and the other three. One, two, three girlfriends, four, five, six—had Kafka been a juggler or did he concentrate on his women one at a time? I turned it all over as I wandered down this hall, around that corner, through this labyrinthine, Kafka-esque divide of former lovers that was making me feel as if I would never see Max or Lily

again and if I did, that they would want neither my fish nor
flowers nor theories of Kafka, Milena, and true love. That
they might not recognize me at all.

Suddenly I found myself at Laurel's kitchen table. She
was sitting with a copy of *off our backs* in front of her,
sipping a cup of tea.

"Oh, there you are. I was wondering what happened to
you. You were gone for kind of a long time." She didn't look
like the friendly Laurel I remembered.

I pulled up a chair and poured myself some tea. "I got
lost"—in among my former lovers, past mistakes, failed
romances.

"Yeah, it's kind of interesting in the bathroom
sometimes."

I stared at Laurel. She looked so very real, with her hair
pulled back and her taped glasses. She looked—I leaned
forward, close to her face. "Can I talk to you for a minute?
About something that's been troubling me?"

She looked back at me with an openness that broke my
heart.

"It's just that—I've been through a most extraordinary
time." I explained to Laurel about Lily and Max and my
recent tour through Robin Zelkind's House of Old
Girlfriends. I felt a great heaviness in my heart as I recounted
my confusion about who was Kafka—Remi or Max, or
me—and who was Milena. And what about Jana—what was
I going to do about her?

"And then what about all the women I'd forgotten
about, like Dinah and Evie and Mara and (it was so hard for
me to say this but I had to) even you—" Now I was
practically crying. I took a sip of my tea and snuffled it
down. "I mean, I thought Mara might kill me." I thought of
Remi, the cockroach, the Czech dictionary.

I was desolate. So when Laurel let out her whinny laugh
and slapped me on the back in that old Laurel way I was
surprised to say the least. A bit hurt. Annoyed, even. "Here I
am telling you what a shit I've been, what a mess I've made
of my life, and you're laughing."

She didn't stop laughing either. In fact she just laughed
harder and harder. She was laughing so hard she hit the table
with both her hands and the teapot shook.

"I'm afraid I don't understand," I said.

"Oh come on, Robin," Laurel said, "it's so easy it's not even funny."

"Then why are you laughing your head off? You of all people. You, who I deserted not two weeks after your brother killed himself in that car."

Laurel stopped laughing for a moment, as if in deference to the memory of her dead brother, Mark, but then a low laugh surfaced again. The light in the kitchen was bright and artificial. Laurel finally got herself to stop laughing.

"The thing is, Robin, you haven't forgotten about any of us. And none of us has ever really forgotten about you. What difference does it make if you thought Remi was Kafka in a past life or you think Max is Milena in this life? The fact of the matter is that Franz Kafka died of tuberculosis sometime early in the twentieth century in Czechoslovakia and you are alive now." Laurel pushed her taped glasses up, leaned forward, and took my hand. "Don't you get it? It's not about Kafka or Milena or me or any of the others. This isn't about malice or revenge."

"My God, it's about identity," I slapped myself on the cheek. "Remi isn't Jewish and you're not and Jana isn't—neither was Milena. But Max and Lily *are*—and so am I." This *was* Kafka-esque.

Laurel started laughing again. "For one of the smartest women I ever met in my life you sure are playing stupid."

"I'm not playing anything. I don't get it." Somewhere a door slammed.

"That's Kit. Do you want to stick around and have supper with us and the kids?"

"Supper?" I looked around me wildly for the fish and roses. They seemed my only connection now to Max and Lily.

"They're next to your chair," Laurel said. "Maybe you'd better head out. The girls get a little manic around strangers, and you look pretty blown-away already."

I was relieved. The thought of watching someone I could have married engaged in domestic bliss was more than I could bear. I felt bereft.

"Could you walk me to the door?"

"Sure," she said. "Don't you want to at least meet Kit?"

"Next time," I said. I didn't want to find out Kit was another lover I'd forgotten.

♦

I embraced Laurel at the front door. She opened it and waited until I hit the sidewalk, then closed it behind me. It was still damp and rainy, just a few very young men and women were sloshing along the sidewalks in brightly colored plastic rain gear. I peeked at my flowers—they seemed as fresh as could be expected under the circumstances. I poked my nose into the fish bag. It didn't smell bad.

I walked past brick buildings and fire hydrants, phone poles with posters on them about this concert and that play. I poked my head into the book and video stores, then I turned left, then right, then right again, and to my great relief, found myself in front of Lily's building. I rang her bell, Lily called down through an intercom, I hollered up, she buzzed me in, and I walked the three short flights to her door and then knocked gently. This was not like the halls and stairs at Laurel's place. This was not like Kafka. What I most wanted now was to see Lily's beautiful face, hear Max say my name with her deep, throaty Israeli voice.

I shifted my packages and held my breath while I waited. The fish and the flowers weren't so important anymore. My truest hope was that the real Lily and the real Max would be there to let me in, that we would light candles for *shabbat*, and that we would, as the good friends we had become, enjoy each other for who we were.

Breasts

Amalia Pistilli

London, 13 February

"Forgiveness is the best revenge, forgiveness is the best revenge": I keep mumbling these words to myself but cannot make them into anything meaningful or real. It's one of the fundamental lines in my Catholic upbringing, but how many people (if any at all) ever manage to make it a reality in their lives?

I try another phrase, instead: "Revenge is sweet." Now, that *does* make sense. Revenge *is* sweet, and probably one of the most natural instincts known to humankind.

And I want revenge, sweet and trickling on my lips like a melting chocolate truffle, like a hot pancake dripping honey syrup.

♦

I can still clearly remember the dream that told me what was going on, except that I did not understand it at the time. It keeps haunting me now.

I was in a darkened house, at the end of a long corridor, and could barely see what looked like a bed at the opposite end. As in a dolly shot of a film, I glided toward the bed—or perhaps only my gaze did—and when I was close enough, I could see that the otherwise very smooth and white cover of the bed was slightly ruffled, like the traces made by a wind blowing on a surface of snow.

I came even closer, and saw that the marks were those left by a body that had lain on the sleek white sheets. Suddenly, through the miraculous power of smooth dream editing, I was in a bedroom with my boyfriend, the beautiful, arrogant, vain, and hung-up Eugene Andersen. He was staring at me, a trickle of saliva dribbling from his gaping mouth. He was particularly staring at one part of my body, below my neck.

I looked down, and to my amazement I saw that I had grown a pair of not just big, but absolutely enormous breasts.

And Eugene seemed to like them very much. We were both naked, and he was sporting the biggest erection I had ever seen on him.

I got closer. What would he like to do with them? I knew, I knew.

I got even closer, bent down, parted my breasts slightly, and welcomed his throbbing cock between them, starting to rub up and down. With a loud groan and a mighty shudder, Eugene came, a volcanic lava jet of semen flooding my cleavage.

And I woke up.

Eugene was sleeping next to me, seemingly untroubled by any dreams, his beautifully thick hair, the color of rusty gold, scattered on the pillow.

I could never stop admiring his beauty: I who had always prided myself on valuing the spirit above all material things, was a slave to a cocksure, immature, flirtatious young man's physical beauty.

♦

In the days that followed, I forgot about that dream. There were too many things to do: running after Eugene in the long, twisted corridors of the film school we both attended, anxiously eavesdropping when he was deep in conversation with one of the pretty young things who

constantly surrounded him in the cafeteria, sneaking up on
him with the excuse of picking up a film spool or a splicer
when it seemed he was too long locked in the darkness of
the editing rooms, finding any way I could to be assigned to
one of the projects he was working on so that I could keep
an eye on him and make sure he wasn't too involved with
any of the women he worked with. I spied on him as if he
were a scientist who had discovered nuclear fission and I was
the secret agent in charge of kidnapping him.

And in all that spying and torturing myself with insane
jealousy, I forgot to do any of my own work. My creativity
was at an all-time low, and I could not function or sleep
properly without worrying that as soon as Eugene turned a
corner away from my eyes, there would be a woman waiting
for him with her arms extended.

And there usually were: not in the obsessive way I raved
about, but he was popular with girls—his half-English
aristocratic, half-Scandinavian good looks made them want
to screw him, and his intellectual arrogance made them want
to mother him, sensing, as all women can, the deep neurotic
fragility his arrogance sought to conceal.

I have come to the conclusion that Eugene was a true
woman-hater: scared of women and their inner power, he
sought to belittle anything traditionally the realm of the
female. Anything that had to do with nature and sensitivity
and the esoteric, he would try and crush under the weight of
his blind faith in illuminist reason.

When we had been dating just a couple of months, and
he hadn't moved in with me yet, we were sitting one night in
his dirty, untidy apartment talking our drunken, exalted talk,
when I tried to do the stupid thing we all try in relationships;
I tried to convert and convince him. Out of my bag I took a
packet and said: "This is for you."

It was Adrienne Rich's *Of Woman Born*, a psychological
and anthropological account of the difficulty, for men, of
acknowledging where they come from: a woman's body, to
which they return every time they make love.

Eugene stared at the title of the book, one brow arched.
"What should I do with this, Mary Ann?" he sneered at me.

I started to feel hot blood running fast through my veins.

"You could read it, you could expand your horizons, you could even learn something from it," I said sweetly, still trying hard not to sound too teacher-like.

"I'm not going to read any of this rabid feminist anti-man crap. . . . Aaaah!"

A large stain of very red blood was widening on his very white shirt, trickling from his forehead where the heavy book I had thrown in his face had made a deep cut.

"Bitch!" he said as he fumbled for a handkerchief to wipe his face with. "You could've blinded me!"

Oh, I should have! How I wish I had!

As it happens, that night he had been reading *Hamlet* to me, his favorite part, from the heavy paperback edition of the *Complete Works of Shakespeare*, which was lying on the coffee table between us, the first weapon my rage had encountered.

Pity it wasn't the leatherbound edition.

I still have that book. But I don't have him. He left. He left me! After all I endured from him.

It is this that really stings. He left *me*. I took no revenge, no satisfaction.

I had thrown him out a few times in my bouts of rage, but I always took him back.

Like when I discovered his porno magazines.

They were hidden under the bottom of a drawer I happened to pull out during one of my tantrums, wanting to throw away all of his stuff. And I got a lot more than I'd bargained for.

I can't remember exactly what they were like or how many—five or six I think—and mostly rather soft except for one anatomical magazine dealing with larger than life close-ups of swollen female genitalia and blow jobs.

I did not linger on them. My rage and outrage exploded at once. Eugene was watching this, fear and shock on his face, which was pathetically squashed against the glass of our ground-floor bay windows.

I had already pushed him out the door and locked it on him; then I grabbed an armful of the magazines and threw them out into the street where he was standing and slammed the door back on his face, howling abuse at him. "You filthy wanker! You disgusting little piece of shit!"

By chance, one of the magazines remained behind in the flat, hidden under a pile of other papers scattered on the floor. I found it later, after he had gathered the clothes and things I had hurled at him through the window and exited with as much wounded dignity as his arrogance could summon.

I was left behind, in the awfully silent flat, to weep on my ignorance, to ask myself all the questions without answers. To clear up the mess, as usual, while crying over spilt blood and papers and the contents of drawers.

I still keep that one magazine, a small, ridiculous booklet full of tacky photographs of rather ugly women carrying monstrously inflated breasts; some are rather fat and maternal looking, their breasts drooping on the floor as they squat in comically unerotic poses, with varicose veins showing on breasts and legs; others are more the business, bodies as taut and breasts as firm and perfectly round as the highest-fee plastic surgery will allow.

Since then I have confronted myself with these pictures, telling myself this is what I lack, this is why he cannot really love me. I've used them to torture myself countless times, dwelling on those images, feeling a disgusted fascination for them, angered and amused by their banality, their cheapness, their appeal to a sexuality I recognize as infantile, facile, unimaginative, but which I cannot dismiss or hope to change.

I was scarred by it. I developed an insane obsession for other women's breasts, observing them in the streets, tirelessly comparing them with my own, and always finding mine wanting. Even when they were smaller than mine, I told myself that the shape, the consistency was better. How could I have grown so obsessed with something I scarcely noticed before? It is this I find particularly frightening about obsessions: they wipe out everything else and grow in your mind like worms, eating its contents from the inside, so that one day you wake up and there is only this big obsession staring at you. It *becomes* you.

◆

Days and days went by.

I moved as if in a daze. I kept going to the film school and meeting Eugene in the twisted corridors. We exchanged cold glances and did not speak to one another.

Like the victim who has developed a pathological dependence on her torturer, I started to miss him.

I began to spy on him again, suffering when I saw him chatting with pretty girls in the cafeteria, elegantly waving his beautiful hands in the air. It was unbearable not to possess him anymore, not to have the right to break into his conversation and thrust my arm around his waist in a gesture that would say to the other young women, "See, he's *mine*."

I did not feel flattered by other men's attempts to come after me once everybody had realized Eugene and I had broken up. I ignored them, too wrapped in my obsession to care about anything else.

We were coming to the end of term, and I was getting desperate. I would not see him for three weeks; meanwhile, he would find another one to love, to cherish, to torture.

I had to do something. I had to get him back.

On the last day of school, there was to be a big party in the main film studio. We had no classes that day but were all recruited to clear the studio of flats, redheads, stands, dolly tracks, and bits and pieces belonging to former productions that lay scattered about the huge floor.

Eugene, as usual, was working very little and talking very much, a court of girls hanging on his every word.

I went casually up to him and delivered the note I had compiled days earlier, torn into pieces, rewritten, torn again, and so on. He took it with a slight hesitation and a bit of a smirk. The note invited him for dinner just before he was due to leave to go visit his parents in the country.

That same evening he phoned.

"Why do you want to see me, Mary Ann?" He sounded suspicious.

"I'd just like to say goodbye in a more civilized way, you know."

"Ha! Talk of civilized! You stomped on my glasses, you smashed my typewriter, you threw me out into the street, and you've still got most of my things at your place."

"Well, come and get them then, and stay for dinner. *Please*, Eugene."

"Okay," he said in his most condescending tone, which normally would infuriate me but in my withdrawal state sounded like a blessing from the Pope.

I prepared myself very carefully. I had bought some sexy, black lace underwear, film for my Polaroid, oysters, champagne, and caviar for dinner, and some highly intoxicating hashish which I took some drags on before Eugene's arrival to give myself courage.

He arrived, looking on guard. He wasn't going to admit he'd been wrong or a jerk. He was going to play hard to get, and I went along with it. We ate dinner, smoked a joint and another and another, got very drunk, and ended up in the bedroom doing all sorts of kinky things with a cucumber and the Polaroid camera.

After the holidays, he came back to live with me. I remember one day taking the Polaroids out of the bedside drawer and seeing that a couple of them were smeared with an unmistakable sticky substance.

I thought I had the edge on his pornographic fantasies; in reality I had just bowed down to them.

25 February

Today I was walking back home from shopping, and on the corner where the street girls usually stand was one I'd never seen before. She wore high black boots and a very short miniskirt, and had a pair of breasts that burst out of her low-cut, tight-fitting red top.

I felt revulsion and hatred, still my usual reaction to big tits. But her face looked nice, open and smiling. She asked me for a cigarette.

"Sorry, I don't smoke. You must be cold, dressed like that."

"Not too much. It's the business suit, ha, ha! Nice of you to worry about it. Most women around here are stuck-up bitches. Bet they all signed the petition to get the council to clean up the streets."

"Oh, well, personally I don't mind you being here. It's your punters I don't like much."

"D'you think I do? It's just work for me. I do it quick and I do it safe. I ain't got a pimp, you know. I'm totally independent, but then, I don't need one, 'cause I don't do drugs and stuff. Some of the young girls I see these days, they're just hopeless. I really feel for them. I've got it all planned, I'm just saving the money to buy my own place, then I'll quit."

"I see. Well, good luck. See you around."

"See ya."

It was the first time in my life I had ever had a conversation with a prostitute. She was nice, I thought, as I fumbled in my handbag for the keys to my front door. As always, my eyes fell on the label inside the bell plate that reads "E. H. Andersen-Mary Ann Jones." As always, I thought: "I must change that." But one of the screws holding the clear plastic cover is rusty and has been resistant to any screwdriver I could find in my not-well-stocked toolbox.

I am hopeless at doing anything with my hands, apart from editing film and cooking. Eugene used to mock me for that. Eugene used to despise me for not having a technical mind.

He thought of himself as a sort of super human, the Nietzschean creature he was so fond of reading about. Someone who was not only versed in the classics, who could read three languages and knew all about the Vikings and the ancient Anglo-Saxons and the Romans, but who could also repair a faulty appliance, rewire a telephone extension, and do decorating work.

I, of course, cannot do any of these things, and I don't know about history and ancient literatures. I am the person who is capable of trying to unravel a ball of string by pulling at the outside thread, but I am also the person who can unravel the much more tangled ball of string of somebody's mind. I know about the people I see around me; I detect things in their faces that sometimes they are not even aware are there. Frowns and lines on their faces tell me about their inner life.

But Eugene said this *intuition* (he used the word disparagingly) of mine wasn't real knowledge; it could not be imparted, shared, tested, verified.

And yet I had that dream, just a short time before I
unearthed his dirty little secret. . . . But Eugene never
accepted this knowledge of mine. He shrugged it away with
his aloof contempt. Eugene Eugene Eugene . . . Oh, his blue
eyes, the color of Scandinavian lakes! Oh, his thick, sensual
lips that belied his absolute frigidity!

Yes, beautiful Eugene Andersen was useless in bed,
selfish and quick and incapable of letting go. I don't even
think he liked sex; he just lusted after images of naked
female bodies. He liked the idea of sex more than the
practice. He did not like physical contact much, except when
rendered fragile and childlike by being excessively stoned
and drunk. Then he would come and cradle in my arms,
seek my caress and my approval.

Oh, God, I am crying again.

8 March

Today it has been one month since he left. It is
International Women's Day. It is Claudine's birthday.

A fitting epitaph.

Claudine, my ex-neighbor, the bitch who made
everything explode. How can I ever trust a woman again
after what she did to me? Calling herself my friend! I realize
I'm just ranting and raving. I'm becoming mad. I dreamt
about him again last night. Of course, in my dreams he was
wonderfully sweet, considerate, and faithful.

God! I can't even remember a single day, out of three
years of relationship, when he was really, completely faithful.
Of course, he always denied that anything was going on,
each and every time I caught him too close and cozy with a
girl. "You are a frenzied, hysterical paranoid!," is what he
used to say to me.

But he couldn't deny what happened with Claudine. It
happened right in front of my eyes. And her husband's.

It still hurts so much, I cannot bear to think about it.
How all the time she was claiming to be my friend, yet when
the four of us were together, she was always flirting with
him, her long eyelids fluttering on a pair of
oh-so-sweet-and-innocent blue eyes! How she gratified him
by hanging on his every word when he talked about
anything at all. Nothing could be more flattering to Eugene's

insecure big ego, and I wasn't providing it anymore. After three years of listening to his ranting monologues, I had become more than just a little jaded about the breadth of his knowledge.

But Claudine behaved as if she thought he was a hero, a prophet, and a genius all rolled into one. This might irritate Oliver, her husband, but he was used to her flirting and didn't think much of it anymore.

Why is it that women are always more jealous?

I remember the music playing that night exactly a month ago: Oliver had put on James Brown's "Sex Machine" as the evening veered toward its conclusion. We all had had quite a lot of wine with the meal I had cooked and brought upstairs to their place because Claudine's allergy to my cats did not allow her to spend too much time in my flat.

I stood up to dance in the small living room, and so did Claudine. For a little while I danced with my eyes closed. Then suddenly I opened them and turned around and saw a scene I will never forget: Eugene was kneeling at Claudine's feet, arms around her waist, she was still dancing, then she leaned down to kiss him on the mouth. Oliver was lying on the sofa looking at them with disbelief, doing nothing.

In memory it all seems like an eternity, their position, their kiss, Oliver's face, my reaction. But it was only a split second.

I walked over to them, pushed her away, pulled him up on his feet, screaming in his face: "That was interesting. Would you like to show me again?" Then I slapped him as hard as I could and stormed out of the room, running downstairs to my flat.

I went to bed, pulling the covers tight over my eyes.

The doorbell rang several times that night while I lay awake in bed, but I never got up to answer.

I was still awake when a long time later Eugene slipped into bed next to me, but I pretended to be asleep.

And the next morning he was all wounded pride again and said he was going to leave—"this time for good."

I don't think I really believed him at the time. He'd done it so often and always come back.

But he hasn't, and I don't think he ever will.

18 April

I haven't opened this diary for ages. What is there to say? I still miss him, I'm still ashamed of it, I still can't help it. I've met the prostitute a few other times. We always have a chat. Her name is Maria. She is thirty-five and has a young daughter who stays with her mother at night. Maria's mother thinks she works in a night club, a bit sordid perhaps, given the kind of clothes Maria has to wear, but she imagines nothing like what Maria really does.

I like Maria. I would like to invite her in for a coffee someday, but I'm a bit reluctant to do it. My middle class prejudices, I guess. And her big breasts.

They still make me uncomfortable. Sometimes I find myself staring at them. I hope Maria doesn't think I'm weird.

Of course, Claudine had big breasts.

I remember when I threw a garden party for my birthday, and the weather was unusually hot. Claudine showed up in a black linen sleeveless dress that revealed about half of her breasts; even more when she leaned over or bent down to pick up something. I surprised Eugene staring at her tits several times during the afternoon. That spoiled my birthday. I was very short with Claudine that day, and she never even guessed why.

It is now seventy days exactly since Eugene left. I am pathetic, counting the days like this, still hoping for his return, but why? I *know* I'm better off without him, of course. I can be free, I can be myself, not living in constant fear of betrayal, stifled by the killing power of jealousy, crushed by the weight of my own inadequacy. But I am unable to regain myself. Perhaps I am lost forever. Perhaps he burned me to ashes in the fire of his immense ego in those three years of violence and pain.

But something else is surfacing underneath the heartache. A rage so red and raw that it even scares me. I am starting to get angry, very angry at him. Maybe it is a symptom of recovery?

9 May

Eugene is thirty today. As if he could be any more grown up!

Where is he living now? What does he do? He's probably wasting his days in an alcoholic daze, reading *Hamlet* out loud to himself, wheezing and coughing in his sleep when his bad asthma avenges itself of his reckless daytime smoking. How he used to keep me awake at night because of it! And I put up with it like a mother puts up with her baby crying all night.

What an image.

Yesterday I met Milko, Eugene's friend at the film school. He invited me to somebody's party, but I declined. Milko stared hard at me, then said: "Still aching, huh?" When I nodded, he went on: "He was no good for you, Mary Ann."

I know. I fucking well know. That doesn't stop the aching.

But the rage is growing. It is swelling up inside me.

How I want to hurt him now!

14 May

This morning I went to the West End to have a look around the second-hand bookshops, which of course reminded me of Eugene and his endless book collection. He would come back with a new book literally every day and wave away my petty female concern—"Where are we going to put all these books?" What did it matter to him if my shelves were overflowing? Such a meaningless problem could certainly not arrest the development of his culture.

I think he read so much because he did not want to see the world around him; even though he also read the newspaper every day, he did not see the real world.

I remember a photograph his mother showed me when I was visiting their wealthy country house. In the frame was a large gathering of relatives all scattered about some elegant living room, seated and standing, all looking at the camera with various expressions, and in the middle of all this an eight-year-old Eugene sat in his habitual cross-legged position on the floor, reading a book, his head sunk into the pages, totally unaware of the situation surrounding him.

At the time, I remember smiling in tenderness: it was so typically him!

Later on in the relationship, of course, I became
unnerved by this habit of his. Sometimes he wouldn't even
reply when I talked to him and he was reading, or he shooed
me away with the contempt reserved for a very annoying fly
that keeps buzzing around your face.

But now that he's gone my bookcases look very empty
and sad, so I went and bought myself a few books, even
though I'm often so depressed I can't even read. On the way
back I passed through Soho and caught sight of the
pornographic cinema Eugene confessed he had once gone to,
with a man and a woman from his class. He had laughed off
my anger at hearing this; he thought what he'd done was
very amusing and naughty. Nothing wrong with it!

How I hated that woman! I remember debasing myself,
asking if she had been masturbating them both while they
watched the film. He said I was the one with a filthy mind, a
real dirty person.

We had a screaming fight. One of many.

The Astral Cinema was showing a double bill of Russ
Meyer films. Just Eugene's cup of tea, with Meyer's
obsession for oversized breasts.

It reminded me of that morning when the film society at
our school showed *Faster Pussycat! Kill! Kill!* and Eugene,
who was sitting beside me, halfway through the film had this
sudden urge to get up and leave.

"I remembered there's something I need to do in the
sound department," he whispered as he brushed past my
knees.

It has just dawned on me that he might have become so
aroused by the sight of all those enormous breasts that he
just had to go to the toilets and jerk off. Yes, I think that's
what he did. Or am I the pervert for thinking it?

I can't take this anymore. I am destroying myself, going
round and round in endless circles of hate and despair,
turning memories into knives that I plunge into my flesh.

20 May

Today I took the pornographic booklet out of the
drawer where I keep it, hidden from none other than myself
under a pile of jumpers.

As I looked at those inflated appendages again and again, a strange plan started to form in my mind.

But I don't know where he is living now.

I suppose I could always ask his sister, pretend I just found something of his in my flat.

I have to talk to Maria. Would she agree? I could not pay her much. . . .

And would he take to her, a stranger? Well, she is an older woman with big breasts, his pathetic maternal stereotype. Yes, he would try with her. He'd try with anyone, just to flatter his vanity.

24 May

I have the address. His sister was glacial but obliging. Of course all his family think he's a model boy and I'm the nasty bitch who threw him out into the cold. Apparently he's living alone. Good, he will be sozzled and stoned most of the time. He never could stand loneliness, needed to have an audience all the time. He hated to be confronted with just himself.

I have spoken to Maria. Surprisingly, she agreed to do it. She said to me that she hates men. "Filthy little boys, all of them, the young and the old. What's this boyfriend of yours like, is he cute? Good, at least it won't be so disgusting. You wouldn't believe the things I have to stomach."

I guess I wouldn't. Or perhaps I would.

"Only a little squeeze, eh, Maria, just so that he'll go out of breath a bit, feel dizzy and get scared, maybe faint. And then you leave. He'll never find you. It's miles away from your patch."

"Of course, love, of course."

She is almost maternal to me, now.

1 June

I bought clothes for Maria, revealing but not too scant. Eugene would not like her if he suspected she was a prostitute. He only likes them in magazines. And I directed her to do a much lighter make-up job.

She looked good, fresh, younger.

I gave her the Shakespeare book Eugene left behind, not sure if he had intended to give it to me or not. As they do in the movies, I wiped it very carefully of my fingerprints. It is fitting that it should be this book again...Hamlet the avenger! This time it's Ophelia's revenge instead, for the madness you poisoned her sleepless nights with!

Maria has gone to deliver my rage, and I am waiting by the phone, a head full of fantasies.

What will he say when he sees her, sees her breasts?

♦

At midnight the phone finally rings, after hours of agonizing waiting.

Maria's voice is chillier than I ever heard it before.

"I'm afraid there was a little bit of trouble, love. I overdid it a bit. It didn't seem he was really breathing when I left. I hope you're not too upset if he's . . . well, he was a bastard, wasn't he? Anyway, I was careful not too touch anything. I never took my gloves off even when I got his dick out; I think he liked that. He went for my tits like a hungry baby and started sucking. Of course he was totally drunk even before I rang the bell. You should have seen the place. What a filthy mess! And this guy was from a good, rich family, huh? Jesus, they are all the same shit. Anyway, love, gotta go. I'll be lying low for a little while, just in case. Guess you'll see it in the paper if . . ."

She hangs up. She has been talking so fast, I have not been able to say a word. I've just been listening with fascinated horror.

This goes beyond my wildest dreams of revenge.

Or is it what I planned all along?

3 June

It's in the paper. Only a small article in the back pages, but he made the national one, courtesy of his rich family, no doubt.

The coroner said he died from suffocation "as if his head had been squeezed between two pillows or some equally soft objects."

The police are puzzled as to a possible motive. Well, I guess they would be.

They haven't ruled out some sort of "autoerotic asphyxiation." And why not? It is, after all, a common pastime of the English upper classes, isn't it? It fits in with his bookish culture, his arrogance.

Soon they will come to talk to me, his ex-girlfriend. But how can they trace my steps to Maria? She won't talk, and nobody else knows.

And I will be inconsolable when they come to tell me. I will scream and shout. I will cry and sob and despair. And some of it will be from the heart, that place right between my breasts.

ACCESS DENIED

Diane DeKelb-Rittenhouse

Load. Aim. Squeeze. *Bang.* "Access denied," she said
softly.

Load. Aim. Squeeze. *Bang.* "Access denied."

Marlene found the repetitive tasks and the chanted
mantra soothing. She could understand NRA supporters,
now, could count herself among them. As she focused on the
stationary target and prepared to squeeze the trigger one
more time, she decided she would have to spend her last
paycheck on a hefty donation. After all, she was no longer
responsible for the kids, and rent was no problem, either.
There simply wasn't anything better to spend her money on.

Load. Aim. Squeeze. *Bang.* "Access denied."

Marlene sighed as the bullet went wide and hit the wall
behind the target. She was missing more times than she was
hitting, but this was the first time she had used the gun,
which had only been in her possession for a little more than
a day. All in all, she wasn't doing too badly; her first shot,
dead on target, had been wildly lucky. She couldn't
complain. For the first time in a long time, Marlene Johnston
really could not complain.

Matters had not been so simple in years. Not since her
father had died, and her mother had begun dying, when
Marlene was sixteen. Certainly not the next year when she

had dropped out of high school to take work in a factory when her mother, debilitated by cancer, had been forced to leave her own job. Nor had the succeeding years been any simpler, as Marlene gradually assumed more of the responsibility for parenting her younger twin siblings, Jesse and Amy. When, at twenty-one, she had buried her mother and moved her small family from their rural home town to the city of Centreville, matters had become as far from simple as they could get. Marlene had juggled her night-shift job waitressing at a diner with parenting Jesse and Amy while first getting her high-school equivalency diploma and then taking classes at the community college. Determined to transfer to Centreville University where courses in computer studies could virtually guarantee well-paid employment for the rest of her life, Marlene had found little time for a social life—and little money to pursue one. She had dated only two men and one woman in the four years since she had arrived in Centreville, all of them people she had met at the diner. She hadn't found true love, and she hadn't found security—though, until a few days ago, she had been working toward both. Instead, what she had found were complications.

Load. Aim. Squeeze. *Bang.* "Access denied."

Losing her job waitressing at the Centreville Diner six months ago had been the lowest point in her life. It had been a pivotal event, her start along a road leading to this precise, serene, and tranquil moment of respite.

Load. Aim. Squeeze. *Bang.*

♦

There had been just enough time before her appointment for a stop at the restroom to wash hands, brush hair, and straighten clothes. Marlene had dressed her brother and sister in what their mother would have called their "Sunday best." Jesse uncomfortable but strikingly handsome in a charcoal-gray suit that made his black hair and dark eyes look even darker, Amy in a buttercup-yellow dress that warmed the deep olive tone of her skin even as its princess lines flattered her developing fifteen-year-old body without making her look like a teenaged tart. Marlene's own dress, a soft ivory sheath with a knee-length hem and boat-neck collar was just as flattering and just as modest. Marlene hated having to ask anyone for help, let alone having to apply to the Department of Public Assistance, but the twins' welfare came before her own pride. Still, she wanted to impress upon the caseworker that they weren't deadbeats looking for a free ride, but hardworking, decent people trying to get past a rough spot.

It was, as it happened, exactly the wrong thing to do.

Mr. Simmonds, the caseworker—a middle aged man with thinning ginger hair, a receding chin, and an expanding waist line—had taken one look at them and decided that they didn't qualify for benefits. Marlene could read it in his face, in the narrowing of his watery blue eyes and the tightening of his already thin lips. His glance—not completely impersonal but holding some indefinable unpleasantness that made her tug self-consciously at her hem—had slid over her appraisingly. She knew that he saw not hardworking and proud, but well-enough off and lazy. Even his perusal of her file was no more than perfunctory, his gaze flicking over the exhaustively detailed forms just long enough to register that the younger Johnston children had a Social Security stipend from both deceased parents and that Marlene had earned decent money during the prior year.

He disposed of her hopes in few short sentences. "I'm sorry, Ms. Johnston, but I can't see anything here that justifies giving you access to benefits. Your salary from last year alone puts you over the limit."

"But that money is gone!" Marlene explained, trying to keep the panic from her voice. She leaned a little forward in the cracked vinyl seat that graced the small, hot office where this harried and judgmental man was casually dismissing her last hope of help. "Tuition, rent, books, food—there's nothing left!"

"You should have put aside some savings," Mr. Simmonds said primly, now almost glaring at her—her youth and attractiveness solid marks against her.

"The savings I put aside," Marlene said with a calmness she did not feel, "have been supporting us since I lost my job."

The job in question would still have been hers had not her former boss retired and the new one possessed some twisted ideas about what "service" meant. In particular, the new manager objected to Marlene's girlfriend, Cynthia. He did not like women who swung both ways unless they swung in his direction as well. Marlene refused. He fired her and then lied to the Unemployment Board about his reasons when they investigated her claim for unemployment benefits. Without a witness to his advances, Marlene's appeals had been denied. She doubted any of this would matter to Mr. Simmonds. Riffling through the paperwork once more—for effect only, not for information, she was sure—he said, "Funds are tight. We have to reserve them for those who are *truly* in need. Your request for access to benefits is therefore denied. I'm sorry. You'll just have to try a little harder."

Marlene thought of the long, hot walk from their apartment to the DPA office, a walk taken because she didn't have money for the bus; of skipping her own breakfasts to make sure there was enough for the kids. Just what did this Mr. Simmonds, with his comfortable middle-aged paunch and his secure government job, know about being *truly* in need? She left the office before the desire to shove his paperwork down his throat could swamp her instincts for self-preservation. She paid little heed to his final words about her right to appeal. From her unemployment case, Marlene knew they'd starve to death long before a hearing date was set.

A stop at a nearby ATM to tap the one, rarely used, credit card she owned proved fruitless. Her last emergency, Jesse's broken wrist, had put her over the card's meager limit. As she watched the glowing green letters flash across the black screen, she decided that their "Access Denied" message pretty much summed up her life.

It was a long, hot walk home.

♦

If anything, matters were worse the next day. She had walked to the community college to sell her old texts at the bookstore and had gotten less for them than they were worth. At least it gave her money for a few weeks of groceries and carfare to get to the job interviews she had set up from the weekend want-ads. But none of the interviews had panned out, and her carefully planned food budget was being done in by frost on the east coast and insect predation on the west. She was tired and discouraged, and her arms hurt from carrying heavy grocery bags up three flights of stairs. She dropped the bags on the landing and sat beside them to take a breather. The twins weren't due home from school for hours. She had time to put away the groceries, start dinner, and comb the day's paper for any new listings that looked promising. Absorbed in her thoughts, she paid no attention to the sound of descending footsteps until a familiar voice said, "You haven't called."

Fabric rustled as the speaker knelt behind Marlene. The touch on her shoulder was gentle as a slim, pale hand stroked back a lock of Marlene's night-black hair. A second hand joined the first and both began to knead the tension out of Marlene's shoulders. She closed her eyes and leaned into that touch.

"I was too depressed. I didn't want to depress you, too," she admitted.

"Listen, Iron Maiden, sharing problems is supposed to *lighten* the load," Cynthia scolded her. "If you can't dump on your friends, who *can* you dump on?"

Marlene laughed ruefully and accepted Cynthia's help with the bags. Cynthia was a willowy blonde who had swept into the diner one night and into Marlene's life. A fashion and merchandising major at Centreville University, she was putting herself through college as a stripper at Dreamtime, a local club. Marlene had never understood how Cynthia could stand taking her clothes off in front of a room full of drooling men. But nothing seemed to daunt Cynthia Driscoll—not working late hours in a dangerous part of town, not coming out to her family and being cut loose, not even stripping her way through college.

As they put away groceries in the kitchenette, Marlene told her lover about the job hunt, the bookstore, and the fiasco at the DPA.

"I have enough cash for food for three or four weeks. I don't know where next month's rent will come from, and

God help me if another emergency comes up. I am as desperate as I have ever been in my life."

"What about the stipend?"

"It's barely enough to cover utilities and maybe half the rent."

"So, skip the utilities, pay the rent."

"And starve," Marlene said bitterly. Cynthia came over and slipped her arms around Marlene's shoulders.

"Not if I can help it," Cynthia said softly. They stood that way for a few moments, Marlene drawing strength from Cynthia's closeness, neither of them speaking. Cynthia kissed her, gently at first, but Marlene needed the comfort of passion and let the kiss intensify. They made their way to the bedroom Marlene shared with Amy and settled onto Marlene's narrow twin bed. Their lovemaking was sweet and slow, and tender, allowing Marlene to forget every other aspect of her life save that moment. But when she surfaced from the brief slumber of satiation, she confronted all the old problems once more.

Cynthia read her mood instantly. She leaned up, resting her head on one hand, and stroked Marlene's hair back from her temple with the other. "I know you aren't going to want to hear this, but—"

"I am *not* going to strip at Dreamtime," Marlene said abruptly, knowing where the conversation was going.

"Damn it, will you just listen?" Cynthia's own temper had sparked.

"We've been *through* this!" Marlene pulled away, got out of the bed, and began to pull on her clothes. "The kids will be home in another hour. Let's clean up," she said brusquely.

"We've *never* been 'through this' because you never want to hear what I have to say!" Cynthia was not about to be sidetracked, even as she moved to dress and help make up the bed. "I know you don't like what I do, but you really have to get over it. It simply is nothing like you think."

"Okay," Marlene shot back, "how isn't it like I think? Tell me that when you get up on that stage all the men in the audience aren't imagining that they are fucking you and that you can't see it in their eyes.".

"All the men in the audience *are* imagining that they are fucking me and I *can* see it in their eyes, and it will always and only ever be in their dreams until and unless *I* decide I want to fuck *them*." She pounded a dilapidated feather pillow into shape and threw it on the bed.

"That's supposed to make me feel better about what you do and about what you want *me* to do?" Marlene treated the pillow's mate similarly, turned on her heel, and left the room.

"It's supposed to make you think about your options!" Cynthia followed her lover into the living room. "Marlene, what happens at the club is no different than what happens when I go to the beach. I wear something skimpy, men come on to me, and I ignore them. Hell, sometimes I end up wearing *more* in the club than I do in the water! The big difference is that I don't pull down four hundred a night at the beach."

That stopped Marlene. It had to. She had been lucky to bring that much home in a week of twelve-hour shifts. She slumped down onto the sofa. "That has got to be an exaggeration," she said. Cynthia sat next to her.

"Four. Hundred. A. Night."

"Every night?"

"No. Mainly Friday and Saturday. On a slow night like Monday I usually get between two and two-fifty, but it's more than enough for my apartment, tuition, the whole nine yards."

Marlene sighed and put her head in her hands.

"I just don't know if I can do it."

"Look, you are making way too big a deal about this." Cynthia slid nearer on the couch and began to rub Marlene's back soothingly. "It's not all that different from what you go through every day of your life. You know what I mean! The guys who honk their horns at you and swerve near the sidewalk when you walk down the street. The idiots who pinch your butt on the subway just as you're walking out the door and can't stop them. Let's not even talk about the creeps who try to follow you home. When I used to come around to the diner, how many times did we have to talk some fool out of coming on to us? Every night?"

"That was different."

"If you mean you weren't getting paid to deal with the come-ons, damn straight it was different! But the fact is that you are young and pretty. Men are going to fantasize about you, if you do nothing more than walk out your front door. You might as well make them pay for it."

Another time, Marlene might have argued, might have said she didn't need to legitimize the fantasies by catering to them, but she was too tired and too discouraged. Cynthia's words seemed like basic common sense.

"Okay, say I decide to give it a shot. What makes you think they'll hire me?"

"Darlin' have you looked in a mirror lately? Seriously! The club is always looking for new talent. You're bright, articulate, and lovely. And with your coloring, you're an exotic, not easy to type. Dreamtime is all about fantasies, and you could make just about any fantasy work. Arabic harem girl, English aristocrat, Indian princess—you could be any or all of them."

Marlene flushed at the term *exotic* but wondered if it wasn't time to make racism work *for* her for once.

It took a while, but Cynthia talked her around. She set up an interview for the next day, and it went well. Marlene was hired to begin work the following week. She made arrangements with one of her neighbors to look out for the kids on the nights she would be working, and Cynthia loaned her the money to have a few costumes made by a seamstress who did work for the other dancers at the club. Cynthia also helped Marlene pick out music and develop routines.

"No, no, no, you're too stiff. These guys want to be teased and coaxed. Play to them."

"I don't know. . . . I don't *like* this," Marlene complained.

"Pretend you're stripping for me."

Marlene cringed, but Cynthia drove her relentlessly. By the time Marlene's first work night came around, Cynthia was confident that her protégé would do her credit. "You look delicious. Didn't I tell you that white lace was just the thing? Against your skin it looks like whipped cream on café latte—good enough to eat."

"Cynthia!"

"Well, maybe later," she grinned. Marlene shook her head. Cynthia was teasing her to distract her from the nervousness and rising nausea as the time for her first performance approached. Marlene's throat was dry and her stomach was rolling. Her act was up next and she frankly dreaded it. It was a Friday, one of the club's busiest nights; all the tables were taken and men stood three-deep at the bar. Every man out there watched with greedy eyes as the girls performed, wanting a beautiful woman to make hot, adoring, exclusive love to him. Marlene had to slither out on that stage and convince each one of them that, with her dancing, she was doing just that. She wasn't sure she could pull it off. Cynthia, however, had no doubts at all.

"Just think of the money and keep pretending you're dancing for me."

If Marlene couldn't quite pretend that her audience was Cynthia alone, the customers at Dreamtime didn't notice any problem. As she stepped onto the back bar of the catwalk, a growl of masculine approval came up over the stage like a wave at high tide. The lights were dim and the atmosphere murky with cigarette smoke. She could barely see a yard past the foot lights, and that helped. The men she could see watched her with avid, greedy eyes. She met their glances and told herself that it was okay, that they could look all they wanted and never touch. And why shouldn't they pay for the privilege of looking? She smiled at those whose glances she caught and let her own eyes promise wonders she would never be required to perform. The audience responded; more approving catcalls roared from the bar and tables. Marlene's frozen smile relaxed a little. She could do this, she realized. Even hating it, she was a success.

Cynthia was waiting back stage when she finished, and hugged her enthusiastically. The manager was also there and gave her a thumb's-up sign.

"Very nice," he said. "Cynthia told me you were special. I'm glad I listened to her."

The rest of the night passed quickly. Marlene received invitations to have drinks from nearly every table. Cynthia helped her choose which tables to visit, joining her at the first one. By the time they split up to work different ends of the room, Marlene was more comfortable. It really wasn't

terribly different from a night at the diner; she made polite
small-talk, was gracious where she could be and flattering
when it seemed necessary. She made it seem, when she
turned down the offers for "dates," that she did so with real
regret. The trick was to remain unattainable while seeming
available. It was a fine line, but she knew she could walk it.

She had to.

Cynthia declared the first night a real success. Counting
her cut from the evening, Marlene was forced to agree;
Cynthia hadn't lied about how much she made on a good
night.

Marlene enjoyed a number of good nights after that. The
new girl, she seemed to have caught on at the club. But
although the money was good, her expenses managed to
keep pace. Some of her salary had to be reinvested in
costumes and music, and taking cabs home on the nights
Cynthia couldn't give her a lift wasn't cheap. Marlene
decided to put some of the money away for a used car, but
that would cost a few thousand. And there were the usual
emergencies—the twins kept growing and needing new
clothes, and her landlord upped the rent when the lease
expired.

Still, with her new "salary," by the time the school year
was out, she had put away enough money to enroll Amy and
Jesse in a summer enrichment program for gifted students.
Her fall semester tuition at Centreville University wasn't due
until August, and she was making enough to save up for
that, get herself the car, and begin to put aside an emergency
fund.

Centreville University did give her a few bad moments
when she went to register for classes. She discovered that the
school had joined the growing number of institutions
requiring all students to have their own computers as a
condition of admission. Systems had to be compatible with
those in use at the university, and the cost of such systems
could be considerable.

"I don't have that kind of money," she told the
admissions counselor anxiously. "My parents are dead, and I
support my sister and brother." The counselor gave her a
fatherly smile and some reassuring information. Centreville
U had a computer lab for working parents which Marlene

might be eligible to use. Another office and three forms later, she got the welcome news that she did qualify for lab access. During the first week of classes, she was to report to the lab and set up a schedule.

With her acceptance to the lab program established, Marlene calculated that if she kept working at Dreamtime, by the time she graduated she would have enough of a nest egg to start the twins at the community college. It would be tough, but that was nothing new. She could manage the finances—if she could stick it out at Dreamtime.

For all the monetary security her job brought her, there were times when she wondered if she really could handle two years in the place. The longer she worked there, the more she became aware of the club's seamier side. Despite management's official position on prostitution, Marlene constantly overheard coy conversations between the dancers and the customers as they arranged "dates." She also noticed coke residue from time to time on some of the small hand-held makeup mirrors, and at least one of the girls used heavy body makeup to camouflage needle tracks.

Cynthia seemed oblivious to the tawdrier aspects of the job, just as she was oblivious to the moves some of the more determined customers tried to put on Marlene. So far, Marlene had managed to extricate herself from the situation each time a would-be Romeo seemed about to cross the line, but it was increasingly hard to smile and be charming when she wanted to slap their faces and tell them off.

◆

Matters didn't get easier when she started classes in September. Marlene arranged as many of her courses for afternoons as she could, but one of her required classes was only available in the morning. She tried to arrange her work schedule so that she wouldn't be on the nights before classes met, but it wasn't always possible. By October she was exhausted more often than not, and, to make matters worse, Mr. Simmonds had turned up at the club.

Marlene had been asked to join a table where a fairly rowdy bachelor party was in progress. Simmonds was one of the group. His gaze was more openly lascivious this time.

"Well, Ms. Johnston, I see you found work when you had to."

Marlene curled her hands into fists to keep herself from slapping the leer off his face.

"I do what I have to," she returned coolly.

"I'll just bet you do," he laughed unpleasantly. Marlene excused herself and mingled with the other members of the party, but Simmonds turned up again the next night she performed, and again a few nights later. Invariably, he would ask her to join him; invariably, she would either decline, or spend no more than a few brief moments.

"He makes me so damned uncomfortable," she complained to Cynthia as they sat at one of the long backstage mirrors putting on makeup.

"Don't sweat it. He's probably harmless," Cynthia told her.

Some of the other customers weren't. A dancer complained she had been followed out to the parking lot. A few nights later another woman's purse was snatched. They complained to management and an additional bouncer was hired to keep an eye on things, but the situation was uncomfortable. One night Cynthia showed up with a book and tossed it onto the dressing room table in front of Marlene.

"Honey, it is time you got religion," she said with a grin.

Frowning, Marlene opened the Bible. She found the book had been hollowed out to form the perfect hiding place for a small handgun. Extra cartridges of ammunition fit neatly beneath. Marlene slammed the cover shut.

"This has got to be the stupidest stunt you have ever pulled!"

"Calm down. You're always complaining about how late we work and how vulnerable you feel. Well, here's an equalizer."

They had their biggest argument since Cynthia had gotten her to take the job. Cynthia refused to take the gun back, assuring Marlene that if she would just keep it for a week, to get used to it, she would see the value in having some protection. Marlene swore and dumped the mutilated book and its contents into the overnight bag with her makeup and costume accessories. A handgun wasn't exactly the kind of item she wanted to leave lying around the club, or any place else for that matter. It did not make her feel any safer, and she was not remotely tempted to use it, although Mr. Simmonds's continued pursuit of her did begin to push her limits.

One night, she found him waiting by her car when she left for the evening. Cynthia had one more set to go, and they had just kissed goodnight at the door leading from the backstage area to the lot.

"Well, that explains why you're the only whore in that cathouse who doesn't screw around." The words were vicious, and they stopped Marlene cold.

"What the hell are you doing lurking around out here?" she demanded.

"Thought you might be a bit friendlier away from that place. And you are, at least with your girlfriend." He smiled, and Marlene repressed a shudder. "Didn't figure you for that kind, but you never know about people. Not that I mind. Opens up all sorts of interesting possibilities."

Marlene glared at him in disgust and yanked open her car door, throwing her bag onto the seat.

"There are no possibilities, Mr. Simmonds. You denied me benefits when I needed help and told me to get a job. Fine. I did just that." She slid behind the wheel of her car, slammed the door shut, and rolled down the window for a parting shot. "Whatever else I do or do not do is none of your concern." She burned rubber out of the lot.

"Isn't it though?" Mr. Simmonds whispered venomously.

A few days later a social worker showed up at Marlene's apartment, along with two police officers with court papers remanding Jesse and Amy Johnston to the custody of the Child Services Bureau. Centreville had suddenly developed serious doubts about her parenting abilities. Marlene was shaking with rage as she read the documents. She wanted to fling them in the social worker's face, slam the door on the cops, and drag Jesse and Amy onto the first bus back to their home town. She had no such options. Amy and Jesse were upset, and she had to be strong for them. She had to remain a good parent.

"It's okay," Marlene said as she helped them pack their suitcases. "I can afford a lawyer. We'll get this mess straightened out. I swear, I will do what it takes to get you back as quickly as possible." Tears filled her eyes as they were led away—Jess sullen, Amy obviously terrified.

As soon as the door closed, Marlene was on the phone to Cynthia, and then to a women's rights group. She was referred to a lawyer specializing in child custody cases. Cynthia drove over immediately and went with her to see the attorney.

Elizabeth Blair frowned as she reviewed the court papers. A trim brunette in her thirties, she wore a red wool suit and very little makeup. Her office was small but well organized—no files spilling over her desk and no coffee rings on her blotter. She gave the impression of crisp efficiency, and Marlene felt confident the attorney would help her.

Ms. Blair's first words, however, were not reassuring.

"I have to say that the fact that you are a sibling and not a parent is one strike against you. You might be considered too young to deal with the responsibility of raising teenagers. Your job is obviously another, and the biggest strike against you is the accusation of lewd behavior."

"Stripping?"

"Lesbianism."

"This is nuts," Cynthia said, half out of her seat. "Marlene has done a great job with Amy and Jesse. She's been raising them since they were eight years old, by herself since they were twelve. She's kept them clothed, housed, fed, and out of trouble. They're both honor students, for God's sake! What more proof does the city need that she's a fit parent?"

"Look, Ms. Driscoll, I understand your viewpoint," the attorney responded, "I don't disagree. But the fact is that we are dealing with law here, not opinions, not rationality. Under Centreville's existing city statutes, lesbian relationships are illegal, and defined as immoral."

"So I have to stop seeing Cynthia if I want my brother and sister to come home?" Marlene asked.

"It will give us a better shot at *getting* them home," Blair cautioned. "It's no guarantee."

"What *would* guarantee getting them home?" she demanded.

"Ms. Johnston, I understand your anger and your frustration, but if you want to pursue this case, you must understand, there are no guarantees." Blair went on to outline the steps Marlene would need to take: quitting the job at Dreamtime, getting more conventional employment, and ending her relationship with Cynthia, at least for the time being. "The fact that you're a college student is a plus. It shows that you're trying to improve yourself."

"Ms. Blair, if I give up my job at Dreamtime, I won't be able to remain a college student. For that matter, I won't be able to support Jesse and Amy, so there will be no point in winning back custody."

The lawyer spread her hands expressively. "I'm sorry Ms. Johnston. You've paid me to advise you, and this is the best advice I've got. If you want your sister and brother back, you'll follow it."

Marlene agreed to try, and left with Cynthia. She cried all the way home. Cynthia put on a pot of tea and tried to reassure her. "You have tuition for next term? Good, enroll. It will help your case. I'll take the term off and give you my tuition. That should be enough to keep you going for a while."

"Even if we're not seeing each other?"

Cynthia smiled ruefully, reached out a hand and stroked Marlene's hair. "Look, they'll be eighteen in two years, right? We'll manage."

Marlene couldn't see how, but she hadn't the heart to argue. She put her own hand over Cynthia's. "I want you to know something. For the past ten years, my life has been about taking care of my family, about being strong, about succeeding. You have been the one thing I have had for myself—water in the desert and shelter from the storm. I love you. It's not something I say easily or lightly, but, God, Cynthia, I do love you. Losing you will be like losing a part of myself."

They kissed and made wild, bittersweet love. When Cynthia left an hour later, Marlene did not know when or if she would see her again. She couldn't bear to go to her classes that afternoon, and there was no question of her working that night. Determined to follow Elizabeth Blair's advice, she dragged herself to the university the next morning, hoping to work on a term paper.

Settling behind one of the terminals, she punched in her code and frowned as the "Access Denied" message came up. She shrugged and reentered the information. When it came up again, she tried another terminal, with no better result. She sought help from one of the lab aides, who checked her student ID against his clipboard and told her that the program director had left word to send her to his office.

Marlene knew it would not be good news, and she was right.

The thin, elderly man looked distinctly uncomfortable as he waved her into a computer chair in front of his desk.

"Ms. Johnston, the child welfare people have alerted us to the fact that they've removed your siblings from your care. Because of the nature of our grant funding, we have to terminate your access to the program."

"In the middle of the semester?" she cried in dismay.

"I'm afraid so."

"How am I supposed to finish the term?"

"Perhaps one of your classmates can let you share their hardware. Some of the student bulletin boards may help." The director was clearly distressed by the situation, but he claimed the program funding could be jeopardized by allowing Marlene to continue. Marlene left his office and phoned Elizabeth Blair, leaving a message with her paralegal to have the lawyer contact her as soon as she returned from court.

With no other options, Marlene checked the bulletin boards for shared access. There were a few notices, all of them charging hefty hourly fees. At this rate, she'd run through her savings long before her custody case was ever heard. In disgust, Marlene left the university and went back to her apartment.

The loneliness hurt. It wasn't like the times when the twins were in school. The rooms seemed sentient, aware that Amy and Jesse would be gone for more than just a few hours. There was an echoing emptiness to each step Marlene

took, and the rooms seemed a few degrees cooler than usual.
Marlene decided that if her custody battle was going to go
on for any length of time, she would have to find another
place to live.

She was searching for the Sunday paper to go over the
job and apartment listings when the phone rang. Elizabeth
Blair suggested they meet in her office at 5:30.

The news wasn't good.

"I think you might want to reconsider this fight."

"My brother and sister are all the family I have. Why the
hell wouldn't I fight for them?"

"Because the city is putting on the pressure. Children's
Services has filed papers to permanently terminate your
guardianship and deny you visitation rights."

Astonished, Marlene could only stare at her.

"Why?" she finally asked.

The attorney shook her head. "I don't know. Maybe
because it's an election year, and we have some 'family
values' politicians who see this as a chance to score points
with the electorate. There are a lot of people in Centreville
who consider clubs like Dreamtime to be a blot on the
community, people who think that a stripper has no business
raising children and that a lesbian is an affront to God. We
can fight for custody, but it could take years. Jesse and Amy
might be old enough to live on their own by the time we get
a decision. Right now, I think you should consider putting
your efforts into trying to maintain contact and preserving
visitation rights."

"'Maintain contact.' 'Visitation rights.' Ms. Blair, do you
understand that my whole life has been about caring for my
brother and sister? Do you have a clue what it is like to be
told that you should give up hoping to be reunited with your
family and that you should settle for trying to 'maintain
contact'?"

"I'm so very sorry," the lawyer said softly.

That night Marlene went to Dreamtime to hand in her
notice and collect a few personal items. She left her costumes
in the dressing room; they were the last thing she needed to
see. Cynthia was not working that night, which made it a
little easier, but not much. The manager told her he was
sorry about how things had gone and assured her that she

was welcome to return if her situation changed. Marlene thanked him and left.

Finding Mr. Simmonds in the parking lot seemed almost anticlimactic. The host of evils swarming about her rendered his presence almost benign.

"Sorry about the kids," he said with patent insincerity.

Marlene frowned. "How the hell did you know about that?"

Simmonds laughed. "Boy, you are one dumb cunt."

At that precise moment Marlene remembered Cynthia's exhortation to get religion.

Load. Aim. Squeeze. *Bang.* "Access denied."

It was near dawn when one of the neighbors, awakened by the constant repetition of gunfire, finally contacted police. By the time an officer gently removed the gun from her grasp, she was nearly out of bullets. One hundred and thirty-eight slugs were eventually recovered from the pieces of Simmonds's body she hadn't blown away outright. She was vaguely sorry to lose the gun and the solace of her repeated target practice, but she supposed that was all for the best. Other routines would rule her life now. She understood that. But she would take comfort in the sameness of her days and her surroundings, and forgetfulness in surrendering herself to the endlessly repeated patterns. There was nothing left to struggle for, nothing left to win.

Access, irrevocably, denied.

THE DEATH OF
THE SUBJECT

Ruthann Robson

"not only is the bourgeois individual subject a thing of the past, it is also a myth; it never really existed. . . ." —Fredric Jameson, in *Postmodernism and Its Discontents*

"Useless; there is no god of healing in this story." —Cassandra, in *Oresteia* by Aeschylus

The smell and sound of the sea. The taste of salt. The feel of my skin stiffening from too much sun.

I crave sensations that are not anchored by the albatross of the visual.

Certainly I am grateful for my sense of sight. That's how I earn my living and it is a comfortable one in the scheme of things. But like all work, mine has its own peculiar curse. Relentlessness. I never have a day off, never a night of relaxation. Not just because my girlfriend, Agnes, is a detective with the police department and is always cajoling me for clues. The curse of her own work, I suppose. But even curled next to Agnes after some sweaty sex, listening to her breathy contentment, I am on duty. I can close my eyes, but I cannot escape.

I'm a seer. A see-er. They call me the fortune-teller of
Surf Palace. My rates are considered reasonable. My
predictions are considered accurate.

You can believe whatever you desire; people always do.

Another sort of curse, I suppose.

Their curse, not mine.

I do not believe in belief.

Desire, of course, is another story. Everyone's story. Even
if I did not have my visions to assist me, I could work the
tourist trade at Surf Palace. All people expect is a hand
sparkling with a few silver rings and some sympathy toward
their thwarted desires. A little hope is a bonus.

I take her fingers in mine. I point to the array of tarot
decks and instruct her to select one. The round women's
cards. The Knight-Rider deck. The Native American
medicine cards. The PoMo Tarot. She never picks PoMo—
the Post-Modern deck alienates her with its images of
televisions and Elvis Presleys—although it is my favorite. She
finds it too familiar, too mundane. She doesn't realize that it
doesn't matter. The cards are a ruse. I watch her as she
shuffles the cards, but what I see is a technicolor pastiche.

My struggle is articulation—the translation of pictures
into language. It is as if I am a foreigner who understands
what is being said but cannot make herself heard. It makes
me envy the psychics who hear voices and need only repeat
the words with cautious and important tones. I can only
hope for a word or two to appear among the shifting shapes,
a piece of text pasted on the messy collage that zips through
my mind.

My struggle is isolation—the segregation of information.
My perception is a conglomeration, a chorus of pop-art
derived from a million sources. Which fragment from this
animated junkyard will touch her heart? As if there is only a
single segment, as if she is not as assorted as my
kaleidoscope. Like everyone else, she thinks she is so special,
so unique, such an individual.

I will tell her she is so different, so wonderful, such a
good lover—if I decide to touch more than her fingers. If I
kiss her. If I lick her breast, lightly with a flicker before
becoming more serious.

I will not tell her what happens. How the images become almost unbearably intense. How the video brightens and sharpens and achieves a speed faster than comprehension. How her life passes behind my eyes as if she is falling from Thrasher's French Fries, the highest building on Surf Avenue, atop which the time and temperature pulsate in blood-colored digits. I will not tell her this: at the moment of her orgasm I see her last moment. She is old or she is not; she is in a car crash or in a hospital bed; she is sliding into the darkness or she is fighting. She is, but she will not always be.

I will not tell Agnes about her, *any* her. My girlfriend, the detective, is the jealous sort. Possessive. "Love is singular," she says. She acts like a charter member of the monogamy society. Except when it comes to her former lovers, especially Clementine, who seems more "lover" than "former" most of the time. It's a false intimacy, certainly, or so I tell Agnes who does not believe me. Agnes tells me I am "jealous."

But jealousy cannot account for my visions. No translation, no isolation, is necessary: they fuck in my head whenever Agnes is late for a date with me. Clementine is always on top and quite passionate in a vicious sort of way. What I cannot see is whether this is reality or simply Clementine's projections.

My clients are my retribution for Clementine. Or perhaps being physical with some of my women clients is simply another aspect of my occupation. The boundaries between mind and body are obsolete, aren't they?

Once in a while, I meet a woman who actually does seem different, a bit wonderful, and not half-bad as a lover. What sets her apart from the others is that she is not entirely self-absorbed; that she is not always looking at me to figure out what I see about her and her meager little life. Though too often even a woman who does not seem self-centered starts asking me questions as if she is interviewing me for a role in the movie she mistakes for her life. "Have you lived in this resort a long time?" "And when did you become a—ah, um, oh—a fortune teller?" "Is your name really Cassandra?"

I parcel out fragments from my autobiography. Possessing a name such as Cassandra, I explain, tends to limit one's occupational opportunities. Excluding dentistry, for example. She always laughs at this and usually licks her teeth. Also excluding architecture and social work. Hotel/motel management, hair styling, and waitressing are more plausible, but ultimately unsatisfactory. The only truly suitable occupations for someone named Cassandra, I tell her as she nods her head, are exotic dancing and fortune telling. There are certainly similarities between the professions, but in the contest between being called a stripper or an oracle, I had no choice but to choose oracle. I have lopsided hips; a congenital condition which prompted several childhood operations, all of them painfully unsuccessful.

I weave my strands into a falsely coherent narrative. I tell her that it was during one of my long recoveries that I started having visions. I thought they were dreams at first, although they did not feel like I was dreaming them. Rather, they felt as if I was participating in someone else's dreams. I knew what my mother had dreamed about me, and not knowing that I shouldn't know something like that, I would talk to her sometimes about the dreams, recalling them as if they were not her dreams at all, but something we had experienced. She was obviously a little confused at first, I suppose she thought that perhaps her own dreams were not dreams after all. And her dreams about me were of the most obvious sort. I was her child, after all, and I was suffering through surgeries because of my misshapen pelvis. She was contorted with guilt. For there had to be some explanation and she was the most likely suspect. That glass of gin? Those cigarettes? Or most probably, some over-athletic sexual position.

My client-lover will then steal a glance at my crotch, which she had thought was perfectly normal, and perhaps even normally perfect. Now—coincidentally enough—it does look as if it tilts to the left. Or the right.

When she leaves, she thinks she knows me. I become a story she will tell to her future lovers, always carefully considering whether or not to include the portion about the asymmetrical pelvis. And once in a while, when she has had some wine, she'll embellish it for a few of her friends. Perhaps she will even guess at some of the details I omit.

That the images crowding my head made me crazy throughout my adolescence, until MTV went on the air and I understood my visions as music videos without the music. That I'm terrified of doing drugs and will not even swallow a white dot of ibuprofen. That I majored in Classics in college and even went to graduate school and started a thesis on Post-Modern Parodies of Greek Tragedies. That my mother and I no longer speak, although I know she is now a feminist therapist practicing in Aspen. Or maybe she does not guess at such details; maybe she is not even interested in them.

Even Agnes does not guess, is not interested.

Agnes is only interested in solving her crimes. This newest one is a bit of fag-bashing on Surf Avenue. Blood and a baseball bat, no stitches and no suspects. No one has been murdered, but Agnes is taking it personally, of course, and has gotten herself assigned to the case even though there is no homicide. At least not yet. Agnes is almost as serious about her lesbianism as she is about her police work.

Clementine is organizing a protest and advocating that we arm ourselves against the marauders who would destroy our queer-positive resort. Clementine prides herself on her politics as well as her aggressive sexuality. She vociferously proclaims to me that she is not sufficiently appreciated for either; "Even by Agnes," she adds for effect. This usually leads to her harangue about Agnes' job having "killed" Agnes' dyke politics. I'm more interested in the part about "aggressive sexuality," but I also hope she doesn't elaborate on that. I think I've already seen more than enough.

I am sitting in Surf Palace, shuffling the PoMo Tarot, waiting for a client on this hot and humid summer afternoon. My silver rings swell around my fingers. I turn over a card and then another, inspecting my own fortunes. The suit of guns dominates. It would be gentler in the women's deck (wands) and more medieval in the Knight-Rider deck (swords), but I suppose the message would be the same and that message is not good. But we make our own fates, don't we? I can choose from all the illustrations that crowd my consciousness; I can select the discourse which will construct my life. Representation equals reality. All prophecies are self-fulfilling.

I am surrounded by slogans: "Divers do it deeper."
"Save the Whales." "Shop Until You Drop." "Visualize
World Peace."

I am surrounded by airbrushed animals: Every breed of
dog and cat. Endangered species of the rain forest. Marine
mammals, including manatees.

I am surrounded by portraits: Trucks. Motorcycles.
Rock stars, preferably dead. "Kurt Cobain died for your
sins." The silkscreen is of the lead singer of Nirvana holding
a gun to his head.

I am in a T-shirt shop. Or if not me, at least my
perceptions.

There are at least a dozen such shops on Surf Avenue. I
never walk through their thresholds; I do not need to. Their
window displays reach out and harass me as I pass, walking
to the bank, the post office, Surf Palace, or to meet Agnes.
And now, I am surrounded in my reverie. The suit of guns is
on the table in front of me, but I am whirling through my
visions. It isn't a trance, it's just a different way of seeing.
Until I can't see at all. A sudden blackness. A blindness. This
has never happened to me before. And it keeps happening.
Every time I see all these T-shirts, my seeing soon stops.
Making me more nervous than the suit of guns.

What if I lose my second sense of sight? I could continue
my occupation, certainly; I could join the ranks of the
charlatans. Become more of a therapist, taking after my
mother. Agnes would probably leave me because I wouldn't
be able to help her solve her crimes. But I could get another
girlfriend, couldn't I? I would still be me, wouldn't I? Just a
different me, a person not cursed with the video version of
the gift of prophecy. I could close my eyes and it would be
dark; I'm sure it wouldn't be so fearful after a while. I could
kiss a woman and stay inside myself; I'm sure it would be
quite enjoyable.

It's really passé to have an identity crisis, Clementine
would say. She is flashing through my visions wearing a
T-shirt that declares "Hate Is Not A Family Value." We are
standing on Surf Avenue and the lights pierce the night,
carousing around her as if she is the most popular dyke in
this summer's trendiest club. Above her, the neon time and
temperature sign flashes, framed by the Thrasher's French

Fries logo. It is seventy-five degrees. Temperature is very important in a resort town; the vacationers dote on it. It is eleven fifty-nine. Time is illusory; we all pretend it does not matter as the season clicks toward its conclusion.

"This PoMo Tarot has got to go," I say. No one is here to hear me, but it does seem to clear the air. I breath deeply. I smell my own sweat. I should just close my curtains. Take a walk next to the ocean. Rid myself of these visions. Dive underwater and swallow some salt water.

I should not just sit here and wait for a client all afternoon. Although I'm not really waiting for a client, I'm waiting for Agnes. She was supposed to stop by and bring me some French fries. She always nags me about eating the fries; says Thrasher's are little bullets clogging each of my arteries; says Thrasher's only changes the oil on Memorial Day and Labor Day; says the cholesterol will kill me. She doesn't know that I won't be dying in any hospital bed. She doesn't know that she won't be either. "Relax and have a few French fries," I want to tell her, but I never do.

Agnes doesn't show up until late afternoon, just as my business is picking up. She is wearing white shorts and a hot pink T-shirt without any slogans or pictures on it. She wants to go boating, believe it or not. "A sunset cruise, just the two of us. I've borrowed a little sunfish."

"It does sound romantic," I concede, "but I've got to work."

She sighs. She doesn't really believe that telling fortunes at the Surf Palace is work. Unlike chasing murderers, or even fag-bashers.

"What if I told you that this would be work?"

"A workout?" I laugh, planning to act more like I visualize Clementine as being. I reach for her ass.

"No, real work. Like snagging the fag-basher."

"On a boat?"

"At the pier."

"What, we're not going to take the sunfish into the water?"

"No, we will. But we'll also be decoys."

"Decoys? For a fag-basher?"

"Don't worry. We'll have back-up." She misconstrues my concern. "Some undercovers will be positioned around the pier. We'll be perfectly safe."

"But it doesn't make sense." I wave my hands as if to explain that we are lesbians, which might not necessarily be appropriate bait.

"If you don't want to, I'll understand." Agnes looks at me and I can see the image of Clementine behind her eyes. I think that this means that she will ask Clementine to go if I decline. So I agree.

At the pier, Agnes is holding my hand and kissing me every five seconds. I think that she is happy that we are going boating, until I recall that she is trying to attract the attention of a homophobe. It makes me a little crabby.

Out on the ocean, I'm in a better mood. The dolphins are dancing to the sunset. Surf Palace, the suit of guns, and the sudden darkness all seem very far away. I'm relaxing so much that even the images whirling in my head are soothing, rocking me gently like a tide. Agnes opens a bottle of wine. I feel like a pampered mistress.

"So, can you describe the basher?" Agnes asks.

"No," I answer honestly.

"Are you losing your powers?" she teases.

"No."

"Then what's wrong? Too many pictures?"

"No."

"Too few?"

"None."

"None?"

"I can only see the victim."

"Are you sure it's him?"

"The red haired one with less freckles than I'd expect, right? The one you introduced me to?"

"That's the one. But is he alone?"

"Not exactly."

"Then?"

"I'm not sure I want to tell you. I know what you'll say."

"I won't say a thing. I promise."

"With Clementine."

Agnes smiles. "You just need to adjust the time frame, darling. Clementine was the first one on the scene. She's the

one who dialed 911. She just happened to be there. She's
friends with the shop owner and has been checking on the
place after closing because he is taking care of his sick lover."

"What a Girl Scout."

Agnes frowns at me.

"That was a lot of blood for such a small cut, don't you
think?"

"He was lucky. Clementine found him and scared off the
basher. She took him in the store and cleaned him up and
bandaged him."

I close my eyes and see Clementine and the victim. She is
pouring blood on him. He is laughing. They are kissing.
They are fucking. This time, Clementine is not on top.

"Isn't he the head of some anti-violence thing?"

"Yes, but what are you saying, Cassandra?"

"I'm saying what I'm saying."

"You've never liked Clementine."

"What's to like?"

"I can't believe you. You're letting your personal feelings
interfere with the investigation of a crime. You aren't being
objective."

"Objective? I don't really assist you by being a paragon
of rationality, now do I?" I feel snotty and want her to
know it.

"But you are implying—are you not?—that there is
something fishy about it."

"Hey, you said it, Ms. Detective."

"Let's go back," she says, sharply enough to let me know
that it is not simply a suggestion.

She navigates us back toward the pier. The shore gleams
like an ancient island, beautifully raw. It has been
almost-dark for a while; twilight lingers in summer. The sky
is seared with lavender.

I can almost see the Thrasher's French Fries building. I
can see a T-shirt shop. I can see Clementine waiting for us,
near Surf Palace. I can see the suit of guns, cards tumbling
across Ocean Avenue. I can see Agnes. She is falling. I can't
see. That darkness again, complete and so solemn.

"Let's go for a walk down Surf Avenue," Agnes is
solicitous again once we are on shore and the boat is
bedded. She takes my hand for the benefit of the basher. I

look around for someone who looks undercover, but I'm not
sure I can trust my own perceptions.

"I am going blind."

"Don't be dramatic, Cassandra." Agnes is annoyed, but
she keeps holding my hand. How did I expect her to be
sympathetic? I am a captive princess to my prophecies, a
seer, a woman with a gift of a goddess. And she is a damn
cop. I'm not sure how we ever got together.

The temperature is seventy-nine degrees.

"I'd like some French fries," I tell her.

"You should think of your arteries."

"I'm not going to die from my arteries."

"You think you know everything."

"And you aren't either," I add, just to be mean. "You
should have a few fries. They won't make a difference. Clean
arteries aren't going to prevent you from dying a violent
death. That's your fate, you know."

"Oh, the soothsayer speaketh her amazing prediction! I
mean, I am a police officer, after all, so I'd say the odds are
pretty good."

"Then why not have a few fucking French fries?"

"Because no bet is a sure bet."

"People believe what they want to believe."

"They sure do," she smiles sarcastically, "even you,
Cassandra."

Clementine is the last person I want to see, but there she
is standing outside of Sea Shore Tee Shirts. Her own shirt
reads "Hate Is Not A Family Value." I blink my eyes
against her.

I am filled with desire. For the life that is slipping from
me. I want to be back in Surf Palace, shuffling the PoMo
Tarot, or better yet, shuffling the women's deck, those round
cards shimmering like gold in my hands. I could touch the
fingers of a client. Touch her hair, which would also
shimmer like sunlight against my tan hands.

I am in a restaurant with Clementine and Agnes. Not
sure how I got here. They are eating meat. I am having
pasta. They are talking, laughing. I am silent. They are
drinking. Gin and tonics, I think. I am quiet. I am watching
the last few hours skulk by.

We are on the street again. Surf Avenue. We walk past
the bank, past the post office. We are outside of Sea Shore
Tee Shirts. Clementine is giddy, rude and loud. The street
lights flirt with her. The shops are closed. It is dark but the
Thrasher's temperature flashes its red proclamation:
seventy-five degrees. The Thrasher's time is eleven fifty-one.

Clementine opens a door with a key. "I just to have
check something," Clementine says. I can smell French fries,
the grease so seductive. I linger at the threshold, but then
follow Agnes into the shop.

I am surrounded by slogans: "Divers do it deeper."
"Save the Whales." "Shop Until You Drop." "Visualize
World Peace."

I am surrounded by airbrushed animals: Every breed of
dog and cat. Endangered species of the rain forest. Marine
mammals, including manatees.

I am surrounded by portraits: Trucks. Motorcycles.
Rock stars, preferably dead. "Kurt Cobain died for your
sins." The silkscreen is of the lead singer of Nirvana holding
a gun to his head.

I am surrounded. By Clementine. By Agnes. By that man
with the red hair and not enough freckles.

I sense the gun. Not the gun that Agnes carries strapped
uselessly to her ankle. Not the gun from the PoMo Tarot
suit. But the gun that I have seen over and over and over.
The gun that I cannot see because it is at the back of my
head. What I can see is the Thrasher's French Fries neon time
reflected through the windows. Eleven fifty-eight.

"You are such a slut," Clementine hisses at me.

"What?" I want to turn around and face her, but don't.

"You heard me, a slut. Seducing everyone with your
so-called powers. Stealing Agnes from me. As if she was
worth stealing. And then stealing all the tourists from me,
taking them to bed with you when they should be with me."

I feel a movement that is Agnes, bending toward her
ankle.

I see a glint, a shimmer. It is not silver or gold.

I am dead, I think. But it is Agnes who crumples. Blood
oozes onto the cement floor under her. It is my blood, it is
her blood. The distance between us is invisible now. The
remnants of all the stories arrange themselves into

understanding. It is a sorrow. It is treachery. It is unbelievable, acceptable only because I do not believe in belief. Clementine is a killer who fancies herself a hero. She will possess individual glory as a champion of the cause. She desires, what? Fame? Or something less complex? It will never belong to her, I curse her. And what I see—without the benefit of a curse—is that she too will be covered in an ugly spurt of red.

"Mark my words, Clementine, this will be avenged. You will die a death more brutal than you can imagine."

"You are such a fraud," she says.

"Hurry up and pull the trigger," he says.

There is no final image. Only

NEGATIVES

Nikki Baker

I

Cassandra Hope is late for her annual physical at Dr. Wilson's down on 95th. She takes the chipping concrete steps at State and Lake Street two at a time, jogging toward the rumbling she thinks is her train, and slings her briefcase over a shoulder so she can make better time. The battered leather case is a style called "Wall Street," a present to herself for finally making detective. Cassandra's come back to Town Hall Station in triumph with a $250.00 hunk of cowhide, amazing herself by signing her Field's card for three bills, handing it back across the counter to the blue-haired lady who looks over her frameless half-glasses to check the signature against the card. Cassandra believed somewhere in the back of her head that she'd amazed the stiff white lady behind the counter, which is maybe the satisfaction for which she'd bought the bag—for somebody she didn't know, the world. Six months later and the soft brown leather is a mess of water stains. Amazing how effortlessly she has grown used to nice things after all those years of her mama buying Maxwell Street underwear and hand-me-down shoes.

At the subway entrance, she turns the gold-tone button that closes her bag and tosses open the flap with one hand,

fumbling with the other for her dollar-fifty. The rumbling of
the train grows louder; Cassandra catches her reflection in
the glass of the fare booth, touches the bang of her thick,
processed hair: a small, smart black woman buttoned up in
an off-white trench coat. Her lips curse softly as Cassandra
gives the turnstile body English, briefcase catching
momentarily on the metal tines. Pushing free and running
down the last flight of stairs, she poises a hand above either
rail in case she slips, imagines herself as the woman she once
saw slip here, in a hurry one afternoon, sliding on her butt
down the slick dirty steps. An ambulance had to be called.

I'm going to make it. Cassandra rolls a shoulder under
the bag, settling it again, only trotting now through the
white tile cave of the Lake Dan Ryan train. As she turns the
corner, Cassandra nearly steps on a homeless man sacked
out on the concrete floor of the corridor. A three-day beard
grows over his chin, sparse in places like scruffy weeds in
knots on the side of the road. A headful of matted hair peaks
out the side of a bandanna dirt-dulled to the color of brick.
His hair is not deliberate enough to be dreadlocks—naps is
what Cassandra's mother called them when her brother
wouldn't comb his hair.

When the man catches an eye, he snaps to attention as if
someone pulled a string at the top of his head, jumping up
like those old-fashioned wooden dolls: two arms, two legs
strung together with twine through a painted peg body. The
nappy-haired homeless man is upright and begging, singing
out, "Yo, yo, brother, bro-THAH," at the people passing,
"spare some change so I can get me somethin' tuh eat?" He's
selling his misfortune, cocky and sure it's something you
might really want to buy. Catching Cassandra's eye, he's
asking, "Spare some change, sister?" as if the color of their
skin makes them family. Cassandra wants to push right by
this guy and get lost in a crowd, but at three o'clock in the
afternoon there is no train-hurried crush of people to propel
her through the station. The beggar grins, showing broken
teeth—he's got her, now.

"No. Now, nu-huh, pretty sister, don't be pretendin' like
you don't see me, now." Cassandra is looking to her right
and left, but there isn't any use in it. He's saying, "Yo. Yeah,
I'm talking to you, girlfriend. You know you got some

change in that nice bag for old Joe. Now give it here." Hand
out as if the money is already his. He is propped, dirty back
against the red graffiti; looking past the dirty clothes, he
looks like everyone else, almost. The slowing of her step
makes him even surer, extending his cup a little further from
the breast of a filthy sweatshirt. The sweatshirt says, "Don't
worry, be happy." His hand shakes. Cassandra's own hand is
fishing in her trenchcoat pocket, looking down at her steady
palm for what it has brought up. She counts three quarters,
two nickels, and seven, eight pennies, shrugging as she
jingles the change into his cup.

"Yes, sister. You keep on keepin' on." Cassandra stiffens
at the familiarity, reminded of Solange who insists on calling
her, only half joking, *fine sister*. Cassandra starts as the
concrete is moving suddenly under her feet, the rumbling of
the train coming from somewhere in the dark. The shaking
that had started in her shoes is moving up through her body
and Cassandra thinks the color in the begging man's face has
begun to fade, as if she is looking at him straight into a
warm summer sun that's washing out the colors, until he is
only shape, light, and shadow.

The rumbling of the approaching train has given way to
a faint buzzing like the sixty-cycle hum of high voltage. The
man's expression and his outstretched hand quick-frozen, as
if Cassandra's brain has stopped them in time. Then the look
on his face fades into something blank, still, and quiet as
Gail Paskie's face was in the photo of her that Gary Lally
was showing around Town Hall Station, the Medical
Examiner's morgue photo.

Which is how it started, with Gail Paskie's telling
Cassandra that she can't go on much longer with her
husband—Steve, another cop at 19th—that she moved out
because all Steve wants to do since he started working
narcotics is go to Dragamento's with his buddies. He slaps
Gail around when she complains. "He doesn't mean it." Gail
says that he's always really sorry after. Cassandra has just
been transferred to Town Hall, working Property, barely
knows this big blonde chatty beat cop, Gail Paskie, from
Eve. But she's met Steve Paskie, knows him to speak to from
a stint at 19th District two years ago. Cassandra remembers
a wiry guy with short man's disease, furious sharp blue eyes,

as if they are very hot or very cold, and always on the edge
like just a little more will freeze them up or boil them over.

Gail tells Cassandra, "Steve likes you," as if being likable
to Steve is doing Gail a very big favor, as if this is why she
confides in Cassandra that Gail can't stop Steve from hitting
her. And Gail wants to die, is going to psych services, as if
this is a secret from anyone now that they've put Gail on
restricted duty and taken away her service revolver. Everyone
can tell she's having problems just by looking at her stuck on
a desk assignment with an empty holster. "I'm not crazy,"
Gail insists, "just depressed." And Cassandra thinks,
nodding, *Isn't everybody*—everybody over thirty anyway.

After she's moved out, Gail's all the time saying, "I can't
live with him and I just can't stay away." Cassandra tells
Gail she's been there too, but she wonders. And Cassandra's
new friend, Lonnie Hudson, a detective doing homicide, says
that's the difference between a black woman and a white
one, "Little guy like that come after a sister and she'd whip
his scrawny ass." Then Lonnie's laughing, big belly laughs,
"You'd whip him, wouldn't you, Cassie?"

Wouldn't you? Lonnie likes to kid her, likes Cassandra.
She knows he has from the minute she transferred into Town
Hall, like a big brother showing Cassandra the ropes in
Property, nothing sleazy about him.

Lonnie says, "Anyone mess with you, you tell me, and
I'll whip him myself," making a face like he means it,
protective. But Cassandra can take one look at Gail, big as
she is, and tell there's nobody to whip Steve Paskie for her.

While watching Gail talk, Cassandra sees the light
around her get shimmery, wavy, and all the colors look
backward for a while, before Gail's face comes into focus
again, making Cassandra wonder if the bad feeling about
Gail Paskie she can't shake anymore isn't something the
matter with her head.

That's before Steve puts the gun in his mouth and before
there were even photos of Gail's place for anyone to show
around. Before Gary Lally showed Cassandra the photos of
Gail on her kitchen floor. Cassandra thinks of the shimmery
light and the moment when Gail's face seemed to freeze
mid-sentence into something like a photo negative.
Cassandra thinks the empty look on Gail Paskie's dead face

is just the same, something Cassandra imagined long before Gary Lally showed it to her.

◆

    Cassandra has always had hunches. Cassandra's mother says her Aunt Elaine has second sight. Nothing like this; Auntie Elaine just knew when the phone was going to ring. A few seconds before it would happen, Cassandra's aunt would say, "There it goes."

    When Cassandra's cousin Jimmie died, Auntie Elaine was all alone. No one came around, and she would get to thinking she could hear Jimmie talking to her. She could tell when the phone was going to ring, but she wouldn't answer it. Auntie Elaine calls her spells when she can hear Jimmie *petit mals*, *Pet-tee Malls*. A little, bad thing. Sounding to Cassandra as if there is just something minor wrong with Auntie Elaine's brain. Cassandra's mother called it "Pure dee crazy. Nothing pet-tee about that."

    The train station is fading away, all but the shaking, and everything that was black is white. Everything that was light is dark, and everything in between, the shades of gray stay gray but are not quite right in no way that Cassandra can identify. Cassandra thinks, *There it goes.* People caught for a second of their lives, the colors of their faces all turned around and then floating back up again out of the dark as if from a photographer's tray of developing fluid, the images swimming onto the paper. Only these images are coming out of Cassandra's head. Cassandra hears herself breathe out into the rush of air that the train leaves behind, each car sliding into the station, stopping, its smooth steel body sighing as it fills the gully of track.

    Cassandra can hear the man calling up from the floor, "You makin' it, sister? You don't look so good." She can hear the sound, but his face stays stuck for a moment longer before it comes back to life again. Cassandra is still shaking; she can tell by her hands, which seem to her like someone else's. She takes hold of one hand with the other and the shaking stops. Then she puts her hands in her pockets as the homeless man watches, his expression odd and sorry for her. Cassandra wonders if, coming home to her empty apartment

at Regents Park, she's not as crazy as Gail Paskie coming
home to a man who beat her just because, walking every day
closer to the kind of ending the ME needs to photograph.

Cassandra turns away from the beggar and steps off the
platform onto her train. As the door closes, she can hear him
calling, "You okay now, sister?" as if she is the one who
needs taking care of.

The seat on the train is cool and black and smooth.
Auntie Elaine needed taking care of. As the train comes up
from the underground and rumbles south toward Stoney
Island, the edge of Hyde Park where Cassandra has a flat,
she looks out the dirty windows, thinks maybe she needs
taking care of too. Luther Payton tells her once a week,
"You need someone to watch out for you, girl. How are you
going to watch out for yourself?" Once a week he offers to
be that someone, with his sly, back-handed offers. He has
two tickets to the Bulls—does she know of anybody who'd
like to go with him? Daly's people are having a reception
and he doesn't have a date. As if Luther Payton has ever had
any trouble finding a date. It has been a long time since
anyone has taken care of Cassandra, not since Lynette
Devereaux, her high-tone experiment with a woman lover.
"I'm teaching you self-love," Lynette Devereaux would say.
Lynette, who taught her how to let herself be taken care of,
taught Cassandra ambition and lust for all those nice things
she has now that seem so ordinary.

II

Lonnie is shaking his head over a dossier of pictures
spread out on his desk, lips pressed tight together. Lonnie is
a big, broad-faced man; his disapproval broods around him,
closing things in. Cassandra has watched it roll up like dark
storm clouds coming over the flat, open spaces outside of the
city. She has known Lonnie more than just to speak to for
only six months. In this time she has found him to have only
two moods he will articulate: grim-stoic and jolly. Any other
emotions that go on in his great bear head remain
unexpressed. She has never seen him angry. Lonnie does not
dream, except perhaps for his son, whose picture with his
wife sits on the desk by his phone. If Lonnie dreams of his
wife, he doesn't say so. All he talks about is his son who

plays basketball and studies communications at Villanova.
Lonnie waves a hand at the case file on his desk—a homeless
man someone found dead in the doorway of the First
Chicago branch on Michigan Avenue by the old Watertower.
He says, "Jesus, it'd be all right with me if I didn't have to
see another dead brother." Cassandra nods as she picks up
the ME's picture. The face looking back at her is strangely
familiar, different from the way other dead brothers—shot in
a drive-by, shot in a gang war, dead wherever—look familiar.
Still it takes a while for memory to put the name in her
mind. *Joe. You know you got some change ta give ta old Joe.*
The week-old jangle of three quarters, two nickels, and
seven, eight pennies falling into a crumbling Styrofoam cup
comes back out of nowhere, making Cassandra's stomach
lurch.

Lonnie's still shaking his head. Cassandra would like to
tell him how she met this man a week ago at Lake Street and
how his face changed suddenly into the photo she's looking
at now, but Lonnie would think she was crazy—and after
Gail Paskie everybody knows where crazy gets you.
Cassandra puts the photo down, turns it facedown on the
desk.

Lonnie's stoic face is jolly again, laughing at her
squeamishness. "Girl, you are going to have to get yourself a
stronger stomach," he advises her, "if you want out of
Property." Even so, Lonnie gathers the pictures and slips the
pile of black-and-whites back into the manila case folder.
Maybe it's because Gary Lally's headed across the office
toward them. Lonnie thinks Gary Lally's got *too* much of a
stomach for the kind of tragedy the pictures show and won't
keep his mouth shut. "More lip than sense," is what Lonnie
says about Gary, mostly laughing, sometimes not. Gary
Lally's taken the sergeant's exam five times and still hasn't
passed. He says, "Fuck that shit about unfair to minorities,
doesn't look like being white has helped me any."

Gary's walking a beeline to Lonnie's desk. He's grinning,
got his two sons with him and his hand thrown up in the air
before he gets there, shouting "Upstairs, man." White boy's
high five. Gary grew up in Terre Haute, Indiana. They say
"upstairs" there, all the lanky farm boys practicing with
hoops nailed to oak trees in the middle of nowhere. Gary

says there they are serious about basketball, even
high-school ball. Lonnie says there's only one reason to put
high-school basketball on television: 'cause there ain't
nothing else to do. Twenty-two years ago Gary's high school
went to the Indiana state finals and Gary was on television.
Gary says, "Nah man, that's not it at all." They talk about
Lonnie's son, who is on television now, and Gary says he'd
like that for Trent, his oldest boy, who's going to Purdue in
the fall and now plays basketball for Lane Tech. Gary
squeezes the taller boy's shoulder muscle and the boy recoils
from his father's affection, ducks slightly to get out from
under his arm, looking surly. The shorter one watches his
brother and puts on the same expression, bored and
embarrassed.

"Sport gives a guy balance," Gary says to Lonnie, claps
the taller boy on the back, "Huh, huh, am I right or what?"
and Lonnie agrees silently in a language of admiration that
only men seem to speak to each other. Gary and Lonnie
speak it now as if Cassandra and the boys are not even
there, the way foreigners speak their language on the
subway, their secrets insulated by culture.

Gary's youngest is too young for high school, but he
plays in junior high. Both boys are standing there behind
Gary now, leaning really, backs propped against the wall,
their lanky legs pushed out in front of them to keep from
sliding down the dirty taupe paint, sullen hands smashed
down in the pockets of their dungarees. The hands come out
to sweep the traces of their wispy hair off their foreheads
and then go right back in the pants pockets. Rocking back
on the heels of their space-age looking hightops, the boys let
their eyes run all over everything, antsy to go, somewhere,
anywhere but where they are.

"So, you-all got tickets to the Bulls tonight," Lonnie asks
as if he'd ask Mary to give him another son, young enough
to be still at home to take to the game, then answers himself.
"Well, all right."

"Yup, going to see the Bulls." Gary's confirmation,
"Right boys," seems to prod them into motion. They push
themselves off the wall, pull their hands out of their pockets
just long enough to give Lonnie one "upstairs" each,
hopping slightly when their palms slap even through Lonnie

hasn't gotten out of his chair. As the older boy's hand meets Lonnie's, the air around his body begins to wiggle like the air above a car hood on a hot day, as if the clap from "upstairs" has shaken the air, left it vibrating even after the sound is gone, faded off into a high-pitched whine. The air is shimmering at the corners of Cassandra's eyes and the oldest boy's haystack hair begins to darken, almost imperceptibly at first, then like some crazy time-lapse from dishwater to brown to black. Cassandra looks away and back and his blond hair is black. His face is black too, and all around the outline of his head the air shines as if he is silhouetted by a hot sun pouring light around him. Just the older boy; the younger one looks the same as he always has, head down and sneaker toes kicking at nothing on the floor while Lonnie and his daddy talk rebound statistics. After a while the shimmering stops; the older boy, Trent, is back to normal. Cassandra wonders how normal she is, puts a hand on the desk to steady herself, but everything's shaking still.

Lonnie's looking at her hard. "What the hell's the matter with you, Cass," Gary laughs, "Looks like you've seen a ghost."

◆

Monday, it's three days later and Cassandra Hope puts the Fitzhugh file on the stack with all the others—stolen cars, break-ins—and picks up her cup and heads for the coffee room to dump the film that riding on top of her coffee. In the coffee room Lonnie is pouring out the end of his last decaf, lumbering, broad, built close to the ground. Even with nothing but a ceramic mug and a plastic stirrer, Lonnie manages to bang things around.

Lonnie's face looks grim. "Hear about Trent Lally?"

Cassandra hasn't.

"Dead. Sunday. Bee sting," says Lonnie, shakes his head.

"The older one?" Cassandra asks, thinking of how his face turned. *Negatives*. It almost makes sense to her. First, Gail Paskie, then the transient, Joe, and now the boy, as if she's taking their pictures like the ME will do later. Taking their pictures and watching them develop in her head. Lonnie tells her that the boy was allergic and nobody knew.

But I knew. Cassandra thinks of what she's hearing now in her head. The ringing comes up, it seems, from nowhere, getting louder until it's not the background anymore but the main thing going on inside Cassandra's head.

"Just fell over," Lonnie's saying, "shooting hoops in his driveway." Gary had called Lonnie at home. The paramedics were too late. "Damn shame," says Lonnie, but Cassandra can barely hear him. "Senseless thing, a kid like that."

"How's Gary doing?" Cassandra manages to ask.

Lonnie shrugs. The boy was everything to Gary. Lonnie, grim-faced, looks down at the floor, then up again. Cassandra imagines he's thinking of what it would be like to bury his own boy. "Gary's not so good." *Who would be.*

Cassandra's not so good herself. First Gail, then the homeless man, and now Trent Lally. Cassandra has taken all of their pictures with this peculiar lens of her mind's eye, seen them all change from flesh and blood into two dimensions.

"I'm going over there tonight," Lonnie says, looks at the wall clock. "It's quittin' time, anyway." Quittin' time—Cassandra's face makes an almost smile, in spite of herself, in spite of Gary, thinking of the epic of the Old South that Lynette Devereaux made her watch years ago in Philly and deconstructed later over fancy coffee, years ago before *latte* or *deconstruct* were words anybody would use.

"I'm through for today," Lonnie says, shaking his head from side to side, meaning more than just with work. "Damn shame."

When he turns with the empty mug in his hand to face Cassandra, Lonnie's eyes are red-rimmed. They seem to fade to black like the storms that used to come in suddenly, black clouds from far in the distance across a long, flat plain, and it's as if the world has slowed down, slower, slowest, stopped. And the light begins to change in tiny increments. Cassandra knows it's happening again. The neat, close fringe of fine gray hair softened from age to kinky spider webs around Lonnie's receding hairline grows black again. The whites of Lonnie's eyes go black, the pupils white, the brown irises an intermediate gray. The white wall behind him, black. Lonnie's face is quick-frozen in its sad, stiff expression

for a moment, colors queer and backward, before it goes
blank, dead, and peaceful.

Now Cassandra's hands are shaking. They drop the cup
and the pieces shatter on the floor. The crashing sound
brings the world solidly back to normal—black hair, brown
eyes again. The spell is there and over so fast Cassandra's
not even sure it's happened, long enough to notice, like the
flash of light she sometimes sees at the corner of her eye but
can't ever catch.

"Hey, Cassie, are you all right?" Lonnie's got a hand
underneath her elbow.

Cassandra tells him, "Sure, fumble fingers."

"Guess we all need a rest," Lonnie says, smiling at her,
worry-faced.

Not sleep. Cassandra's toe scuffs at broken pieces of mug
and Lonnie bends to pick them up.

"I've got that," Cassandra tells him. They are both on
their knees. He places the broken pieces he has collected
gently into her cupped hands.

"You know," Lonnie says, "I could drive you home
before I go to Gary's."

But Cassandra knows it's out of his way. She just needs
to cool out, she says, just for a little while. Lonnie eyes her
skeptically before he lets her trudge back down the hall to
her desk in the bull pen.

◆

The phone is ringing. "Hope," Cassandra says when she
picks it up.

The voice on the line is laughing. "Yeah, hope," it says.
"That's all I ever do," and then, "Hi, Babe." It's Solange.

Solange Orlowski is a med tech at the ME's office, a
tough little dyke—or at least that's what everybody says, as
if everybody has slept with her. *Solange.* It has been a year
since Solange started calling Cassandra, casually enough,
about a case they were both working on at the 19th. Very
easy and then Solange had another question a few weeks
later, casual but just as easy. So now once a week Solange is
calling to chat, suggesting lunch.

"Tomorrow? Then what about the day after? Next week?" For months she was right there whenever Cassandra turned around, smiling that peculiar little knowing expression that's not quite a smile, odd and crooked, between her pale, thin lips.

One night when an off-duty lunch at Dragamento's has gone long, Cassandra is feeling tipsy. "Honey, you're plowed," Solange pronounces, all the time smiling her crooked smile. Cassandra's too drunk to make it home. "I'll take you," Solange says, even though it's out of her way.

It seems better to Cassandra than leaving with one of the guys, who are eyeing her like wolves eye their prey. If a man fucks a woman he works with, he's made a conquest. If a woman fucks a man, she's been made one, and Cassandra is too ambitious to let herself be reduced to locker-room bragging. Riding with Solange is better. Safer, maybe, if only politically. Somehow they never go back to Cassandra's place.

Now whenever Cassandra looks at Solange, she's looking back. Even when she isn't asking the question, it's in her look, asking when the next time will be. Cassandra doesn't know, has contrived to be politely busy. Cassandra thought the last time was with Lynette Devereaux, years ago. No use getting into that again, especially since there is something she likes about Solange, likes especially.

"So, Dragamento's?" Solange is offering. Dragamento's, down by Juvenile Hall. It's the PD hangout, way across town from Town Hall Station, where Cassandra works now.

"I don't know," Cassandra hedges. Both the big and little hands of the clock on the wall across the room are on the six. "It's late and I don't have my car tonight," she lies.

"Half an hour," Solange says. "Come on, I'll even pick you up."

Cassandra feels unsteady. The ride sounds good. The ride sounds indispensable under the circumstances. Her hands are still shaking and Cassandra would rather not be alone.

"I'll pick you up," Solange says. "Ten minutes."

Between Cassandra's office and the front door nobody's face freezes or changes color.

John Win turns and catches the door as Cassandra opens it, holds it as well for Booker Robie, who's walking with

him. Booker smiles wide when he sees her stop to wait by
the curb.

"Waiting for a friend," Cassandra explains and Booker
raises his eyebrows, teases, "Lucky guy," walks off toward
Irving Park and the train, slowly.

"All work, no play." Cassandra wants him to be gone
before Solange gets there, especially Booker. She doesn't
want the ribbing. Cassandra crosses her fingers as her eyes
search Addison Street. *Thank God.* It's just like Solange to
be late. Cassandra watches Booker's figure getting smaller in
the distance, trenchcoat blowing open; the belt in the back
swings back and forth and the air behind him seems to
shimmer strangely. Cassandra watches the air wave until
Solange taps her horn a second time.

Solange has reached over and pushed the passenger door
open before the car stops rolling. She calls to Cassandra
through the open window. When Cassandra's inside Solange
makes a tight, fast U-turn on Halsted Street heading south
and laughs as Cassandra looks queasy. They don't talk;
Solange just smiles all the way to Western Avenue, wearing
an expression as if she has a mouth full of something sweet.
Dragamento's is south, miles away, but Solange turns left on
Fullerton and pulls the car into a bus stop.

She looks at Cassandra, "I don't really want to go all the
way down to Dragamento's, do you?"

Solange's apartment is on Sheffield, and somehow they
end up parked down the street from the walk-up where
Solange has her little flat with a view of the rooftops and,
from a narrow window in her bathroom, of downtown. The
city lights take the place of stars, Solange puts the stereo on,
and Billy Holiday moans "Blue Moon" out of the speakers
on Solange's mantle—so corny, it's sweet. Sweet how hard
Solange is trying for something—romance, but Cassandra
thinks what's the point when they both know where this is
going. *Blue Moon.* Cassandra is thinking maybe this is what
she needs, it's been a long time.

Cassandra is thinking about the words to the song,
thinking about having someone to care for. Through the
pass-through that separates the galley kitchen from the main
room, Cassandra watches Solange break a tray of ice cubes
into a white plastic bin, take out three squares, and clink

them into a short, fat glass. She pours three fingers of vodka
over the ice and walks it over to Cassandra on the couch, a
futon that unfolds into a bed. Cassandra remembers the bed,
the old stuffed tiger on the empty side of the bed. Most of
all, Cassandra remembers Solange's touch as she drops next
to her, sighing, "I've been thinking about you since March."
Solange is blushing, confessing what Cassandra already
knows.

What surprises Cassandra is how pleased she is to know
it. Solange kisses her neck with soft, open lips. Solange, who
told her in whispers that she never had a black lover. Solange
says carefully, "African-American," conscious of their
differences, as she says how she is thrilled by the color of
Cassandra's skin, rubs Cassandra's back until she dozes, and
then kisses Cassandra awake enough to make love again.

Cassandra is awake and screaming into Solange's open,
puzzled face. The three deep lines in Solange's forehead are
moving now in an upside-down smile toward the widow's
peak of her hairline. The face is now Solange's again, her
thin blonde hair hanging forward above Cassandra.
Straddling her waist, Solange catches Cassandra by the arms
and holds her still, wrists pinned down to the sides of her
head. Now Solange's face is animated, concern forms in its
peaks and gullies, the flesh is flushed red and the mouth is
whispering, "Cassie," softly. "Cassie. Whoa." The thin pink
lips plant feather kisses on Cassandra's eyes.

"Was it nice for you?" Solange asks. Wishes for what she
wants it to be. The hard face seems unused to saying naked,
needy words. "I wanted it to be nice for you." They do not
talk about love. Purposefully. Rather, they talk around it and
around the subject of who Cassandra is and who Solange is
to Cassandra.

"It's always nice." Cassandra isn't lying. "Very nice."
She watches Solange bend her face into a smile, always
surprised that it takes so little.

"Are you sure?" Solange asks, insecure since the last
time, the time that was supposed to be the last.

It is ten o'clock. Cassandra says she has to go; she has an
early meeting, volunteers to call herself a cab. But as she
goes to stand up, the colors in Solange's face begin to change

and she lets Solange pull her down again on the bed, wrap
her up safe in her legs and arms.

◆

"I didn't think you'd stay," Solange is telling her the next
morning, pleased. Cassandra doesn't tell Solange she didn't
expect it either; it's 7:15 and she's got a meeting with a
state's attorney down on 26th and California, a trial left over
from her stint at the 19th. Luther Payton is the prosecutor.
"Sweetness," the women cops call him, like Walter Payton,
the football player. He's bigger than Walter, but the girls say
he's just as fast. Cassandra wonders if she can avoid Town
Hall Station all day so no one will know she's wearing
yesterday's clothes.

"There's a toothbrush in the drawer below the bathroom
vanity," Solange tells her. Cassandra takes a green one in a
box that reads, *compact head, soft,* from a pile of five,
maybe six, other new toothbrushes, thrown in the drawer as
if Solange is used to impromptu company. Cassandra opens
the medicine chest, takes the toothpaste from the little shelf
behind the mirrored door. She bends at the sink, turns the
porcelain faucet handles marked "H" and "C," and rushes
her hand underneath to catch the water. The water spills
over her palms. She would like to let it run and run over her
wrists. Instead, she takes what she has caught and splashes it
toward her face, eyes closed, and then opens them, looking
across at the mirror. The round globe lights make the room
too yellow, she thinks. As she closes the medicine cabinet
door, the three vanity light bulbs begin to waver, Cassandra's
face begins to change. She closes her eyes so she doesn't have
to see and when she opens them again her face is the same as
it always was, staring back at her from behind the mirror. A
blue-and-white line of toothpaste has squeezed out into the
sink. Cassandra takes her hand and wipes the cool white
sides and smears the toothpaste in the running water, until
it's thin enough to wash away down the drain.

Cassandra lays the toothbrush on the side of the sink.
Solange picks it up, drops it in a hole beside her orange one
in the pink ceramic toothbrush holder set in the speckled tile
above the faucet.

"In case you need it again," Solange says, seeming to
Cassandra both sweet and sad. The fact of Solange's orange
toothbrush, the bristles splaying slightly from weeks of use,
makes her seem now as if she's made of glass instead of piss
and vinegar.

Solange walks Cassandra to the porch to meet her cab,
reversing the route they took last night to Solange's small
fourth-floor apartment, down the short, carpeted steps
through the locked inner door, and out into the tiled foyer
before the unlocked outer door. Solange opens it, lets
Cassandra out into the pale fall light, hiding her legs, naked
under a T-shirt, from the morning behind the opening door,
and kisses Cassandra goodbye in the thin little shaft of warm
air that wafts from the foyer. Cassandra thinks of the skinny
legs, the petite frame, and the small hands that push the door
closed behind her. Cassandra used to think Solange was
indestructible; now she knows differently. Cassandra
wonders what will happen to her, thinks, *What accident?*
Cassandra counts the possible catastrophes.

"Call me," Solange says, "Soon. Okay?"

"Take care," Cassandra tells her. Means it.

III

It's a long cab ride to the criminal court at 26th and
California, a building complex in two parts: a squat, old
graystone from the 1920s attached by a walkway to a thin,
modern box of concrete and glass. Cassandra flashes her
badge as she walks past the desk guard and around the
metal detectors, through the side door for employees of the
court, and toward the elevators that take her to Luther
Payton's office in the administration building. Luther's door
is open; she can hear him talking before she gets there and
stands for a while in the doorway before he looks up. When
he sees her, Luther's out from behind the desk, phone in one
hand and free hand out. He squeezes her palm, smiling.
"Detective, we've got to stop meeting like this," and the
smile spreads wider as if he's thinking of all the other places
they could meet.

Luther Payton is confident, with a line of patter so
smooth he can shrug off her habitual rejection. Cassandra's
loss. *Maybe not.* Because every time Cassandra strikes him

out, Luther's back in there pitching. *In there.* Cassandra can
hear them joking, Luther and his cronies in narcotics asking,
"Did you get it, man?"

She can imagine what Luther would say, shit-eating grin,
"Yeah, I was in there."

He pulls back the heavy chair in front of his desk for her.
"Have a seat." Cassandra sits, pulls on the heavy wooden
arms of the chair, scooting it closer to the desk, and crosses
her legs. The hearing Luther is preparing for is late, more
than six months after the bail was set, high. The defendant
was holding too much coke for recreational use. Luther's
joking, "more like a cottage industry," and with intent to
deliver. Now it's Luther who wants to get the trial over and
done with and the defense attorney who wants his client's
guaranteed jail time put off until God-knows-when. So here
they are, six months after Cassandra's left the 19th, and she
can barely remember what the guy looks like.

Luther's bitching, "so much for a speedy trail," when his
phone begins to ring. He picks it up, turning slightly toward
the console, two lines of buttons and light. "Excuse me," not
like he's asking but telling. "Is that right?" Luther's saying to
whoever is on the phone. He's giving Cassandra the benefit
of his tight-pored brown skin and sharp features in profile.

After a while he hangs up, smiling faintly at good news
he doesn't bother to explain. "Nothing to do with this case,"
Luther mumbles over Cassandra's report, questioning her on
the points, reminding her of them. After an hour and a half,
he's sure there will be no inconsistencies that could foul them
up. "Four gold stars," Luther tells her, pompous. "You're a
quick study, Detective." He stands to let her out of his office,
throwing banter again, "I wonder what other tricks you
know?"

Cassandra tells him nothing he hasn't already seen
before and he grins his vague, good-news smile again.

"I can't say I'm sure about that now," he says. But
Cassandra is already down the hall, halfway to the elevators.
As the elevator doors close behind her, Cassandra's ears
begin to ring, and when they open again on the ground floor
the walls have begun to bend, the grooves in the floor tiles
begin to wiggle, bend, and straighten. Above her the
fluorescent lights are wavering; they seem to strobe over the

hall and below them people's faces begin to change, black to white, white to black, and Cassandra wonders if she isn't crazy. Thinking, everybody knows crazy runs in families. Now Cassandra's thinking she knows when someone is going to die, knows because of the way the air shimmers and the sound starts in the back of her head, sounding like it's far away, like the sound of the background music of a song when the radio is barely on.

Cassandra would like to run, but she can't move, can't even breathe until the humming is over and the light stops moving and the color in the hallway has settled down again. When Cassandra hears her name, she's standing there in front of the elevators, people flowing around her as if she is a rock in the stream of their motion. Cassandra doesn't know how long she's been standing there, but it's been long enough that Luther has come out of his office for lunch.

"Waiting for me?" he asks, looking pleased. What can Cassandra say? He lets her go out the double doors first, giving one of them a push and holding it open for Cassandra before he takes his natty, double-breasted jacket out after her. Luther's mentioning the meeting he's got at Daly Plaza, cryptically, dropping the name of a mayor's aide as if he'd like Cassandra to ask what he's been tapped for now. Cassandra doesn't, so instead he suggests Greek Isles, asking her to lunch at the place on Halsted with the mood lighting and the wrought-iron rails partitioning the tables, the vested waiters who shout "O-pah" when they light the flaming cheese.

Somehow even with all that "after you," Luther reaches the curb three steps ahead of her; he's got his arm up, hailing a cab before Cassandra can answer. He opens the dirty yellow door for her, polite hand on her elbow, motioning her to slide across the seat before him. She's nodding, "All right," halfway into the cab, acquiesces feebly, as if to re-assert that her agreement is still necessary. In case he's forgotten that. *All right.* Cassandra adds, "If you're buying," thinks Luther looks a little too smug as he scoots in beside her, pulling the cab door closed behind him.

The cab smells like old cigarettes even though the sticker on the Plexiglas partition behind the driver says "Thank you for not smoking." The cabbie is a black man wide enough to

fill the dirty cloth driver's seat and make its back sag toward
Cassandra's knees. He looked her up and down at the curb.
Cassandra pulls the oil-stained seat belt across her while
Luther tells the cabbie, "Halsted and Adams." The driver
turns the cab in a U, heading down California toward the
Damen on-ramp to the Stevenson Expressway, talking,
talking, talking. Luther, gabardine knees spread wide,
sloughed back with an arm across the seat back, in his
hundred-dollar Matisse-print tie, meets the cabbie's
familiarity with a cool *noblesse oblige*, as if to say *I'm riding,
you're driving, but let's pretend*. Luther's letting the cabbie's
opinions run over him, slide off his back like water, with no
more resistance than a nod or an uh-huh. Luther lets a
hairpin turn slide his pant leg against Cassandra, where it
stays, feeling warm and soft against her own. Luther wants
to get Cassandra to a close, dark table at Greek Isles and
work his rep, work his rap, because either one should be
enough for a Maxwell Street girl like her.

The cabbie turns his shoulder, swiveling his head around
to make his unwanted conversation through the partition
window, and fills in the gaps on Luther's side of the
conversation with a deep laugh that dies into sputters when
Luther's doesn't join in. Luther just lets the cabbie talk. The
hanging silver buckle at the end of the driver's seat belt
makes a clicking rhythm against the door as the old Chevy
engine vibrates, a tambourine played under the driver's
topic, now Mike Tyson, just in jail.

The cabbie is saying, "Girl ought to have knowed better
than to be up there in his room at no twelve o'clock
midnight," voicing male black outrage at "cheap females
bringing our heroes down." He's turned clear around in his
seat, head facing backward, making his appeal to fraternity,
his laugh starting up like a pull-cord lawn mower. All the
way across the Chicago River on the trestle bridge and onto
the Stevenson Expressway the cabbie's turned around,
explaining, "Mike Tyson, I mean, I mean, he a man," one
hand hung over the steering wheel and the other slapping the
dirty Plexiglas partition for emphasis. Cassandra wants him
to watch where he is going, wants him to stop gesturing and
put his hands back tight on the nubby black wheel cover.
Through the metal girders in the bridge the sunlight comes

in streaks, shining through the rusty lattice and then blocked
out as the car passes each support. As the cab speeds on, the
light seems to strobe on and off, and the air outside begins to
shimmer and hum.

"Uh-huh," Luther nods, noncommittal.

"What's a man supposed to do?" The air around the
driver's head is glowing.

"Keep his pants on," Luther says and the cabbie
belly-laughs.

"I'm saying," the driver's round head is bouncing up and
down, neck turned, his fingers playing again with the edges
of the fare-window. "Man keep his pants on unless she want
it. Now, she don't want it, man's supposed to keep his pants
on. But don't no girl go up to no man's hotel room at
midnight without knowing something is going to happen."

Through the front passenger window, the air outside has
begun to waver like hot air over a summer sidewalk, even
though it's cold enough to see your breath. Cassandra
watches the driver's fat palm slap the pilling blue seat beside
him, watches it rise and fall, then rise again, suddenly
white-skinned, as if the lattice streaks of light have washed
all the color out of him. The cabbie's saying, "Woman use a
man to get what she wants if he's not careful," mouth open
to show black teeth and a flash of pale tongue wagging.
"They all set him up," the cabbie's saying, "see, don't
nobody want to see a black man get nothing. They want
Tyson to stop fighting 'cause can't nobody beat the man,
see."

The cabbie is weaving through the traffic on the
Stevenson Expressway, and Luther's nodding, uh-huh,
shoulders tight. Cassandra can feel his foot tapping against
the floor, counting the exits. When the cabbie's eyes turn
back to the road, Luther turns to Cassandra, smiling, and
rolls his eyes.

The cab is flying across four lanes of traffic, and the
cabbie's got himself turned clear around again, this time
checking his blind spot. He's talking conspiracy theory at
Luther, saying, "Man's so hot in the ring, got to put the man
on ice," oblivious to everything but Mike Tyson's injustice.
Cassandra's watching him come up fast on the rear end of a

Pinto but can't say anything, like she couldn't say anything to Gail Paskie running headlong into something bad.

In profile the cabbie's face is white, his black hair whiter. The blue interior of the cab is off somehow. She can't say anything, opens her mouth to tell Luther something's wrong, but he looks just the same. The Matisse dancing girls on his tie are browns and easy bright and pastel blues, but the sky outside has turned a funny shade. The world is humming. Cassandra hears the high, thin squeal of brakes and then she's screaming too. The cab has stopped but she's still flying forward, feels the lap belt catch her, stop her face just short of the Plexiglas partition and the sharp edges of the money pass-through. She hears Luther swearing, outraged, before the belt boomerangs her back against the seat, sends her sideways, head banging against the side of the door. The back seat collapses in against her, and far away there are sirens, coming closer, until their crying fills up her ears.

After that there's Luther's voice speaking softly. When she opens her eyes he's asking, "Cassie, are you all right?" She can hear him saying, "We're all right," as if he's pinching himself out of a bad dream. He's saying it to the people opening the cab door for her, firemen cutting the steel with whirring saws. Then he's saying it to her again in a voice that seems to echo. Cassandra's looking into a face that's the same as it always was, red-brown skin and strong sharp features. *We're all right.* He's smiling, strained, but the same, white teeth, brown eyes, black hair.

"Everything's going to be okay," Luther says as the crumpled cab door is pulled away and sunlight, bright in a clear, blue sky, floods in on her, spilling onto her arms and legs, illuminating everything in what's left of the back seat of the cab. Cassandra holds her breath, but the colors stay that way, warm and comforting, like the sun and Luther's voice. She closes her eyes, the sun blazing orange against her tight-shut lids.

CONTRIBUTORS

AMALIA PISTILLI, born in Naples, Italy, has lived in England since 1984. In Italy she was active in fringe theater and performance art, exhibited mixed-media work, and conducted a radio program. After moving to England to study photography and filmmaking, she has worked as a freelance translator and photographer and has exhibited her jazz photography at several venues. She writes poetry and short stories; this is her first published work.

BETH BRANT is a Bay of Quinte Mohawk from Tyendinaga Mohawk Territory in Ontario, Canada. She is author of *Mohawk Trail* (poetry and prose), *Food & Spirits* (short fiction), *Writing as Witness* (essays), and editor of *I'll Sing Til the Day I Die: Conversations with Tyendinaga Elders* and *A Gathering of Spirit: A Collection of North American Indian Women*. Recipient of an Ontario Arts Council award, a Canada Council Grant, and a National Endowment for the Arts Literature Fellowship, she has taught Native women's literature at University of Toronto and has been a writer-in-residence at Trent University and Claremont College. She is a mother and grandmother and lives with her partner of twenty years, Denise Dorsz.

DIANE DEKELB-RITTENHOUSE's shady past includes stints as a factory worker, tarot card reader, medical technician, designer of telecommunications terminals and, in a dark and desperate hour, candidate for political office. A native Philadelphian, she abandoned a flourishing career in Manhattan as an unemployed bellydancer/actress/punk-rock lyricist for the joys of wife- and motherhood. Author of numerous science-fiction and fantasy tales, she lives with her husband, underground comic book writer W. E. Rittenhouse, and their daughter in Levittown,

Pennsylvania. Her day job is on the staff of a local college, where she also leads a union and teaches courses in genre writing.

HELENA BASKET was born in a Maryland snowstorm in 1965.

J. D. SHAW was born and raised in Michigan and has lived in many areas of the U.S., from New Orleans and Chicago to Pine Bluff, Arkansas, and Enid, Oklahoma. She now lives in Philadelphia. She is author of *Provenance of a Murder* and is currently working on a novel about murder in Maine.

JOANNE DAHME is the author of two science-fiction novels, and her short stories have appeared in several anthologies, including *Thirteen by Seven, Out for Blood,* and *Night Bites.* She heads the Public Affairs Division of the Philadelphia Water Department and lives in Philadelphia with her husband and son.

JOYCE WAGNER is a writer and actress, formerly of Chicago. She now resides on Martha's Vineyard with her symbiont, David Wilson. Her short stories have appeared in *The Joy Page, Perihelion,* and in the anthology *Night Bites.* She is currently at work on her first novel.

JUDITH KATZ is author of *Running Fiercely Toward a High Thin Sound,* which won a Lambda Literary Award for best lesbian fiction. Her work has appeared in *The Original Coming Out Stories, Tasting Life Twice, Night Bites,* and *The Penguin Book of Women's Humor.* She teaches at the University of Minnesota and Hamline University. Her second novel, *The Escape Artist,* is forthcoming.

JUDITH M. REDDING (coeditor) is a Philadelphia-based independent filmmaker and writer. Her video *Mondays* won third prize/experimental in the 1994 Visions of U.S. Home Video Competition. Her work has been shown at festivals in the U.S., Canada, England, and the Netherlands. She is the film and video editor for *Curve* magazine and writes about film for many national publications. Her fiction most recently appeared in *Night Bites.*

LINDA K. WRIGHT's short stories have been published in several anthologies, including *Out for Blood* and *Night Bites.* Her work has also appeared in *Murderous Intent, Echoes,* and *The Maryland Review.* Winner of the 1995 Charles Johnson Award for Fiction, she is vice president of the Delaware Valley chapter of

Sisters in Crime. She lives in the Philadelphia suburbs with her husband.

LISA D. WILLIAMSON's novel, *The House that Jake Built*, featuring sleuth Valerie Duncan, won awards at the Philadelphia Writers Conference, as have several of her other works. Her writing appears in *Out for Blood* and *Night Bites*, as well as *Belles Lettres* and *Death Knell II*. President of the Delaware Valley chapter of Sisters in Crime, she currently lives in the Philadelphia suburbs with her husband and two sons.

MABEL MANEY is a writer and book artist residing in San Francisco with her companion of ten years, Miss Lily Bee. She is the well-groomed author of the Nancy Clue series and numerous short stories. She is at work on a novel, *A Way With Men*.

MEREDITH SUZANNE BAIRD is the author of the satiric novel *Romancing the Romaine: The Adventures of Valentine Willowthigh*. Her short stories have appeared in several anthologies, including *Out for Blood* and *Night Bites*, and she has won numerous awards for her short fiction at the Philadelphia Writer's Conference and flash fiction at the Mid-Atlantic Mystery Conference. She is an active member of Sisters In Crime and Mystery Writers of America. A twenty-two year resident of Southern California, she is currently decompressing in Malvern, Pennsylvania, with her husband and seven cats.

NIKKI BAKER is author of the Virginia Kelly mystery series, featuring the first African-American lesbian detective. Her novels *In the Game*, *The Lavender House Murder*, and *Long Goodbyes* have all been nominated for the Lambda Literary Award for Best Lesbian Fiction. Her short fiction and nonfiction have appeared in numerous anthologies. A lifelong Midwesterner and former resident of Chicago, she currently lives in the San Francisco Bay area.

RUTHANN ROBSON's work includes the novel *Another Mother*, two short story collections (*Cecile* and *Eye of a Hurricane*), and a book of lesbian legal theory, *Lesbian (Out)Law*. Her forthcoming work includes the novel *A/K/A* and a book of theory, *Sappho Goes to Law School*. She is a professor of law at the City University of New York School of Law.

TERRI DE LA PEÑA spotted a lone dragonfly earring at an outdoor jewelry display. Abashed at being unfamiliar with the Spanish word for *dragonfly*, she asked the vendor who responded, "*caballito del diablo.*" In that instant, Terri bought the silver earring and found the title for her story. She is the author of *Margins* and *Latin Satins* and is currently working on her third novel.

TONI BROWN is an African-American lesbian writer. Her work has appeared in the journals *Sinister Wisdom* and *Common Lives, Lesbian Lives* and has been anthologized in *The Poetry of Sex: Lesbians Write the Erotic, The Body of Love, Lesbian Writers*, and *Night Bites*.

VICTORIA A. BROWNWORTH (coeditor) is a columnist for *Curve* magazine. Her work appears in many national publications, including *The Advocate, The Village Voice, Poz, Ms.*, and *Out,* She teaches writing and genre fiction at several Philadelphia-area colleges. Her previous anthologies include *Out For Blood: Tales of Mystery and Suspense by Women* and *Night Bites: Vampire Stories by Women*. Her most recent book is *Too Queer: Essays From a Radical Life*.

Other Books from Third Side Press

MYSTERIES

Out for Blood: Tales of Mystery and Suspense by Women Victoria A. Brownworth, editor
Fifteen previously unpublished stories by beloved and soon-to-be-beloved mystery writers. Tales of humor, terror, and otherworldliness, you'll find them creepy, scary, funny, nerve-wracking, horrifying, relieving, and memorable.

> *"Irresistible! From the evocative 'An Evening Out' by Victoria Brownworth to the delicious 'The Confectioner' by Meredith Suzanne Baird, this anthology sizzles and snaps with mystery and wit."* —Ellen Hart

$10.95   1-879427-20-6

Timber City Masks by Kieran York. Royce Madison is a major threat to some people in Timber City, Colorado. The question is, which people? The softspoken deputy, and only woman on the sheriff's department roster, has her work cut out for her. In *Timber City Masks*, the first in the series, she must find the murderer of her lover's best friend and, in the process, explore her feelings about the death of her father in the line of duty.

$9.95   1-879427-13-3

Crystal Mountain Veils by Kieran York. In *Crystal Mountain Veils*, it's the murderer of gossip monger Sandra Holt that Royce Madison is after, and motive is the key: everyone hated the tabloid columnist, but who hated her enough to kill her, and why?

$10.95   1-879427-19-2

EROTICA

Speaking in Whispers: African-American Lesbian Erotica by Kathleen E. Morris. Unflinchingly non-PC, yet occasionally vanilla, erotic short stories celebrate the diversity in shape, style, and manner of loving among lesbians.

> *"Takes us where we want to go."* —Jewelle Gomez

$11.95   1-879427-28-1

NOVELS

The Sensual Thread by **Beatrice Stone.** The simple
story of Leah Kirby's awareness of the beings on earth around her
and how that love transforms her sense of self. Being empathic
gives making love a whole new dimension.

> *"An incredibly romantic love story about two women who are*
> *committed to the life of the land, in every way. It is a*
> *fantasy, but fantasy so close to possible experience for many*
> *women that it becomes heartbreakingly real and desperately*
> *longed for. . . . This book is a real treasure." —Women's*
> *Books Online*

$10.95   1-879427-18-4

Entwined by **Beatrice Stone.** More magical realism from
Beatrice Stone. In this case, the truth is that what happened to
Lottie Mower really happened; the magic is that the mystical
connection between Lottie and Charly made a difference in the
end.

> *"Intrigue, romance, wonder, searching, pain and finally,*
> *triumph. Guaranteed to slightly shift your sense of reality*
> *and help you to appreciate the power of dreaming."*
> *—Amazon Bookstore News & Notes*

$10.95   1-879427-21-4

On Lill Street by **Lynn Kanter.** Margaret was a young,
radical lesbian-feminist in the mid-1970s, her credentials
unblemished, her ideals firm, when she moved to a mixed-gender
house on Lill Street.

> *"Watching everyone struggle with her/his feelings, politics,*
> *impulses is truly engrossing and a joyful experience."*
> *—Bay Windows* $10.95   1-879427-07-9

Not So Much the Fall by **Kerry Hart.** Through a fog of
angst and chemically-induced confusion, on an odyssey from
Memphis to Portland—and back again nine years later, Casey
glimpses the consequences of her lifes actions.

> *"This collage of one woman's life, memories, and twisted*
> *revelations takes readers on a road as winding as any*
> *Kerouac ever explored." —Nisa Donnelly*

$12.95   1-879427-24-9

AfterShocks by Jess Wells. Tracy Giovanni had a list for everything, but when the Big One hit San Francisco—8.0 on the Richter scale—her orderly world crumbled.

$9.95   1-879427-08-7

"This book kept me up all night."   —Kate Millet

AMERICAN LIBRARY ASSOCIATION
1993 GAY & LESBIAN BOOK AWARD NOMINEE

Hawkwings by Karen Lee Osborne. A novel of love, lust, and mystery, intertwining Emily Hawk's network of friends, her developing romance with Catherine, and the search throughout Chicago for the lover of a friend dying of AIDS.

$9.95   1-879427-00-1

AMERICAN LIBRARY ASSOCIATION
1992 GAY & LESBIAN BOOK AWARD FINALIST

DRAMA

She's Always Liked the Girls Best by Claudia Allen. Four humorous, heart-warming lesbian plays by two-time Jefferson-award-winning playwright. $12.95   1-879427-11-7

AMERICAN LIBRARY ASSOCIATION
1994 GAY & LESBIAN BOOK AWARD FINALIST
LAMBDA BOOK AWARD 1994 FINALIST

STORIES

The Dress/The Sharda Stories by Jess Wells. Rippling with lesbian erotic energy, this collection includes one story Susie Bright calls "beautifully written and utterly perverse."

$8.95   1-879427-04-4

Two Willows Chairs by Jess Wells.
Superbly crafted short stories of lesbian lives and loves.

$8.95   1-879427-05-2

The Country of Herself Karen Lee Osborne, editor.
Questions of identity—cultural and personal—abound in this collection of short fiction by Chicago women writers, including Carol Anshaw, Sara Paretsky, Maxine Chernoff, Angela Jackson, and others. $9.95   1-879427-14-1

HEALTH

Cancer as a Women's Issue: Scratching the Surface
Midge Stocker, editor. Very personal stories explore how cancer affects us as women, individually and collectively. Includes multiple perspectives on dealing with breast cancer.
> "If you are a woman, or if anyone you love is a woman, you should buy this book." —Outlines
> "An explicitly feminist perspective." —Sojourner

WOMEN/CANCER/FEAR/POWER SERIES, VOLUME 1
$11.95   1-879427-02-8

Confronting Cancer, Constructing Change: New Perspectives on Women and Cancer
Midge Stocker, editor. Confronting myths about cancer, presenting options for responding to a cancer diagnosis, and provoking political action to clean up the environment and reduce risks. Includes information about lesbians and cancer and about ovarian cancer. Features writing by feminist cancer movement organizers around the U.S. and an introduction by Sandra Butler.
> "Questions the usual, concealed reactions and advocates a more open, woman-centered, political stance." —Booklist
> "Read it and reap." —Chicago Tribune

WOMEN/CANCER/FEAR/POWER SERIES, VOLUME 2
$11.95   1-879427-09-5

Alternatives for Women with Endometriosis: A Guide by Women for Women
Ruth Carol, editor. Nutrition therapy, acupuncture, chiropractic, biofeedback, and massage therapy are a few of the available alternatives to relieving the pain of endometriosis without having a hysterectomy, taking toxic drugs, or getting pregnant when you don't want to.
> "I highly recommend you read this book. It can open some new doors for you." —Endometriosis Association Newsletter

$12.95   1-879427-12-5

MENTAL HEALTH

Beyond Bedlam: Contemporary Women Psychiatric Survivors Speak Out

Jeanine Grobe, editor. Up-close and personal writing by women who have survived psychiatric abuse on psych wards and in mental hospitals.

> *"Could be the book that awakens the world to the ugly reality of loony bins. . . . It's a book we'd like to publish in our pages, month after month, telling not just of shipwrecks on the ragged shoals of psychiatry but of reconstructing meaningful lives in the aftermath." —Mouth*
>
> *"an immensely powerful contribution to the contemporary psychiatric literature." —Dendron*

$15.95   1-879427-22-2

SomeBody to Love: A Guide to Loving the Body You Have by Lesléa Newman.

Forty-two ways to rethink how you relate to what you eat and to people around you. Speaking from her own experience, Newman guides women toward a new view of ourselves, as beautiful, powerful, and lovable, regardless of our size or shape.

> *"a moving experience and a practical tool." —Eating Disorders Digest*
>
> *"funny, touching, and totally unique approach." —Many Hands*

$10.95   1-879427-03-6

Coming Full Circle: Honoring the Rhythms of Relationships by Nancy VanArsdall.

Personal, political, and spiritual, this guide works from the premise that to have healthy relationships we must honor the waxing and waning, the rhythmic cycles, in each of us and in our intimate relationships. Examines the cycles of individuals as those cycles play into and intertwine in the cycles of relationships.

> *"Years of perceptive insight and intuitive empathy as a therapist have provided Nancy VanArsdall with a deep understanding of the cycles of relationships. Now we can all receive the gifts of her wisdom on the pages of Coming Full Circle." —Merlin Stone*

$15.95   1-879427-25-7

AUTOBIOGRAPHY

Enter Password: Recovery **Elly Bulkin.**
Autobiographical book about transforming the self through
language details with uncommon courage the author's experiences
with trashing in the feminist community, facing memories of
childhood sexual abuse, exploring Jewish identity, and ending a
long-term relationship.
> *"A rich and challenging book, one that will inspire a lot*
> *of healing." —Feminist Bookstore News*

$7.95   1-879427-10-0

BUSINESS

The Woman-Centered Economy: Ideals, Reality,
and the Space in Between **Loraine Edwalds and
Midge Stocker, editors.** Principle-centered business and right
livelihood? Feminists have been practicing them for 25 years.
Creating and operating businesses and organizations based on
personal beliefs is what the woman-centered economy is all about.
Sonia Johnson, Mary Kay Blakely, bell hooks, Phyllis Chesler, and
others examine the women's community from an economic
perspective, presenting case studies of real women's businesses and
discussing how and why those businesses fail or succeed.

$15.95   1-879427-06-0

To order any Third Side Press book or to receive a free
catalog, write to Third Side Press, 2250 W. Farragut,
Chicago, IL 60625-1802. When ordering books, please
include $2.50 shipping for the first book and .50 for each
additional book.

Third Side Press
because every issue has more than two sides.

The book you are holding is the product of work by
an independent women's book publishing company.